Arguer's Position

Arguer's Position

A Pragmatic Study of *Ad Hominem* Attack, Criticism, Refutation, and Fallacy

DOUGLAS N. WALTON

Contributions in Philosophy, Number 26

GREENWOOD PRESS
Westport, Connecticut • London, England

Library of Congress Cataloging in Publication Data

Walton, Douglas.
  Arguer's position.

  (Contributions in philosophy, ISSN 0084-926X ; no. 26)
  Bibliography: p.
  Includes index.
  1. Reasoning.   2. Logic.   3. Fallacies (Logic)
I. Title.   II. Series.
BC177.W32   1985   165   84-8971
ISBN 0-313-24439-1 (lib. bdg.)

Library of Congress Catalog Card Number: 84-8971
ISBN: 0-313-24439-1
ISSN: 0084-926X

First published in 1985

Greenwood Press
A division of Congressional Information Service, Inc.
88 Post Road West, Westport, Connecticut 06881

Printed in the United States of America

10 9 8 7 6 5 4 3 2 1

For Amy Merrett, without whose help I could never have finished all the books and articles written over the past fifteen years, perhaps even my doctoral thesis at square one.

Inconsistencies of opinion arising from changes of circumstances are often justifiable. But there is one sort of inconsistency that is culpable: it is the inconsistency between a man's conviction and his vote, between his conscience and his conduct.

Daniel Webster (Quoted by J. F. Kennedy, *Profiles in Courage;* New York: Harper & Row, 1956, p. 59)

Criticism invariably consists in pointing out some contradiction. . . . But criticism is, in a very important sense, the main motive force of any intellectual development. Without contradictions, without criticism, there would be no rational motive for changing our theories: there would be no intellectual progress.

Sir Karl Popper, *Conjectures and Refutations* (London: Routledge & Kegan Paul, 3d ed., 1969, p. 316)

It is better for me that my lyre or a chorus I directed should be out of tune and loud with discord, and that multitudes of men should disagree with me rather than that I, *being one*, should be out of harmony with myself and contradict *me*.

Socrates, *Georgias* (trans. H. C. Helmbold; Indianapolis: Bobbs-Merrill, 1952, p. 50)

Contents

Preface

Increasing concern over the past two decades about the
study of argumentation in natural language has recently
peaked with the appearance of such works as Informal Logic:
The First International Symposium, edited by J. A. Blair
and R. H. Johnson (1980) and Argumentation: Approaches to
Theory Formation, edited by E. M. Barth and J. L. Martens
(1982). The contention of some exponents is that a new
field, variously called informal logic, practical logic,
or argumentation, has been identified. Bits and pieces of
this field appear to be found in the various disciplines
of logic, rhetoric, linguistics (especially pragmatics),
English composition, speech, communication studies, cognitive psychology, and educational studies. The leading
characteristic of this new area of emphasis is a concern
for the reasoned evaluation of actual arguments, realistic
commonplace arguments as they occur in a natural setting,
whether that setting be science, public affairs, the consumer marketplace, or even the most ordinary dispute or
conversation. Inspiration for this new style of approach
to argument study has been given by philosophical works of
C. L. Hamblin, Henry W. Johnstone, Jr., Stephen Toulmin,
and Chaim Perelman, each of whom, perhaps in different
ways, tried to grapple with a theoretical understanding of
some practical conception of argument.

The historical sequestering of pragmatic studies of realistic arguments from the field of formal logic came as a
result of the mathematization of formal logic which esca-
lated at the beginning of the twentieth century. Studies
of the evaluation of realistic argumentation have henceforth been dumped into the pragmatic wastebasket of so-
called informal fallacies, a field left more or less
stagnant since Aristotle's account of it (aside from the
enthusiasm with which it was occasionally pursued in the
Middle Ages). But since the 1960s, there are signs of
rising concern that this neglect of the applied dimensions
of logic should not be continued, that the area of practical argumentation is worthy of sustained scholarly interest
in its own right.

Recent trends in linguistics, especially in the area of
pragmatics, have also pointed in the same direction of
practical emphasis through an awakening interest in the
concept of action in communication. For example, speech-
act theorists have concentrated on studying conditions for

the successful performance of an action in order to understand promises and other kinds of performative utterances.
Pragmatic analyses of argumentation like that of Frans van
Eemeren and Rob Grootendorst (1983) can go forward on the
assumption that certain inferences in natural language may
fail to be carried out successfully for reasons other than
violations of truth-conditions in a set of statements.

These circumstances suggest the deeper interest within
certain types of failure of correct inference in argumentation that occur in an apparent inconsistency of some
sort between a proposition asserted and the performance of
an action. Chief among these is the circumstantial ad
hominem argument where a participant in argument advocates
some proposition as true, but then acts so as to bring
about the very opposite of that proposition. Can conditions be formulated to rule when such instances of seeming
hypocrisy fail to be, in some sense, correct or successful
arguments? This is our question.

Other developments as well suggest the importance of
addressing this question of practical or pragmatic logic.
First, the work of Donald Davidson, Ingmar Pörn, and other
action theorists has been addressed to the question of
whether action sentences have a logical form. It is time
this field of research was related to informal logic
studies, and clearly the point of intersection is the
analysis of the circumstantial ad hominem fallacy. What
needs to be clarified is whether sentences expressing
actions can be inconsistent with or bear other logical
relations to other propositions or other action sentences.
If so, and if such relationships are expressible within a
logical theory, as Pörn and Davidson allege, then surely
ad hominem argumentation must be an important area of
application of the theory of action.

According to Gricean conversation theory, the performance
of a speech act in a standard cooperative context conver-
sationally implies that certain conventions governing
that speech act are satisfied. According to H. P. Grice,
if a person in conversation wanders off the subject, he
violates the Rule of Relevance. Conversation theory has
indeed provided a stimulus to renewed interest in the
analysis of argumentation, and the Gricean approach
points the way towards understanding why a rule like "Be
Relevant!" is essential to successful communication.
However, Grice's approach needs to be extended in two
ways. First, noncooperative contexts need to be studied,

but disputational contexts are important as well, especially where the informal fallacies are concerned.
Second, Grice limits his study of implicature to the
informal level. Therefore some rapprochement with the
logical structures of Davidson and Pörn would seem to be
a fruitful way to understanding failures of pragmatic
relevance at some adequate level of theoretical precision. It occurs to one that relevance or relatedness
logics must surely have some role to play in such investigations as well. In fact it will turn out to be our
thesis in this book that the structure of action propositions appropriate to ad hominem refutations has as its
core a relatedness logic, a subsystem of classical logic.

A problem for the classically based theories of Davidson
and Pörn as a vehicle for the analysis of circumstantial
ad hominem inferences can be posed as follows. Suppose
a vegetarian and a meat eater are arguing, and the vegetarian advances the conditional claim, "If you ate meat
yesterday, you brought about the death of an animal."
The meat eater defensively replies, "Not so. And anyway
I didn't eat meat yesterday." By the principles of
inference of classical logic, the meat eater's reply has
to be inconsistent. For by the classical (Philonian)
account of the conditional, the statement "It is not the
case that if I ate meat yesterday I brought about the
death of an animal" implies that it is the case that I
ate meat yesterday. The form of inference "⌐(p ⊃ q),
therefore p" is valid in classical propositional calculus. By these lights, the meat eater's reply must be
logically inconsistent. However, it does not appear to
be. Our natural and seemingly reasonable interpretation
is to say that his reply is consistent. How can this
sophism be resolved?

The approach of Gricean implicature has resources to deal
with this problem. Utilizing Gricean strategy, we could
argue that when the meat eater denied the vegetarian's
conditional statement, she was not really negating the
conditional. At least, all she really had good grounds
for denying was the alleged connection between her meat
eating and the bringing about of the death of an animal.
For the Gricean implicaturist, this connection is not
part of the truth-conditions of the original conditional
assertion, but rather an accompanying conversational
implicature. By these lights, the meat eater's statement
is not ⌐(p ⊃ q) but comes to something weaker, namely
this: "Maybe you're right that if I ate meat yesterday I

brought about the death of an animal.   But if I did bring
about the death of an animal it wasn't by means of eating
meat yesterday that I did it."   By the Gricean analysis
then, the asserted lack of this connection is not enough **to**
count as a claim to falsify the conditional.   So classical
propositional calculus is thereby argued to be compatible
with a reasonable account of pragmatic disputations about
the consistency of actions. [1]

It is to this sort of problem that this book is addressed.
We will argue that the Gricean strategy is a favorable
approach as far as it goes.   But we find that by leaving
the account of connections between actions at the informal
level of conversational conventions, it leaves open the
further question of whether these conventions can be
articulated in a more precise manner.   Our explorations
will show how some further precise articulations can be
carried out at the core of action-theoretic reasoning.
But we will also propose an analysis of ad hominem refutation that leaves certain aspects at the informal level, in
keeping with the pragmatic spirit of the enterprise.

Because we wish to emphasize the realities of practical
argumentation, we will analyze a number of actual specimens of argument, in several instances even conducting
detailed case studies.

In analyzing these case studies, we will put an emphasis
on trying to discern the best core structure that is helpful in offering some clear and formally well-written
guidelines to assist in ruling whether the argument is
correct or not.   This strategy flies in the face of those
who see informal logic as essentially and deeply informal,
that is, not being related in any useful way to formal
structures.   On the other hand, we will find ourselves
opposed to those who feel that there is no room for any
realistic application of logic, and that aside from purely
formal logic, the study of informal fallacies is simply
incoherent, or unimportant.   We will argue that there is
some legitimate room for systematic study between formal
logic on the one hand and the appraisal of argumentation
in natural language on the other, and that the question
of how ad hominem reasoning can be fallacious is answer-
able in this pragmatic area.

Our conclusion will be that ad hominem refutations are
sometimes successful and correct as arguments, but that
an ad hominem attack in disputation can turn out to be

fallacious (incorrect) under certain conditions. Thus we
hope to have established the thesis that ad hominem reasoning is not always fallacious per se.

Johnstone (1978, p. 53) argues that no philosophical argument can be valid unless it is ad hominem in Richard
Whately's sense. According to Whately's account, which we
subsequently examine in detail, the conclusion in an ad
hominem argument is established not absolutely, but only
relative to the arguer's own position or conduct. Johnstone's ingenious defense of this thesis makes it clear
that the analysis of ad hominem reasoning has important
implications both for metaphilosophy and for the foundations of rhetoric as a discipline. Indeed, much of our
concern with the ad hominem as an important aspect of the
theory of argument is provoked by Johnstone's work.

Our thesis is that ad hominem criticism is essentially a
form of strategic attack in a logical game of dialogue by
a proponent against the position of his opponent. We will
define the position of an arguer in the context of a game
of dialogue as the set of that arguer's commitments or
concessions relative to the game. One problem for the
adjudication of ad hominem criticisms is that in realistic
cases of argumentation, the position of an arguer may not
be clearly known or articulated, either by the defender or
attacker. In realistic arguments, an arguer's position is
often attributed to him on the basis of his personal con-
duct--that is, on the basis of certain descriptions of
actions alleged to have been carried out by that person.
Whether the cited actions in fact can be fairly justified
as committing the arguer to a definite position is best
treated as very much part of what is at issue in ruling
on ad hominem disputes. Consequently, much of the work of
supporting our thesis must consist in showing how particular act-descriptions can be fitted into a pattern of a
person's practical reasoning about a particular situation
or issue so that allegations of positional inconsistency
can be supported or refuted.

Clearly then the concepts of action and dialogue must be
included within the concept of reasonable argument needed
to support an analysis of ad hominem argumentation. Hence
our study will take us well beyond semantics and syntax,
and into the domain of that branch of linguistics and
logical studies now widely called pragmatics.

NOTES

1. The kind of context I have in mind here is the
following. Suppose the meat eater had set a mouse-trap
in his attic yesterday, and killed a mouse. He concedes
that he brought about the death of an animal (the mouse).
And he is willing to concede that if he ate meat yesterday,
he brought about the death of an animal. However, he
denies that he ate meat yesterday. And he denies that
there is any connection between his eating meat and his
bringing about the death of an animal yesterday.

Acknowledgments

I would like to thank John Woods, Dick Epstein, and Max
Cresswell for various discussions that have been influ-
ential in shaping the goals and methods of this project.
Maurice Finocchiaro, Gary Iseminger, and Henry W. Johnstone, Jr., have been particularly helpful in giving
detailed comments and criticisms of previous drafts.
Among many individuals who have contributed comments or
discussions on particular points, I would especially like
to thank Myles Brand, Jan Crosthwaite, Risto Hilpinen,
Krister Segerberg, John Bishop, Tony Blair, and Lynn
Batten. I am grateful to Gerald McAuliffe, who has given
permission to reprint as an appendix his article "Just
How Ethical Are the News Media?" from Quest, and I should
like to thank Gordon R. Lowe for giving permission to
reprint his review "The Myth of Szasz" from the Queen's
Quarterly. The University of Winnipeg and the Social
Sciences and Humanities Research Council of Canada have
contributed support through research grants and a leave
fellowship. My very deepest thanks are due to Amy Merrett
for typing the manuscript, through many drafts, with
unfailing care. I am indebted to Dave Schultz for com-
posing the index and for some examples and discussions.
Finally, I would like to thank my students, over the past
fifteen years of teaching, who have so often challenged
me to think more deeply about arguments and fallacies.

Arguer's Position

1

The Study of Fallacies

The initial problem with the study of informal (practical,
applied) logic is the questionable presumption that there
is some coherent understanding of what constitutes an
argument or fallacy. There is also the unjustified
assumption that once one has identified an argument, there
is some objective and decisive or at least rational way
of coming to know whether that argument is correct or
fallacious. Such optimistic presumptions about the fallacies are soon exploded by the most elementary probings of
even introductory-level students. How do you determine
when an appeal to authority is incorrect? What is the
difference between a vicious circle and a circular but
benign series of steps of reasoning? What is the difference between a fallacious ad baculum (appeal to force) and
the seemingly reasonable threat of loss of driving privileges to the drunken driver? Where is the fallacy in the
latter? If it might not be fallacious, then just when is
the ad baculum a fallacy, and how can we tell whether one
has been committed? There appears to be no theory of
argument we can appeal to in attempting to even begin to
frame answers to these perplexing questions.

Not only are textbook accounts unclear on characterizing
the fallacies, but they too often persist in a most
naively sanguine expectation that any of them could be
effectively pinned on any arguer who, heaven forbid,
might actually be present to dispute the allegation. Thus
students are too often quite incorrectly encouraged to
identify an ad baculum as soon as any indication of force
or threat is encountered. Or to cite the ad misericordiam
(appeal to pity) as soon as an appeal to pity is made.
Very often, however, such an allegation can be a most
superficial and misleading evaluation. With many an appeal
to pity or force, it is not even clear that an argument--
at least one meeting the minimal requirement of being a
set of propositions--is being put forward. It is difficult
enough in many instances to differentiate clearly between
a threat and a warning. But either of what appears to be
one of these is often put in the form of a command, request,
or other form of nonstraightforward propositional speech
act.

Hamblin (1970a) has ably documented the superficialities

of the Standard Treatment of the fallacies; a basic theoretical problem impeding scholarship in this field is the
seemingly impassable gulf between what is perceived as
(pure) formal logic and (applied) informal logic. Many
textbooks that treat both sides of the subject sequester
them neatly into separate chapters or sections with no
attempt to relate one side to the other. Indeed some
commentators would carry this separation as far as to
claim that (1) formalisms have no place in informal logical studies at all, or (2) broader questions of the evaluations of everyday argumentation have no place in the
purely mathematical discipline of formal logic. The dissonance produced throughout philosophy by (1) and (2) forces
an asking of a fundamental question: What is an argument?
That question is always at bottom of our deliberations on
the ad hominem arguments studied in this book, lurking
darkly, and often surfacing.

WHAT IS AN ARGUMENT?

Mrs. Jones has her attention drawn to the wall adjoining
the next apartment. She hears some tense, guttural pro-
nouncements--a man's voice? Then she hears some higher-
pitched responses that a speech act theorist might describe
as "aggrieved whining." The lower voice now breaks into
loud staccato accusatory stabs of statements. Mrs. Jones
can even make out some unprintable words. The higher voice
now responds with unmistakable screams, audible even to
Mr. Jones, who is trying to read Maclean's magazine. The
crescendo of voices is punctuated by a crash of crockery.
"What's going on over there?" Jones queries his wife.
Mrs. Jones replies, "They're having an argument!"

The paradigm probably most of us have of an argument--at
least those of us relatively uncontaminated by the study
of logic--is that of a verbal interchange between or among
a number of participants with (a) an adversarial or disputational flavor and (b) heightened emotions, very often
anger, being involved. Of course none of these items is
absolutely essential. One can argue with oneself. One
can have a friendly, or constructive argument. And one
can argue unemotionally, in the style of Mr. Spock, the
imperturbable Vulcan. Nonetheless, hot, interpersonal
dispute is among the commonest conceptions of argument.
Let us call this model of argument the quarrel, more
fully exposited in John Woods and Douglas Walton (1981).

According to the much more modest and sober, not to say

austere, conception of argument favored by twentieth-century logic, an argument is merely a set of propositions. This conception strips away the emotion, the interpersonal element, and even the adversarial notion of disputation. By this conception, an argument can even be some chalk marks on a blackboard or ink marks on a page, according to some of the most determined exponents of austerity, at any rate.

If we define logic to be the science of argument, which model of argument is better to start with? The first one is obviously rich in psycho-social information. Even Ann Landers would find lots there to be interested in. The second is very rich in mathematical results. George Boole and subsequent generations of mathematicians have found lots there to be interested in.

It is not too hard to see the fascination of each model for the critic of arguments. The second one admits of formal models that are decidable and complete. You can tell by objective tests which arguments are correct and which fall short of correctness. That is worth studying. The first one gives real-life case studies of actual arguments, refutations, and fallacies. Critics, however, have pointed out limitations of each model. The first model is unstable, subjective, even unruly. Too often it seems impossible to tell who is mostly right or wrong, or even what the argument is. The second model is provably correct as far as it goes, but it is questionable to what extent it applies to lively specimens of realistic argumentation. Are we forced to choose between them?

Sometimes exponents of one model will partially acknowledge the other. Gricean conversation theory argues that classical deductive logic is the right logic, but it needs to be trimmed with conversational niceties in order to approximate the do's and don't's of natural discourse.[1] On the other hand, some who stress the study of real-life argumentation may concede that formal logic has its place. It is just that arbitrary designation of a set of propositions as argument does not go far enough. It is a legitimate--but informal--task to determine what the argument is, even before it gets processed further.

But the question remains whether we have to choose between these two models of argument. Are there other alternatives?

Aristotle, the founder of the subject of logic, distinguished

two models of argument, neither of which is precisely
identical with either of the pair above. Aristotle
defined a demonstrative argument as one in which the
premisses are better known than the conclusion, so that
the conclusion may be established on the basis of the
premisses. That is an asymmetrical model of argument.
If p is a correct argument for q, then q cannot be a
correct argument for p. It is also irreflexive. The
classical inference pattern 'p, therefore p' cannot be
correct according to the demonstrative model of argument.
Aristotle defined a dialectical argument as one in which
the premisses are presumed to be true, or thought to be
true by the wise, or by some source short of guaranteeing
that the premisses are known to be true. These facts
about Aristotle are well known, but they are worth
reviewing because they posit models of argument distinct
from the quarrel or the purely deductive model.   In
modern treatments, the first model is akin to the model
of epistemic logic developed notably by Jaakko Hintikka.[2]
The second has been formalized by the dialectical games
of Hamblin (1970a). According to the dialectical model,
an argument is a two- or many-person game with a set of
rules that defines permissible moves in orderly sequence
and a win-strategy. Each move is a proposition indexed
to a participant.

These dialectical and demonstrative models of argument
are a useful compromise because they capture the personal
element, the give-and-take of disputation, and the directionality of reasoning. But at the same time the rules
are clear, and the model is amenable to decision procedures to determine correctness or failure of correctness.
Saul Kripke has even given an interpretation of the
intuitionistic calculus that would seem to make it a very
good model of one kind of demonstrative argument.[3]

A major problem is that there are many formal models of
dialectical and demonstrative reasoning. So the application problem is very much with us. Which of these is
most applicable to realistic argumentation where fallacies and other good or bad steps of reasoning take place?
The realistic models of the quarrel, or even the discussion, Socratic disputation, or debate cannot be left
behind. Even the model of argument as a set of propositions is incorporated into the dialectical and demonstrative models.

If all four models of argument so far identified have a
legitimate role to play in the theory of argument, do we

not seem to be enmeshed in a hopeless pluralism?--not to
mention the inductive-deductive pluralism. Is there some
common root to these various models? In essence we are
asking, What is logic about? I will not try to settle
this question. Suffice it to say that it is my own
opinion that we will only be able to work towards an
answer to it by means of a more attentive study of the
so-called informal fallacies--traditional, significant
sophisms of argument that provide benchmarks for the
analysis of argument.

Logic, argument, and fallacy--the three concepts are
closely connected. But how closely? John Woods and
Douglas Walton (1976a) and Charles Kielkopf (1980) have
warned that there may be fallacy (at least of the traditional sort, like ad baculum) without argument. But perhaps more narrowly and properly construed, a fallacy
should be a fallacious argument. Certainly logic is
about arguments, and thereby about fallacies. Without
pursuing these interconnections further, let me pose one
problem about them.

Mrs. Jones, her attention drawn to the apartment wall
again, hears what appears to be the higher voice saying,
"George, you're so inconsistent. You tell me not to
back-seat drive, and then the other day you criticized my
failure to signal a turn. You're always lecturing me on
the foolishness of smoking, and you can't give up the
habit yourself. . . ." Mr. Jones looks up, "What's going
on?" Mrs. Jones replies, "She just accused him by means
of the circumstantial ad hominem."

Here we have an argument, and a very interesting one at
that. George stands accused, not of logical inconsistency,
but of an action-theoretic circumstantial conflict that
may, or may not, be reducible to some logical inconsistency.
In a nutshell, he is accused of failing to practice what
he preaches. This lapse, if not defensible, may indeed be
a serious ethical failure or at least evidence of one. But
despite the traditional ad hominem label, is it really a
lapse of logic? Are George's arguments incorrect because
of his actions? If the answer is to be yes, it is equally
hard to see how the argument can be elucidated by any of
the four preceding models of argument. Consequently, the
direction of this book will have to be towards consideration of whether there can be a logic of action sentences
if this possibility of an affirmative answer is to be
evaluated adequately.

George may even admit that he can't give up smoking and
that he is thereby circumstantially inconsistent. He may
still maintain his condemnation of smoking is, in itself,
sound. Is his argument good, bad, or partially both? We
might say that the argument could be correct in itself
even if George's own personal advocacy of it is questionable. In other words, according to one model of argument
--an impersonal one--the argument is good. According to
another model--a person-relative one--the argument can be
criticized negatively. In short, we are back to a rela-
tivity of pluralistic models. Just as worrisome, we are
on the borderline between the logic of argument and the
ethics of argument. It is not entirely clear that the
lapse, if there is one, is a failure of logic as opposed
to a moral incorrectness of George's actions. We shall
have to sort out these problems.

Should the circumstantial ad hominem be taken out of the
logic textbooks and put into the ethics textbooks? We
will argue not--at least not yet, and not entirely. We
will argue that one can follow, at least up to some point,
a tradition in which there is some wisdom, without excluding the ad hominem from logical analysis altogether. For
the moment however, one cannot but suspect that George is
being criticized more for his morals than for his logic.

To gain our initial bearing, let us look at several more-
or-less randomly selected accounts of the ad hominem
fallacy given by current textbooks. In subsequent chapters, we will also look at other examples from the logic
texts.

STANDARD TREATMENT OF THE AD HOMINEM

S. Morris Engel (1976) distinguishes between the abusive
and circumstantial varieties of the ad hominem fallacy,
or as he calls it, the fallacy of personal attack. As
examples of the abusive ad hominem he cites the rejection
of a medical theory because the originator is a known
Marxist and the rejection of a politician's argument
because he has forgotten about his constituents back home.
Interestingly, the third example of the abusive ad hominem
offered by Engel (p. 108) is an argument we will classify
as a circumstantial ad hominem: "In reply to the gentle-
man's argument, I need only say that two years ago he
vigorously defended the very measure he now opposes so
adamantly." At any rate, this third example certainly
conveys the idea that the ad hominem is a sort of allegation

of inconsistency in some instances.

Engel describes the ad hominem as a kind of attention-diverting tactic that often succeeds as a refutation because of its emotional appeal, for example, through humor. It is also mentioned that ad hominem sometimes functions as "poisoning the well," forestalling one's opponent's ability to reply by impugning his character or trustworthiness.

The difficulty of ruling on the correctness or incorrectness of ad hominem arguments is implied by Engel's remark (p. 110) that sometimes it is appropriate to question a person's character: "In a court of law, for example, it would not be irrelevant to point out that a witness is a convicted perjurer or a chronic liar." However, Engel adds, such an assertion would not prove that this witness's testimony was false, even if it would reduce the credibility of the testimony. Is Engel suggesting then that questioning character or past conduct of a witness can be a correct form of ad hominem argument since it is "not irrelevant" as a move in argument? Certainly he is saying that such an argument does not refute the witness's testimony in the sense of proving it false. Or is he rather taking the line that questioning character is not a form of ad hominem argument even where it does reduce credibility of testimony? Apparently, the latter, for Engel seems to hold the general view that all ad hominem arguments are fallacious.

Engel's concluding statement on ad hominem makes the statement that an irrelevance has occurred where the basis of the argument is personal attack or the arguer's position: "As in all fallacies based upon personal attack, any consideration of those who hold a position, or who originated a position, or who are opposed to a position, must be viewed as an irrelevance." (p. 113). This statement seems to take the position that all ad hominem arguments are fallacious, a thesis often suggested by the cursory treatment given to ad hominem in textbooks.[4] At any rate, whether we can fairly interpret it as going that far, the statement itself is open to challenge.

Let us suppose that Amy and Fred are disputing the question of whether smoking is a cause of chronic obstructive lung disease. If Fred points out that Amy is a Catholic, Fred's move may be correctly judged to be irrelevant to the point at issue for the very reasons cited by Engel. Amy's holding of a Catholic position may be viewed as irrelevant.

However, let us suppose that Amy and Fred are disputing
the question of abortion, and Amy argues that in her case
abortion is an acceptable option. Now if Fred points out
that Amy is a Catholic, his move may not be altogether
clearly irrelevant to the point at issue. Suppose that
Fred goes on to remind Amy that she has opposed abortion
strongly in many previous instances from her often-argued
position as a staunch, practising Catholic. Does Fred's
move have to be judged irrelevant to the point at issue?
Some would say not. Amy may try to argue that her own
case is different in some ways from these other cases,
that she is the exception to her own rule, etcetera. But
clearly she is put on the defensive by Fred's ad hominem
(ad feminam) argument, and many would say rightly so. To
consider Fred's argument as having to be altogether fallacious is too narrow as an approach to the ad hominem.

Of course there is an important difference between questioning an argument, arguer, or position, and conclusively
refuting that argument, arguer, or position. But what
this distinction amounts to has yet to emerge. For the
moment, it seems wise to consider the possibility that not
all ad hominem arguments are fallacious.

Another survey of what some standard textbooks say about
the ad hominem, Govier (1983) finds texts enunciating the
principle that claims should be evaluated exclusively on
the basis of the evidence offered in support of them.
These texts take as a corollary that characteristics of
the person who makes the claim should be treated as
irrelevant to the claim. Such personal remarks should
not be counted as part of the evidence for or against the
person's claim,[5] according to these texts. Thus it is a
mistake to connect the content of a claim with the character or situation of the claimant.[6] Govier remarks that
while these sort of statements are commonly found in logic
texts, they are highly implausible and unintuitive, contrary to common practices. For we quite commonly do take
an established record of personal judgement into account
when evaluating advice or recommendations. And as Govier
notes, this practice very often seems reasonable.

It seems then that even the elementary accounts of the
beginning textbooks raise many unanswered fundamental
questions about the ad hominem. Under the topic of the
circumstantial ad hominem, Engel cites this example. "It
is true that several college professors have testified

that these hallucinogenic drugs are harmless and non-
addictive, but these same professors have admitted to
taking the drugs themselves. We should certainly dis-
regard their views." (p. 111). This particular example
is a curious one because it seems partially to involve an
ad verecundiam (appeal to authority), in that alleged
experts' pronouncements are being evaluated. It is a
kind of obverse of the ad verecundiam, however, for the
appeal to authority is not a positive attempt to escalate
credibility, but rather an attempt to undermine the
authorities' pronouncements. Curiously, however, the
argument seems more like an abusive ad hominem argument
than a circumstantial one. True, there is a circumstantial element present. The professors' pronouncements are
being evaluated in relation to certain actions attributed
to them. However, usually in the traditional view of the
circumstantial ad hominem, an action inconsistent with,
or running counter to what the arguer says or recommends,
is cited. By this conception, the right sort of example
(my own) would be this: "These professors testified that
these hallucinogenic drugs are harmless and non-addictive,
but several of these individuals are addicted to them,
and others have been in the hospital due to their addiction." That would be the classic circumstantial ad hominem
of the Standard Treatment. But in Engel's case, interestingly, the action and recommendation of the arguer are
quite consistent! We are left in a quandary to know
whether the example he cites really is fallacious or not.

Howard Kahane (1978) describes the ad hominem fallacy as
an attack on the person argued against, rather than his
argument, citing Nixon's attacks on his political opponents as "pinkos." One might ask precisely what is supposed
to be fallacious about this, and in fact Kahane, like
Engel, cites the legitimacy of the connection between
character and testimony in courtroom testimony (p. 246).
However, Kahane draws the conclusion that not all ad
hominem arguments are fallacious as the lesson of this
courtroom observation, precisely the opposite of Engel's
conclusion. Wisely, Kahane avers that the question of
when an ad hominem argument is or is not fallacious is
"quite complex," and does not try to answer it.

However, he does link the ad hominem with the ad verecundiam in an interesting way. Such an argument can, he
suggests, be nonfallacious if based on a claim of expertise, and in such a case information about the character
of the expert may be "an important kind of evidence"
(p. 246). In appeals to expertise, however, Kahane adds,

the ad hominem argument only cancels the expert's testimony rather than positively showing that what the expert
said is incorrect. Kahane makes no distinction between
the abusive and circumstantial ad hominem, and indeed his
treatment is quite cursory, only taking up the best part
of one page.

Robert J. Fogelin (1978) characterizes the ad hominem as
"an argument directed against the arguer rather than
against his argument or against the conclusion of his
argument" (p. 89). He mentions that the fallacy seems to
involve irrelevance, but that some ad hominem replies are
not without some relevance. The example he gives is this.

> A: It is time for the United States to develop more
>   normal relations with Cuba.
> B: Yeah, so you can make a bundle importing cigars
>   from those Commies.

According to Fogelin, B's reply is not entirely irrelevant
because "he points to a fact that gives us some reason not
to trust A's integrity in a discussion of U.S. relations
with Cuba" (p. 89). Accordingly, Fogelin is led to draw a
distinction between an ad hominem attack, a challenge to
someone's right to perform a certain speech act, and an
ad hominem fallacy, an attack on the truth of what the
person says or the soundness of his argument.

To illustrate the distinction further, Fogelin alludes to
the Lord's answer out of the whirlwind when Job asks why
he should be made to suffer when he was blameless. The
answer consists of questions like "Where were you when I
laid the foundations of the earth?" suggesting that Job is
ignorant. Fogelin, questioning how talk about Job's
ignorance could justify his undeserved suffering, suggests
that this answer must seem like an ad hominem fallacy.
However, he proposes that if we interpret as an attack on
Job's right to ask such a question, then no fallacy is
committed, for the Lord's statements are not meant to be
taken as an answer to Job's question at all.

I will not undertake to provide my own interpretation of
what the Lord meant on this occasion, but merely comment
that the distinction drawn by Fogelin is an interesting
one. We will utilize it subsequently.

A biblical example more representative of the standard
conception of the ad hominem reply could have been taken

from the reply of Jesus to those who would have stoned an adultress: "Let those among you without sin cast the first stone."[7] Jesus' reply shifted the burden of guilt onto the accusers by calling attention to a certain inconsistency implicit in their proposed action. They evidently do not occupy the "moral high ground" that their action might appear to presume. This is to say: "You who accuse this woman of sin are yourselves sinners." If you are prepared to punish someone else by a retribution you might not be prepared to inflict on yourself, you should ask whether your plan of action is really consistent. At least, that is the message that seems to be suggested.

Of course one could interpret Jesus' reply as a fallacious ad hominem argument if his conclusion is meant to be that the accused woman is innocent or should not be punished. Yet it is quite possible to interpret his reply as not being that sort of argument. While not denying guilt or legality of the punishment, the reply may be questioning the consistency of the position of the accusers. If they too are guilty of the same act, then their position is in some sense inconsistent. And that observation is a kind of criticism that appears to have some legitimate force in querying an arguer's position.

David J. Crossley and Peter A. Wilson (1979) divide the ad hominem fallacy into the two traditional categories of circumstantial and abusive. The abusive ad hominem, according to them, "involves personal attacks on an opponent's character, ethnic origins, or other irrelevant features, rather than investigations into and evaluations of the truth and the logical coherence of the argument presented by that person" (p. 42). They note that in the case of the circumstantial ad hominem, argued reasons for a person's proposal may be dismissed on grounds of personal or professional standing. For example, they point out that the position of a local gun club that there should be no restrictions on the sale of firearms should not be rejected simply because this is the type of argument one would expect from gun club members.

A couple of the examples cited are choice specimens of the circumstantial ad hominem. One is a criticism of a woman who is telling other women how to be happy with a housewife's career. It is pointed out that this woman herself is making a vast income on the lecture circuit and as a popular author. According to Crossley and Wilson (p. 44), this criticism is "an illegitimate attack on the person."

Another example mentioned in passing: "Your doctor may
tell you that you are ruining your health by being over-
weight while she herself is obese." Crossley and Wilson
comment that her obesity does not mean that the doctor
cannot correctly comment on her patient's condition (p. 44).
These examples bring out that the circumstantial ad hominem
characteristically involves an ostensible contradiction
between what somebody advocates and how he acts.

FORMAL AND INFORMAL LOGIC

If an argument form is valid, then every argument that has
that form is valid. But if an argument is an instance of
an argument form that is invalid, it does not follow that
the argument is invalid. For example,

   1. If Wellington is the capital of New Zealand,
       Auckland is not.
       Wellington is the capital of New Zealand.
       Auckland is not the capital of New Zealand.

has the form of modus ponens, making it valid. But it
also has the form 'p, q, therefore r' which is not a valid
form of argument. So just because it is an instance of an
invalid form of argument, it does not follow that it is an
invalid argument.

This asymmetry is the basis of the argument of Gerald J.
Massey (1981) that there can be no theory of invalidity
that can provide the basis for a useful theory of fallacies. Massey proposes that a bonafide theory of invalidity
would have to offer a principled account of why an argument
like

   2. If Wellington is the capital of New Zealand,
       Auckland is not.
       Auckland is not the capital of New Zealand.
       Wellington is the capital of New Zealand.

can be shown to be invalid because a valid translation of
it into a logical form that is valid cannot be found,
whereas the same failure for

   3. John took a walk by the river.
       John took a walk.

warrants only suspension of judgment. Intuitively, we
accept 3 as valid even though, excepting certain proposals

made recently by Donald Davidson and Pörn, we have not been able to find a valid argument form of which it is an instance. Whereas with 2, we cannot find a valid argument form of which it is an instance, so we reject it as invalid.

One thing Massey overlooks is that validity is defined for argument forms relative to a given semantical structure. Thus the argument

4. John took a walk.
   John took a walk or bananas are yellow.

is valid in classical logic because of the way validity is defined in classical semantics. However, in a formal structure where validity is defined in a semantics that takes relevance of subject matter into account, as well as truth-values, 4 might well fail to be an instance of any valid form of argument. In other words, by this admittedly pluralistic approach to logical form, just because an argument has a valid form (in some semantics), it need not follow that the argument is in some sense valid, that is, valid in every semantical structure. So validity of arguments is not determined by logical form alone, any more than invalidity is.

Of course validity in a system can be determined by logical form, but that is not to say that validity of an argument (in natural language) is determined by logical form. One also needs the presumption that the structure which is applied to the argument is in some sense the correct or appropriate structure for that argument. But logic has never been an applied (enough) discipline to prove anything like that, at least by any formal method. It is just an assumption that can be defended, or questioned, philosophically.

Massey seems to conclude that since formal logic cannot be applied to fallacies or provide a theory of fallacies, so much the worse for the study of fallacies, a study that probably belongs more properly to psychology than logic anyway.

The force of Massey's criticisms of potential theories of the fallacies stems from the fact that validity, as usually defined, is a positive notion, whereas fallaciousness is a negative one. But is this asymmetry an essential fact about logic? No, it is not. As our subsequent

investigations make clear, analysis of a traditional fallacy turns up correct as well as incorrect patterns of
inference associated with this particular category of
"fallacious" reasoning. So the subject matter of fallacies often begins on a negative note, but requires much
investigation of correct or valid forms of argument as
well. But although the idea of assertion has always been
the theme of logical systems since Gottlob Frege, Jan
Łukasiewicz (1957) introduced a logic based on axioms and
rules for rejected expressions. Thus it is not essential
to logic that a formal system be based on a positive concept of validity.

Łukasiewicz observed that Aristotle proceeds not only by
validating syllogisms by deducing them from other syllogisms accepted as valid, but also by rejecting certain
syllogisms by linking them with others known to be invalid.
Of course, Aristotle most often rejects invalid syllogistic
forms by simple counterexample through concrete instances.
But Łukasiewicz shows that some forms are rejected logically, that is, by basing their rejection on other forms
that are rejected. In fact, he shows that if two particular forms are rejected axiomatically, all the other
invalid syllogistic forms may be rejected by two rules of
rejection (p. 96).

> R1. Rejection by Detachment: if the implication
>   'If $\propto$ then β' is asserted, but the consequent β
>   is rejected, then the antecedent $\propto$ must be
>   rejected.
> R2. Rejection by Substitution: if β is a substitu-
>   tion instance of $\propto$, and β is rejected, then $\propto$
>   must be rejected.

Using this pair of rules as a basis, Jerzy Slupecki,
Grzegorz Bryll, and Urzula Wybraniec-Skardowska (1971)
develop a formal theory of rejected propositions. In
order to develop deductive systems of rejected propositions, they construct a meta-language in which decidabil-
ity, consistency, and completeness are defined in a new
way appropriate to the idea of the demolition of propositions. These developments suggest that the negative
notion of anticonsequence is just as open to formal treatment as the more familiar concept of (positive) implication.

What is the lesson of formal systems of rejection for
fallacy theory? How significant is Massey's criticism

that invalidity cannot be demonstrated in the usual (asser-
tional) formal systems? The lesson is that the positive
orientation of the usual formal logics is no obstacle to
the study of fallacies as a logical discipline. If we want
to stick to the negative element implicit in the notion of
fallacy, we can indeed proceed by Łukasiewicz's method of
linking invalid forms of argument by proofs of rejection.
Formally, as the development of Łukasiewicz's ideas have
shown, there is no obstacle to constructing axiomatic
systems of rejection. However, while this technique may
turn out to be very useful for the systematic study of
fallacies, it is not always required, since it turns out
that the analysis of fallacies tends to require positive
forms of argument as much as negative.

These lessons are vividly brought out by our subsequent
investigations here of the ad hominem fallacy. Without
further theoretical disquisitions, it is better to get on
with the particular study. While it is useful to ask
questions about fallacy theory, it is still better to build
up that theory by looking at the requirements that arise
out of determined attempts to give analyses of particular
fallacies. For ultimately, the reason why fallacies are
so important as objects of study is that they represent
practical errors of argument that really do bridge the gap
between logic as a theory of formal inference and logic as
a tool to clarify argumentation and reasoning wherever it
takes place. The major fallacies, the petitio, the ad
verecundiam, and so forth, represent targets for analysis
that have been acknowledged since ancient times as significant phenomena for analysis of argumentation.

While Massey castigates the study of fallacies for lacking
a theory, Maurice A. Finocchiaro (1981) criticizes the
textbook treatments for being not practical or reality-
oriented enough, and for lacking "actual examples" (p. 18).
Indeed, according to Finocchiaro, the superficiality of the
usual accounts is itself a fallacy "analogous to the inconsistency between what one preaches and what one practices
. . ." (p. 18). This is a good point--more realistic case
studies of the fallacies are clearly a first step towards
their serious study. On the other hand, Finocchiaro's
insistence on "actual examples" can lead to absurdities if
carried too far. The fact that Fred Smith enunciated this
particular argument on October 4, 1980, in Crystal Falls
at the pub at 7:38 P.M. does not somehow magically escalate
it above a fabricated argument that might illustrate the
same point as well or better. Because Fred said it, the

argument does not thereby qualify as a proper object for
logic to study. Despite what Finocchiaro seems to suggest,
actuality is not a sine qua non of the worthwhile fallacy--
instance. Rather, the sample should be realistic enough to
bring out why the mistake is significant as a fault of
argument. Thus case studies of actual dialogues or written
arguments should be encouraged and, as we will see in this
study, are very useful. Idealized dialogues however will
also be used where they bring out, or bear resemblance to,
features of interest in ordinary reasoning.

This bifurcation in the formal versus the informal approaches
to logic has resulted in some truly amazing anomalies in the
core subject matter of both fields. One example is this.
Many of the traditional informal fallacies are thought to
be informal because they are failures of "relevance" in some
elusive sense. On the other hand, there is a whole special-
ized branch of formal logic called relevance logic. Relevance logic has been highly developed and intensively
investigated as a purely formal discipline. Its main problem is that it appears to be foundering for the lack of
some clear practical notion of what relevance is in argument.
I would suggest that the duality of this situation is very
strange. We have a practical problem of clarifying with
some analytical precision what relevance means in ordinary
arguments. And we have the problem of finding some worthwhile applications for a class of formal logics that were
designed with some philosophical notion of relevance of
argument in mind. Why has it occurred to nobody to see the
two problems as part of one single problem? Gary Iseminger
(1980) was virtually the first person to even suggest that
relevance logics could possibly find some practical applications in the traditional ad populum (appeal to popular
sentiment), ad baculum, and other informal fallacies of
relevance.

It is true that Alan R. Anderson and Nuel D. Belnap, Jr.
(1975) distinguish a number of "fallacies of relevance,"
for example, if q is true then 'if p then q' is true for
any unrelated p and q you care to choose (interpreting
'if p then q' as the classical material conditional). But
how this "formal fallacy" is related to the kind of failure
of relevance that is characteristic of an ad baculum or
some other kind of practically significant fallacy of
realistic argumentation is a question that they do not
ever address.

In a mathematics course, it may be quite reasonable to
define stipulatively 'if p then q' for various purposes

as meaning 'it is not the case that p is true and q is
false.' For, as a mathematician might put it: "The
question of the real meaning of 'if p then q' is something we will not take up here." However in a course of
logic taught by the philosophy department, where part of
the objective is to teach students how to evaluate arguments critically, such a response would be an evasion.
And students would be all too likely to sense that evasion.
How well known it is that persuading students at the
elementary level of the reasonableness of the truth-
functional definition of the conditional is a losing
battle. They know it is not reasonable, and nothing you
can say is very likely to persuade them that it is not a
trick.

But then what happens when we come to the section of the
course on informal fallacies, and the students are informed
that certain arguments are bad--like the ignoratio elenchi
(misconception of refutation)--because the premisses are,
in some way, not related to, or disjointed from, the conclusion to be proved. In the previous section of the
course, the part on formal logic, we just told them that
it does not matter whether p and q are in any way related
for the conditional to be true. There the implication
held provided only that you never went from a true p to a
false q, never mind whether they might be completely
unrelated to each other. Earlier, we were told that we
were not to worry about what 'if p then q' really means.
Now we are told that if p is not connected to q in some
appropriate way, the argument is incorrect or fallacious.
Is this equivocation going to give anyone the idea that
there is some sort of coherent or unified field or discipline here that one is to take seriously as an academic
subject? Not likely. Some plumbing of the connections
between formal logic and the so-called informal fallacies
is necessary if logic is to be a coherent discipline.

FALLACY THEORY

What Massey overlooks is that investigations of the fallacies show that a given "fallacy" turns out to have
correct as well as incorrect instances. Sometimes arguments from parts to wholes, and conversely, are incorrect.
But sometimes they are quite correct. So the job of an
analysis of the fallacies of composition and division--
see Woods and Walton (1977c)--is to sort out the correct
from the fallacious. Similarly, sometimes an argument

that goes in a circle in quite nonfallacious, such as an
equivalence proof in mathematical reasoning. On other
occasions circular argument can be fallacious, for example,
if the proof is presumed to be one-directional only as a
condition of the exercise. So what appears to be a
petitio principii can be sometimes a correct type of argument, even though under other circumstances circularity of
argument is rightly condemned as fallacious. The job of
the analysis of petitio then is to sort out these two sets
of circumstances in a general way--see Woods and Walton
(1975; 1977d; 1979a; 1982a; and 1982c). Thus the job of
the investigation of fallacies concerns valid arguments
just as much as invalid arguments.

Why then the emphasis on the negative? Why is it the
study of fallacies, sophisms, and so on that have dominated tradition, rather than the study of nonfallacious
arguments that seem invalid but are really valid? One
factor is that the stress on taking the invalid as valid
is the more worrisome error in much workaday reasoning.
So perhaps the stress on the negative is merely a way of
bringing out the practical emphasis on common and widely
operative types of argumentation that have always been
characteristic of the area of informal fallacies and
sophistical refutations. This area has always been closer
to rhetoric, disputation, debate, and reasoning in natural
language than other branches of logic. Hence it is
natural that it be more tuned in to what seems valid
psychologically, but is not. The psychological element
is not essential to the normative analysis of whether a
given argument is really fallacious or not. It merely
makes a nod towards psychology in order to concede that
this area of logic is supposed to be more applied to the
study of the correctness or incorrectness of arguments--
and not just their forms--than other branches of logic.

But a profound question is raised by these speculations.
If semantical structures and their axiomatizations do not
determine whether an argument, say, in a natural language,
is correct or incorrect per se, how can we ever know that
an argument is correct (incorrect)? In other words, how
is applied logic possible?

Asking this question presupposes that there is some relationship between a logical system with its semantical
conception of validity and some informal arguments or
fallacies that are external to the formal system. Pluralism
in logic is the position that there is more than one correct

system of logic, <u>correct</u> meaning that a system corresponds or bears some relationship to some informal arguments. It is quite unclear however what "corresponds" or "relationship" should mean in this context.

A natural proposal is that an analysis of each informal fallacy gives an informal subject matter against which the adequacy of a given formal system to model this subject matter can be comparatively assessed. For example, classical logic is a relatively incorrect or bad model of the <u>petitio principii</u>. For example, 'p, therefore p' is valid in classical logic--and rightly so, for we can hardly go from truth to falsity if we don't "go anywhere." A better model of circular reasoning--or so it could be argued, as in Woods and Walton (1978a)--would emphasize the directionality of groundedness. That is, if **p** is grounded on **q**, in a sense meant to exclude circular justification, then q cannot be grounded on p.

The particular system we shall propose in this paper as a best candidate for a formalization appropriate to the circumstantial <u>ad hominem</u> is a fragment of classical logic. The position we <u>will take</u> is that classical logic is correct, but it is too coarse as a model of <u>ad hominem</u> reasoning that is very illuminating. We propose as a better application a formalism that requires for p to imply q that the truth-values can be as in classical logic, but that also requires that p and q be related. What we mean by 'related' is given semantically by certain conditions we impose on a relation, r, to be added to the usual truth-valuation, v, for classical propositional calculus. This relation can be defined semantically in different ways, resulting in different logics--see Richard L. Epstein (1979 and 1981). But for purposes of applying r to the practicalities of the circumstantial <u>ad hominem</u> we think of r as meaning "approximately spatio-temporally coincident in an act-sequence." This particular interpretation is a pragmatic one, for space-time relatedness is not usually associated with logic at all. We argue that this logic is the most correct or at any rate best applicable to <u>ad hominem</u> reasoning of all the available candidates.

Some might say that if that is the best we can do, there is no logic to the <u>ad hominem</u> at all. It is a purely informal business, and therefore, some would even say, not a matter of logic at all. Its subject matter, it might be argued, is not logical, but perhaps physical, rhetorical, or pragmatic in some sense.

In fact we shall try to press the study of ad hominem as
a test case for the applied logic of the fallacies. We
show that ad hominem can be defined narrowly with some
success, but that if the traditional conception of the
ad hominem is to be more fully realized as a target
analysandum, we have to adopt a more adventurous formalization that raises many questions about the project of
applied logic. Finally, we go on to argue that if the
analysis is to be fully applied, in keeping with the
demands of the traditional conception, we are eventually
driven beyond logic altogether to factors pertaining to
rhetoric of the audience and interpretation of what a
speaker or writer might have meant as his argument. The
question at this point is not directly whether the argument is correct, but rather more as a preliminary we have
to try to determine what is meant to be the argument. It
eventually becomes clear at this point that we have gone
deeply into pragmatics even beyond practical logic and
into speech-act analysis.

But in the middle areas of our analysis of the ad hominem
there are questions of to what extent formal logics are
applicable to the fallacies. To use the Kantian turn of
phrase, we are asking whether applied logic is possible.
It must remain an open question, but I hope to have pushed
the analysis of ad hominem far enough to sharpen it.

According to the positive theory of fallacies adumbrated
by Massey (1981), a theory of fallacies needs to take into
account the rule repertoire of an arguer, that is, a set
of rules accepted by this individual. Some of these rules
may be formally invalid in a given repertoire. However,
since more than one sequence of rules might yield the same
argument, it will not do to say that an argument is fallacious as proposed by a particular argument simply because
it could be generated by a sequence utilizing an invalid
rule. For the same argument could also be generated by
another sequence of rules that yield the same argument.
That is, typically an arguer's repertoire might contain
several inferential routes to the same argument. Massey
proposes that the fallacy is the invalid rule that is used
in the simplest and most direct route to the given argument.

I would like to remark, however, that this approach to
fallacies, while suggestive, is too limited to be very
helpful, as can be seen by the example of the fallacy of
petitio principii. If a starts with a set of rules and
premisses, and can deduce by various sequences of demon-
strations that some conclusion C follows from this set,

there may be several distinct sequences or routes that a may take. Suppose some of these routes are cycles, that is, suppose some sequences but not all take us not only from some premiss-set to C, but also back from C to one or more of the premisses from this set. When can a be justifiably said to have committed the petitio principii fallacy?

Massey, in line with his theory of fallacies, would seem to be committed to ruling that a commits petitio if and only if the simplest and most direct route from the premiss-set to C takes us back by the rules to some member of that premiss-set. It has been remarked in Lynn M. Batten and Douglas N. Walton (1979) and Walton (1980d), however, that there might be nothing fallacious about such a cyclical inference route per se. Rather, a better characterization of the petitio fallacy is to rule that a commits a petitio if and only if every route from the given premiss-set to C takes us back by the rules to some member of that premiss-set. Our reasons for preferring this definition of the fallacy is that arguers are not always committed to the simplest and most direct route of inference, and the existence of such a cyclical route is harmless provided a noncircular one is available to the arguer. In fact many cyclical routes of proof, such as equivalence proofs, are quite benign. The problem is to sort out the vicious cycles from the benign.

Not wishing to dwell on the petitio, we merely wish to make the point that theories of fallaciousness are best propounded in relation to studies of the particular informal fallacies themselves. Each fallacy, at least of the major ones catalogued by Hamblin (1970a), must be looked at in its own right as a particular guidepost towards the eventual construction of fallacy theory. We hope the study of the ad hominem pursued here will be a help in this overall quest for theory.

MODELS OF ARGUMENT

Certainly any particular attempt to study or analyze an informal fallacy must take as a starting point Hamblin's discussion of the concept of argument in his chapter 7 of Fallacies (1970a). Among the points Hamblin makes are these.

    1.   An argument is more than just any arbitrarily designated set of propositions, for there are

        sets of propositions--'p, moreover q'--that are
        not arguments (p. 229).

2.   The commonplace assumption that an argument can
        be broken down into a one-step sequence of pre-
        misses and conclusion may be an oversimplifica-
        tion for some studies of fallacies. For example,
        petitio principii may be misrepresented if we
        overlook the idea that an argument has a "thread"
        involving a sequence of intermediate statements
        (p. 229).

3.   Not all arguments are deductive arguments (p. 230).

4.   An argument is perfectly good provided that it does
        not allow us to go from true premisses to a false
        conclusion (p. 232).[8]

These sorts of musings lead Hamblin on to ask, Just what
then is an argument? He first formulates what he calls the
alethic model of argument, which has four requirements:
(1) the premisses must be true;   (2) the premisses must
imply the conclusion;   (3) the conclusion must follow
reasonably immediately;   (4) if some of the premisses are
unstated they must be of a specified omissible kind. This
model, according to Hamblin, sets a certain standard of
worth for pure logic, but a logic of practice should also
allow an epistemic model of argument, which has the following as requirements: (1) the premisses must be known to
be true;   (2) the conclusion must follow clearly from the
premisses;   (3) premisses that are not stated must be such
that they may be taken for granted;   (4) the conclusion
must be such that, in the absence of argument, it would be
in doubt. This model of argument seems appropriate if
epistemic fallacies like the ad ignorantiam (argument from
ignorance) and petitio principii are to be amenable to
analysis.

The problem with applying these two models to many of the
fallacies, however, is that they are too strong, for many
arguments proceed on the basis of propositions that are
accepted, but not known to be true. But, asks Hamblin,
is adopting this model of argument a "lowering of one's
sights" as the pure logician may feel? No, he responds,
because one of the purposes of argument is to convince,
and our criteria should say something about this aspect
of argument. How if I wish to convince you of B, and you
accept A and 'A therefore B,' I can use these two premisses
to try to get you to accept B, regardless of whether or not
I myself accept A or B. The argument 'A, and A therefore B'
may be quite a good argument from your point of view if you

accept both these premisses but were not initially ready
to accept the conclusion. And at any rate, if I want to
win the argument, I'll have to start from something you
accept. Hence Hamblin, like Aristotle, feels that there
is a place for a third model of argument called the
dialectical model, with analogous requirements to the
epistemic model except that 'is accepted to be true' is
put in place of 'is known to be true.'

Having proposed these three models of argument, Hamblin
is in something of a pluralistic embarras de richesse.
An argument can be correct from one point of view yet
incorrect in relation to another model of argument.
Another problem is that very little has been definitely
established about the second and third models as regards
their precise logical properties, indeed to the extent
that formal logicians could be very suspicious about them.
How can we proceed to study the fallacies in light of these
problems?

The method Hamblin by and large pursues is to construct
rules and formalisms for dialectical argument that are
essentially game-theoretic in nature. Within this game-
style formulation of rules for the organization of commitments and permissible moves and locutions in dialectical
argument, Hamblin (1970a, chapter 8) utilizes classical
deductive propositional calculus as a basic core language.

Thus we appear to be offered a choice in studying criticisms, fallacies, and other problems of applied logic. We
can focus on the set of propositions that make up the argument, and study the propositional logic of this sort. This
way of approaching the ad hominem fallacy would be to start
from the inside. We could study the logic of inconsistency
involved in disputes about circumstantial ad hominem criticisms. In fact, in the account given in this book, we do
exactly that, arguing that the appropriate propositional
logic is a logic weaker than classical logic. The other
option is to focus on the aspects of ad hominem argument
extrinsic to the propositional logic. This program is the
one Grice (1975) has opted for, and its object is to study
the "conversational trimmings" of basic propositional
inferences. By this approach, rules like "Be Relevant!"
are imposed from outside the logic of propositions. Hamblin
too has adopted this approach of starting from the outside
and working in.

I think Hamblin is basically on the right track, at least
in his general directions and methodology, and in this

analysis to follow, we will follow his sort of program in
general outline. Hamblin's games of dialogue are procedural structures that can be used to model the conversational context of an argument. We will consider the pros
and cons of alternative games of dialogue and eventually
settle on one basic structure that behaves something like
a Hamblin game of dialectic except that, among other
features, it will incorporate as its core logic a nonclassical propositional calculus. In this respect, we will work
from the inside outwards. Yet in generally adopting
Hamblin's framework of considering rules of dialectic as
guidelines of fair argumentation external to a particular
canon of valid argument (like classical logic) in the core
of the game of dialectic, we will also work from the outside inwards. In short, I will work in both directions at
once.

This program for the analysis of ad hominem argumentation
will entail some radical revisions of our concepts of argument and fallacy. The term 'fallacy' will turn out to be
a misnomer, to some extent, because ad hominem criticisms
will sometimes turn out to be fair and reasonable. The
"fallacy" will turn out to be not always fallacious. An
argument will be construed as a set of propositions, as
the textbooks so often state. But that necessary condition does not, by itself, fully characterize the nature of
argument. For an argument should be defined as a claim or
move advanced by a participant, as part of a regulated
procedure, towards the position of another participant in
that same procedure. The procedure in question should be
a game of dialogue with agreed upon rules. The study of
fair and reasonable rules for games of dialogue is what we
will consider to be external part of an argument. Without
studying this external aspect of argument, the inner propositional core of an argument would reveal precious little
of the strategies of move and counter-move so crucial to
the proper study of ad hominem criticisms and refutations.

Like Hamblin, we will accentuate the positive by studying
correct as well as fallacious sequences of reasoning in
dialectical interchanges. The model of argument we will
put forward to study the ad hominem fallacy will therefore
postulate valid (correct) forms of argument, and not be
exclusively negative in its intent, as Massey seems to
think a theory of fallacies has to be.

Perhaps the single most unusual feature of our treatment
will be that partly formalized models will be evaluated
against case studies of actual or, in some cases, more-or-

less realistic sequences of argumentation in natural language. That means of course that the formalisms we will
study will be inadequate for purposes of application to
these case studies in certain ways. Not least, therefore,
we must look at the divergencies between our models and
what it is they purport to model.

Our conclusions will not be the final word on the ad
hominem fallacy. By attempting a rapprochement between
informal case studies and formal models, we nevertheless
hope to make the options for further study clearer. This
pragmatic approach to the subject will lead us towards the
conclusion that ad hominem arguments should most often
realistically be treated more like criticisms than fallacies. The term "fallacy" is a strong form of condemnation
of an argument, implying that the argument is refuted, that
it is deceitful, or that it is badly wrong to the point
where it cannot be repaired. However, many of the traditional "fallacies" are not like that at all, when seen in
a more realistic context. They are more like criticisms
that question some aspect of an argument. In alleging a
"fallacy," the critic is questioning or challenging some
aspect of the argument, and the proponent of the argument
may very often come up with a reasonable reply to the
criticism. Such a reply often serves to partially defend
the original argument against the criticism that has been
advanced by the other party to the argument.

Certainly this more dynamic and dialectical context of
reasonably justifiable or unreasonably aggressive criticisms advanced against an arguer's position more truly
models the real cases of ad hominem argumentation we will
study in the sequel. Hence it may already be helpful to
orient the reader if we suggest at this point that the
term "informal fallacies" might better be rephrased, in
many cases, as "criticisms in reasonable dialogue." It
may be time to recognize that the term "fallacy" is unduly
dramatic. A more sober and mature approach to the study
of the reasonableness of argumentative moves in dialogue
suggests that we try to offer guidelines for distinguishing between justifiable ad hominem criticisms of an argument and unjustifiable ad hominem criticisms. It is not
that the term "fallacy" is always inappropriate, but in
many cases the hasty use of this term turns out to be an
exaggeration.

NOTES

1. H. P. Grice, "Logic and Conversation," in The Logic of Grammar, ed. Donald Davidson and Gilbert Harman, 64-74 (Encino, Calif.: Dickenson, 1975).

2. Jaakko Hintikka, Knowledge and Belief (Ithaca, N.Y.: Cornell University Press, 1962).

3. Saul Kripke, "Semantical Analysis of Intuitionistic Logic I," in Formal Systems and Recursive Functions, ed. J. N. Crossley and M. A. E. Dummett, 92-130 (Amsterdam: North-Holland, 1965).

4. Engel is not exactly stating in this quotation that all ad hominem arguments are fallacious. But he comes close to it, and suggests that thesis by his remark. He hedges his bets by saying that all fallacies of personal attack are "irrelevant." It is certainly safe enough to hazard the "thesis" that if something is a fallacious personal attack it can be dismissed as, in some sense, irrelevant. But, I think, what the reader is encouraged to conclude is that all personal attacks (ad hominem arguments) are irrelevant and therefore fallacious. This thesis really has some bite. I would like to thank Nira Dookeran for drawing this passage of Engel to my attention.

5. Ronald Munson, The Way of Words (Atlanta: Houghton Mifflin Co., 1976).

6. Stephen Toulmin, Richard Rieke, and Allan Janik, An Introduction to Reasoning (New York: MacMillan, 1979).

7. I would like to thank Kent Strang for this example.

8. What Hamblin specifically questions (p. 232) are the two assumptions (a) that a valid argument, even one that has false premisses and a false conclusion, should always be called a good argument, and (b) that if a good argument has true premisses and a satisfactory inference-process, it must have a true conclusion.

2

What Is Fallacious about the *Ad Hominem*?

The traditional informal fallacy of the argumentum ad hominem is standardly described as the fallacy committed when an arguer attempts to refute an opponent's argument by attacking that particular opponent's personal characteristics or circumstances. Certainly attacking somebody on the basis of their personal circumstances can be discriminatory, rude, libellous, or downright curmudgeonly. But it is not immediately obvious that it need be fallacious. Sometimes personal characteristics or circumstances may be quite appropriately and nonfallaciously taken into account in the assessment of arguments. Your previous arrest record for grand larceny might be quite an appropriate circumstantial factor for us to take into account in evaluating your suitability for the position of a judge on the Supreme Court, for example.

Moreover, an outrageously vehement personal attack, culpable as it may be, could be nonfallacious on the grounds that it is not even an argument--that is, a clearly identifiable set of propositions. An argument, whatever else it might be--see Hamblin (1970a, chapter 10) --should minimally consist of an identifiable set of propositions.

These questions concerning precisely what is fallacious about the traditional ad hominem fallacy are shared by the traditional accounts of several other fallacies as well. The ad baculum, ad misericordiam and ad populum appear to fall into a particular pattern or class of fallacies. They are all emotional or personal appeals that somehow function as a distraction or irrelevance from the argument at issue. What appears to go wrong is that the personal individualities of particular disputants somehow illegitimately get bound up in the argument. Take the ad populum, for example.

RELATED FALLACIES

The traditional informal fallacy of argumentum ad populum is standardly characterized as the fallacy committed by directing an emotional appeal to the feelings or enthusiasms of "the gallery" or "the people" to win assent to an argument not adequately supported by proper evidence.

What is thereby characterized certainly finds the mark in
pointing up a widespread ethical deficiency of advertising
practices and a quotidian rhetorical shortcoming familiar
in many aspects of public affairs.   But is it a fallacy?
Specifically what is wrong, as a deficiency of correct
argument, with appealing to popular enthusiasm?   And if
this appeal can be a fallacy, exactly what manner of argument is it that is thought to be incorrect?   In other
words, exactly what is meant in this context by the phrase
"not adequately supported by proper evidence"?   These are
hard questions, but they need to be asked.

We are told by a certain hamburger chain that not buying
their product is virtually an affront to patriotic clean
living, cheerful industrious dedication, and happy family
togetherness.   Wouldn't it be better if this commercial
time were allocated to giving rational evidence that the
food they sell is a good value or has arguable nutritional
advantages?   We are told by an oil company that nature is
beautiful.   Wouldn't it be better if this time were used
to offer some rational assurance that this company is not
destroying nature, or is at least contributing in some way
to the quality of our lives?   If so, then the question
should be asked whether a fallacy has been committed, that
is, whether there is an incorrect argument or whether the
deficiency is a breach of advertising ethics or is some
impropriety other than a failure of correct argument.   But
if the alleged inadequacy is in the argument itself, in
its very logic, then our second question must be addressed.
What precisely is the error?   Is it an identifiable fallacy
that admits of analysis and the determination of rational
guidelines for adjudication?

These questions are worth asking not only because of the
widespread seriousness of the ad populum and related as
mischievous fallacies in practices of the manipulation of
public opinion, but because there is a positive and constructive need to understand the fallacies, how they work,
and when and why they are wrong.   A faith in the power of
argument as an ally of truth and correct argument is the
mainstay of our democratic political institutions and our
adversary legal system.   But in order to understand argument there is the scholarly requirement to bring some
order to the study of the informal fallacies as a coherent
discipline of logic and philosophy.

It is easy to suggest that emotion has no place in logic,
and too often the Standard Treatment of these fallacies

goes little beyond this suggestion in the direction of
venturing a serious analysis of how to sort out the correct from the fallacious. One problem is that many
appeals to emotion are perfectly reasonable, or at least
are not fallacious in any obvious way. Consider the ad
misericordiam. Are there not situations where pity is
legitimate as a factor to be considered in arriving at a
decision on a course of action?

For example, a nine-year-old girl is dying of leukemia.
The doctor knows that she is very near to death and that
there is no hope for her. She is very anemic and pale.
She has been coming into the hospital regularly for transfusions of blood products. She hates the transfusions and
always cries and has to be comforted by her mother when
she has to undergo them. Finally, she refuses to take
another transfusion. Her mother brings her in to hospital
to see if the doctor can persuade her to take another
transfusion.

The doctor tells the mother that if the little girl does
not have another transfusion she will bleed to death at
home in a day or two through massive internal bleeding.
If she takes the transfusion, she will probably live
longer, but certainly will die anyway before too long.
The little girl is adamant. She looks terribly upset,
frightened, and miserable. She does not want the transfusion. She puts her small, pale hand in her mother's
hand. Her mother is crying. What should the doctor do?

Does the doctor commit an ad misericordiam if he takes
his feelings of pity for the little girl into account in
deciding what he will recommend to her mother? I do not
think so.

If such emotional appeals are not always wrong or misguided, we are left with the problem of deciding just when
the alleged fallacy occurs. Kielkopf (1980) reminds us
that too often students are encouraged to acquiesce in the
superficialities of the Standard Treatment by alleging ad
misericordiam or ad populum as soon as any appeal is made
to pity or popular piety, fallacious or not.

Yet students do often perceive a need to understand the
fallacies, but as Hamblin (1970a) has pointed out, the
Standard Treatment largely fails to offer adequate theory
to aid us in classifying putatively fallacious arguments
into correct and incorrect cases. Too often, a putative

fallacy like the ad verecundiam turns out to have instances
that seem to be correct after all, even if the precise
model of argument turns out to be elusive. Yet as John
Woods and I have argued (1974; 1976b), a fallacy, if it is
to command our interest as an incorrect argument, must be
more than a mere behavioral aberration or a shortcoming of
persuasiveness, manners, or morals. It must be a wrong
argument.

A main problem is that once it is perceived that the model
of argument involved in an informal fallacy is not that of
classical first-order logic, the move is either to dismiss
the study of the fallacy as of no interest to the proper
subject of logic or to insist that "informality" must
signal the complete inappropriateness of any structured
decision mechanisms of any "formal" sort. Hence we have
the stultifying bifurcation between formal logic and the
study of informal fallacies that has resulted in the
Standard Treatment.

In this monograph we will try to indicate how that impasse
should be overcome in the case of the ad hominem, by
arguing that formal mechanisms are involved, but that the
logic involved is not standard, and that the role of extra-
logical components must also be brought in and integrated
with the formal elements. Thus it will be shown that what
informality is involved need not require the entire avoidance of logical structures; quite to the contrary. But
the structures involved will not be those of classical
logic.

ARGUMENTS DIRECTED TO SPECIFIC RECIPIENTS

Perhaps what initially seems most wrong or fallacious
about the use of the fallacies ad is that such an argument
is directed to a specific group of actual persons rather
than being an attempt to argue from true premisses. In
arguing ad populum, when one selects premisses, it matters
little whether the premisses are true. The question is
rather one of whether these premisses are plausible and
will be accepted--if possible, enthusiastically--by the
audience that is being confronted. The fallacy here would
be that of throwing concern for the truth aside in favor
of an outright partisan process of trying to convince by
utilizing whatever assumptions, no matter how outrageous,
that one's target audience seems prepared to tolerate.
What seems wrong is that one's argument is allowed to be

subjectively oriented, person-relative, and therefore it
subverts the objective goal of arriving at the truth by
the process of logical reasoning.

In this connection there seems a clear parallel between
the ad populum and the ad hominem. The main difference
is that whereas the ad populum is directed toward the
group, the ad hominem is directed toward one individual.
Of course there is a difference of orientation in that the
ad hominem is negative in its intent to discredit the
individual, whereas the ad populum is positive in its
intent to win the approval of the group. But the subjective element is common to both.

However, the above explanation of what is fallacious about
the ad hominem and ad populum is incorrect, insofar as it
rests on the assumption that the only worthwhile and
legitimate function of argument is to reason from true
premises--that is, to produce sound arguments. A properly broad and dialectical perspective on the concept of
argument and its uses adequate to the study of the fallacies should include argument from premises that may or
may not be true. Can we not argue, for example, from an
opponent's premises, demonstrating that they imply a
falsehood, in order to demonstrate to that person that
one of his premises must be false? Do we not often, in
numerous legitimate contexts of argumentation, work from
premises of uncertain truth value in order to see if
their logical consequences may better enable us to assess
their truth or falsity? If so, it is hard to see what is
wrong in arguing from a set of assumptions that are
accepted by an individual or group, but are not known by
the arguer to be true. I am, of course, referring to the
function of argument called by Aristotle dialectical. As
the philosopher characterizes this notion at the very
beginning of the Prior Analytics, a demonstrative premiss
is one that is simply laid down by the demonstrator at
the outset, whereas a dialectical premiss is one that the
arguer's opponent is prepared to admit at the outset.

What, then, is fallacious about a dialectical argument?
Nothing, per se, we think, though of course dialectical
argument, like any form of argument, is something that
can be abused. So far, however, it is not clear how
either the ad hominem or the ad populum can be located as
a specific and identifiable abuse or fallacy.

To understand the dialectical function of argument we need

to look at real argumentation. Often when we want to
counter-argue against someone's argument, we may lack new
premises, new data to support our side of the argument.
It may be the best we can do, in a situation of this sort,
is to try to refute or undermine or challenge our adversary's initial premises. This form of dialectical challenge functions by challenging or criticizing the adversary's position. Ad hominem criticism is often of this
sort.

Consider as a realistic example the following exchange
recorded in a dialogue from Hansard (Canada: House of
Commons Debates, vol. 59, March 28, 1984, pp. 2510-2511).
The topic is employment and, in particular, a request for
additional funds to create jobs for youth.1

Hon. Roch La Salle (Joliette): Thank you, Mr. Speaker.
        My question is for the Minister of Finance.
        Yesterday, the Minister said that his Budget
        included a proposal to set aside $1.3 billion
        for job creation initiatives intended for young
        Canadians. The Minister is certainly aware
        that under the Canada Works Program, the budget
        for summer jobs for students is providing enough
        funds for only one-third of the projects sub-
        mitted. In view of that, the Minister will cer-
        tainly understand the relevance of my question.
        I would like to ask him whether he intends to
        double this budget so that at least 66 per cent
        of the projects submitted may be approved to
        help young Canadian students.
Hon. Marc Lalonde (Minister of Finance): Mr. Speaker, I
        am sorry that the Hon. Member's Leader has
        decided to leave after his short five-minute
        weekly visit to the House. I would have liked
        him to hear the question asked by the Hon. Member
        and my reply. In any case, I would like to
        inform the Hon. Member that I have added $150
        million to the budget allocated to young people
        under this program. This will bring up to $1.3
        billion the amount set aside to provide assist-
        ance to unemployed young Canadians. These funds
        will be distributed by the Cabinet Committee in
        charge of social affairs, with particular atten-
        tion being given of course to the recommendations
        received from the Minister for Youth and the
        Minister of Employment and Immigration. As soon
        as these decisions are made by the Cabinet

Committee, I am certain that the Ministers will
inform the Hon. Member and the public.

Hon. Roch La Salle (Joliette): Mr. Speaker, the Minister
of Finance will admit that it may be somewhat
difficult to direct questions to the Minister of
Employment in view of his current ambitions.
However, I think that the Minister of Finance is
familiar with the question I want to ask him
today. He certainly knows that the budget available to create jobs for students is definitely
inadequate.

Hon. Marc Lalonde (Minister of Finance): Mr. Speaker, the
Hon. Member is well aware that it is never possible to approve all the applications submitted
by those who would like to help to reduce unem-
ployment in Canada. However, I appreciate his
party's and his own belated interest in issues
which concern young people considering that the
position of the Progressive Conservative Party
has always been to cut back on social programs.
When they were in power for a short stint in
1980, the first thing they did was to abolish the
job creation programs designed to help the unemployed throughout the country, including those
intended for unemployed young people. Even
today, all we hear them say is that we must
reduce our expenditures and the deficit, but at
the same time, they rise in the House to ask us
to double our funding.

Mr. La Salle: Do you want to do anything about it or not?
That is the question.

Mr. Lalonde: I think that the Hon. Member should recommend to his colleagues that they put a stop to
their hypocrisy and make up their minds on this
issue.

Mr. La Salle: It would be indecent if you were not to do
anything!

Mr. Lalonde: Either they seriously want to help the unemployed as we do

Mr. La Salle: If you do not want to do anything, it is
ridiculous then!

Mr. Lalonde: or else they want to mislead the population
as they are trying to do.

Study of the argument posed by this real sequence of
dialogue in parliamentary debate involves looking at the
whole network of questions and answers. Mr. Lalonde's
reply to the question is dialectical in the sense that it

challenges Mr. La Salle's position in relation to the
question. The problem of ad hominem analysis is to give
good reasons for deciding whether such a response is
fallacious or reasonable in a given case.

The first point to be made is that the question asked by
Mr. La Salle can be questioned as a reasonable one. Mr.
La Salle asks whether Mr. Lalonde intends to double his
budget so that at least 66 per cent of projects may be
approved to help young Canadian students. This is a
complex question. If Mr. Lalonde says "no," it could be
taken to mean that he does not intend to help young
Canadian students.

He answers that he has increased the budget, but does not
say, in direct answer to the question, whether he has
doubled the budget by that increase. This is a shift in
answering, but given the aggressiveness and complexity of
the question, we might not want to say the answer is
unfairly evasive.

At any rate, having answered the question, Mr. Lalonde
then goes on--the face of Mr. La Salle's repeated insistence on this line of questioning--to attack Mr. La Salle's
question by means of an ad hominem argument. Mr. Lalonde
replies that the Conservative Party, which Mr. La Salle
represents, cut funds for social programs when they were
in power--including job programs for young people. Here
then we have a classical tu quoque form of the ad hominem
rejoinder. Mr. Lalonde is arguing that the Conservative
Party's past actions and traditional position are in
direct conflict with what Mr. La Salle (a Conservative
Party member) is now pushing for. It is a classical ad
hominem allegation of inconsistency of position. Here,
Mr. Lalonde is arguing dialectically by challenging Mr.
La Salle's own presumptions or premises, and thereby
Mr. Lalonde moves to refute Mr. La Salle's argument
implicit in the latter's line of attack.

The problem for us is to try to work towards some basis
for enabling us to evaluate whether an ad hominem
response, like this of Mr. Lalonde's, is fallacious or
not. In this case, Mr. Lalonde's reply could certainly
be defended, if in fact he is right about the Conservative
position as based on their past legislative record.

Our point for the present, however, is that Mr. Lalonde's
reply has to be evaluated in dialectical context. If it

were fairly taken to be an attempt to evade answering Mr.
La Salle's question, we could have some basis for calling
it a fallacy. However, Mr. Lalonde did give an answer to
the question prior to launching his ad hominem rebuttal.
Presuming the relative nonfallaciousness of the sequence
to the point of the rebuttal, what should we say of the
ad hominem rebuttal itself?

One approach is to claim that Mr. Lalonde's ad hominem
criticism successfully points out a circumstantial weakness in Mr. La Salle's argument. That is, Mr. Lalonde
has successfully challenged Mr. La Salle's line of questioning in light of the assumptions that the latter brings
to the argument as a member of the Conservative Party. Is
it right then to attack an argument on the basis of its
proponent's party affiliations? To some, such a type of
argument may seem questionable. And perhaps it should be
questionable in some circumstances. But here, we need to
appreciate that if dialectical arguments per se can be
reasonable and nonfallacious, then attacking the premisses
that an arguer is prepared to concede at the outset of
argument may be a legitimate and reasonable form of criticism.

The problem posed for this book, then, is the following.
If the ad hominem criticism can sometimes be a reasonable
form of rejoinder in the context of dialectical argument
and realistic dialogue, under what conditions does it
become a fallacy?

Ad hominem, like its partners in crime, ad misericordiam,
ad populum and ad baculum, is often, perhaps usually,
characterized as a fallacy that is essentially emotive.
So construed, it is a questionable move because it attempts
to short-circuit rational argument by jamming it with emotional interference. Why trouble to mount logical arguments if you can arouse your audience so much more directly
and winningly by appealing to their raw emotions? These
fallacies seem to consist in the element of emotional
impact in certain appeals. As Irving Copi (1972) puts it,
"We may define the argumentum ad populum fallacy . . . as
the attempt to win popular assent to a conclusion by
arousing the feelings and enthusiasms of the multitude"
(p. 79). This way of characterizing the fallacy appears
to be adequate to what the logic textbooks want to say
about it, but is it a characterization that can be clearly
understood as an identifiable logical fallacy?

First there is the problem that an appeal to mass emotion
may be an attempt to waive or subvert argument, but it
may not itself be an argument. Where are the premisses
and conclusions to be found? And, indeed, it is by no
means clear at all what is wrong, logically or otherwise,
with attempting to win popular assent to a conclusion by
arousing the enthusiasm of the multitude. Surely if the
conclusion is worthwhile, such an attempt could be, and
often is, highly commendable.

But the overwhelming difficulty with this approach is
that it would seem scarcely credible that there could be
decision procedures or even rational guidelines for
determining that an argument is incorrect exactly when
an attempt has been made to win popular assent by arousing mass feelings. The fact is that any attempt to
define a fallacy in this way would be enmeshed in a hopeless and vitiating psychologism of the worst sort. Once
we start defining incorrectness of argument in terms of
attempts at arousal of mass enthusiasms, we can be sure
that the basic problem of identifying the species of
incorrect argument that constitutes the conceptual core
of the fallacy has become unmanageable. We have pretty
well exclusively gone over into the psychology or
sociology of rhetoric and propaganda. Consequently we
are back to the first problem--where there is no argument, there is no fallacy, because there is no possibility of the notions of correct or incorrect argument being
applicable.

Whether or not individual or mass feelings are aroused
should not be the determining factor in evaluating the
correctness of an argument. The personal enthusiasms
are surely not an element of the argument or a property
that the argument has. Rather they are a property of
the audience, the target group to whom the argument is
directed.

Here we are at the intersection of rhetorical and logical
criticisms of an argument. The problem posed is for us
to see how personal factors relating to the audience or
readership of an argument can play a role in the evaluation of the correctness or incorrectness of that argument.

DIALECTICAL GAMES

Above we referred to the Aristotelian conception of a
dialectical argument. According to this conception, an

argument is to be thought of not just as a set of propositions, but as a two- or many-person disputation between participants in a rule-governed sequence of moves in argument. Each proposition is indexed to a specific individual, representing a move of that individual in the sequence of argument. Can this conception of argument bring in the person-relative aspect of argument needed to support the traditional view of the ad hominem, ad populum, and other emotive fallacies as incorrect arguments? The dialectical model of argument is person-relative while still being a purely normative or conceptual framework. It is not person-relative in the sense of being psychological or sociological in its evaluations. In modern times, dialectic is thought of as a two-person or many-person game of dialogue.

A dialectical game is a regulated dialogue with a number of participants (two, in the simplest case) who take turns speaking in accordance with a set of rules. Descriptive dialectical games draw rules from actual discussions, parliamentary debates, legal cross-examination, or other experientially rich argumentative exchanges. Formal dialectical games consist in the setting up of simple systems of exact but not necessarily very realistic rules and the running of dialogues according to these rules.

In studying a fallacy like the ad hominem, one ideally wants an account that has normative force, that is, an account that will rule that certain instances are correct arguments while others are incorrect by some objective standard of correctness. However descriptive, dialectical games do not by themselves yield up adequate normative standards of correctness. In a debate, an ad hominem argument may be decisively effective in defeating one's opponent and winning the debate, even according to the rules set by the referees or judges, but the argument may be far from correct. Studying debates and other actual argumentative interchanges is necessary for gaining a realistic grasp of the subtleties of how it works in the cut and thrust of objection and reply. But this study, without formal dialectical structure, will not by itself furnish a model that will have normative force in giving objective and reasonable guidelines for correctness or incorrectness.

The analysis of the ad hominem given by E. M. Barth and J. L. Martens (1977) uses the Lorenzen formal dialogue-game logic as its theoretical basis. In a Lorenzen (1969)

game there are two participants. The proponent tries to
defend a certain thesis, and the opponent tries to criticize this thesis. Usually the opponent concedes certain
propositions at the outset of the dialogue. These are
called his <u>concessions</u>. The proponent argues <u>ex concessis</u>,
that is, on the ground of, or by means of, her opponent's
concessions. Thus the game is asymmetrical, the proponent
attacks or criticizes these concessions, whereas the
opponent may not attack his own concessions. Barth and
Martens (1977, p. 83) then define a <u>line of</u> attack as any
set of possible moves made by the opponent. A thesis is
defined as a <u>logical truth</u> if and only if a proponent of
that thesis has a winning strategy against every possible
line of attack of his opponent.

In this framework, Barth and Martens characterize the <u>ad
hominem</u> fallacy as follows (p. 84).

> If P [the proponent] has defended his/her
> thesis T successfully, against O's [opponent's]
> criticism, by arguments <u>ex concessis</u>, then it
> is not yet settled whether T is <u>true</u>, not to
> speak of: whether T is <u>logically true</u> (valid).
> What has been settled is merely that anyone
> who concedes what O concedes (namely O's
> avowed opinions) cannot maintain this criti-
> cism of T.

> Notice that we do not say that such a person
> cannot successfully carry out any attack on T.
> For it is quite possible that, for all we know,
> the same or another opponent making the same
> concessions (and no other ones) can take up
> another line of attack such that P cannot
> maintain T against that attack.

According to Barth and Martens, the <u>ad hominem</u> fallacy is
to argue that a thesis must be logically true simply on
the basis that it has been defended successfully on the
basis of one's opponent's concessions. Just because T is
relatively defensible against the position of <u>this</u> opponent, it of course does not follow that T is absolutely
defensible, against any opponent who makes any concessions
he might care to choose.

Indeed, according to Barth and Martens there are two
different ways of committing the fallacy. First, for T
to be true, that is nonconditionally true, the truth of

the opponent's concessions are required. Hence it is a
fallacy to argue that T is true per se just because T
has been defended on the basis of certain concessions;
these concessions may or may not themselves be true.
But, second, even if T has been successfully defended
against this particular opponent, it does not follow
that T has to be defendable against any opponent who
might make the same concessions yet choose a different
line of attack. Another opponent might make different
moves and successfully overturn that defense.

Barth and Martens's analysis is very constructive and
helpful, for it ties in the ad hominem to a formal game
of dialectic with precise rules and win-strategies. We
are thereby indeed rescued, as they put it, from the
chaos of subjective interpretations of the ad hominem
in quarrels and debates that are not as regulated.
Their analysis moreover does take us to the crux of the
ad hominem fallacy--it is the fallacious move of arguing
that a thesis must be false simply because it conflicts
with the internal position or commitments of a particular
opponent in disputation.

We presume here that Barth and Martens mean by concessions a set of propositions that is not closed under
implication. That is, if O concedes p and p implies q,
it does not automatically follow that O concedes q. In
other words, before P can use q as part of O's concessions, O must specifically concede q itself and not
merely, say, some equivalent of q.

Another question is whether concessions are retractible.
That is, if p is a concession of O, can O at some point
in the game cancel or retract his commitment to p? The
answer is no because the Lorenzen games referred to by
Barth and Martens are essentially cumulative in the sense
that once p is a concession of O, then p remains in that
concession-set of O for the duration of the game.

These are questions about the particular formal properties of different alternative formal dialectical games.
How do we decide which is the most appropriate or best
formal model of a particular fallacy? Which rules are
most helpful? These questions take us back to descriptive dialectical games, back to those pragmatic factors
that can only be determined by detailed case studies of
particular arguments, debates, and dialectical interchanges.

To admit the study of formal dialectical games as an
approach to logic is to admit the possibility of a plurality of different logics, depending upon the particular game one has in mind. Formal development of these
games by Paul Lorenzen (1969), C. L. Hamblin (1970a),
Nicholas Rescher (1977), and others, offers evidence of
a pluralism of legitimate types of games, utilizing
different rules, different connectives, and different
types of logical structures. Formal dialectical games
have clear normative force--they definitely rule on
which moves are allowed or not, and which moves are win-
strategies and so forth. But their rules, by their
nature, are somewhat arbitrary and simplistic in relation to the complexities of actual argumentation. And
their very pluralism suggests that they need to be comparatively evaluated concerning the applicability of
their various structures to realistic features of ad
hominem arguments. Moreover, there are several important aspects of the ad hominem, as this fallacy has
traditionally been conceived, that outrun formal dialectical games as we know them. These aspects have to do
with the action-theoretic and deontic-pragmatic character of many arguments that have traditionally been taken
to be ad hominem disputations.

In short, neither the purely formal nor purely descriptive approach is by itself entirely adequate to gain a
good understanding of why and how the traditional ad
hominem argument is a fallacious (or sometimes nonfallacious) argument. What one needs is an integration of the
two approaches, or a study at a pragmatic level somewhere
between these two extremes.

What would be particularly useful is to take a hard look
at a representative collection of many actual or at least
reasonably realistic specimens of what has been regarded
as the traditional ad hominem argument. We need to
analyze these in the attempt to say just what is supposed
to be fallacious about the arguments that are involved.
This means, first of all, formulating the argument. What
is the allegation? Is it an argument? What are the
propositions that make it up? What is the reply? What
opposition is really involved in the dispute, and how can
some guidelines be brought forward for resolving it, or
at least adjudicating it?

At the same time, we have to ask, given the types of
rules formulated for formal dialectical games, what sort

of rule could be applicable in regulating this particular disputation? In formal games of dialectic with two participants there are, first, rules that regulate permissible moves for each participant. Usually one participant, the questioner (proponent, attacker), formulates questions. The other participant, the answerer (opponent, respondent), puts forward propositions that reply to the question. The game may thus be represented as a two-column tableau, one column containing the questioner's moves, the other the answerer's propositions. There will be a set of formation rules, indicating that only questions and propositions of certain forms will be permissible. Usually the questioner moves first, or initiates the zero-move.

There are also rules to determine when a sequence of moves constitutes a win or loss. There may also be rules limiting how many moves each participant can make. There is very often a strong asymmetry in these rules--that is, the questioner may win if the answerer fails to achieve a certain objection or vice versa. The burden of proof may fall on one participant more strongly than the other.

Clearly there is a good bit of freedom in constructing formal dialectical games and formulating different kinds of rules. It is therefore an interesting and open question to ask what types of rules would be particularly helpful in regulating disputations that turn on ad hominem allegations and arguments. Let us therefore turn back to the ad hominem fallacy as a traditional deficiency of argument. Having cleared away some of the rubble, can we try to obtain some clearer initial grasp of the target of analysis. Some remarks on the historical origin of the term ad hominem could be a place to start.

HISTORICAL AND MODERN CONCEPTIONS OF THE
AD HOMINEM FALLACY

The historical origin of the use of the expression argumentum ad hominem as a logical term with something like its modern meaning is a mystery. However John Locke is generally credited as the first author to use the expression as a technical term for a particular kind of fallacy (see Hamblin [1970a, 159f.] and Barth and Martens [1977, p. 80]). In a famous passage in the Essay, Locke remarked on four sorts of arguments that men ordinarily use to

prevail on the assent, or silence the opposition, of
others they reason with. The first is the appeal to
learned authority, or the argumentum ad verecundiam. The
second way to win over an adversary is to require him to
admit what you allege as a proof or give a better one--
the argumentum ad ignorantiam. According to Locke (quoted
in Hamblin, p. 160), the third way is "to press a man with
consequences drawn from his own principles or concessions."
Locke remarks that this way of arguing is already known
under the name argumentum ad hominem. Then he contrasts
this with a fourth way, called argumentum ad judicium
which he describes as "the using of proofs drawn from any
of the foundations of knowledge or probability." According
to Locke, only this fourth way brings true instruction or
advances the way to knowledge. He points out that bringing
to light a person's own shamefacedness, ignorance, or
internal error, as by the first three arguments, does not
really help him to the truth, even though it may dispose
him for the reception of truth.

Locke's account clearly conveys the basic idea of many
modern accounts of the ad hominem fallacy: just because
an arguer's own concessions, or propositions that are
consequences of them, are shown to be collectively incorrect or untenable, it does not follow that the thesis he
wishes to maintain must be false. If I maintain a proposition T, but my adversary shows that T cannot be consistently maintained along with some other propositions T'
that are conceded by me, it does not follow that T is
false. All that follows is that T cannot consistently be
maintained by me if I insist on sticking to this other
set of propositions T' as well.

But where did Locke get the term ad hominem which he
describes as already known under that name? According
to Hamblin (p. 161), the term originally came from
Aristotle, who, in the De Sophisticis Elenchis (178 b 17)
writes, "these persons direct their solutions against the
man, not against his argument." The Latin translation of
course used the phrase ad hominem, and the same term does
appear in medieval treatises like the commentary of
Albert the Great on the De Sophisticis Elenchis.

This is not to say that Locke may not have picked up the
term from later sources. Finocchiaro (1974) suggests
that he may have gotten it from Galileo. Whatever the
philology of the term, Locke certainly had the basic
idea of many modern interpretations of the ad hominem

argument.

However, we have to be careful in making the leap from what Locke writes to modern conceptions of how ad hominem is a logical fallacy. We should remind ourselves that the type of argument Locke describes as the ad hominem need not in itself be fallacious or incorrect. Criticizing the internal dialectic of someone's position is not in itself fallacious. As Socrates and many other philosophical critics have often shown, criticizing the internal logic of an arguer's concessions can be a very valuable and enlightening process of reasoning. It can be over-indulged or abused, in various ways, but is not in itself categorically wrong as a form of argument.

Johnstone (1970) in fact describes the argumentum ad hominem as a correct form of reasoning, and indeed ventures the interesting thesis that all philosophical reasoning, presumably much of it perfectly sound, is essentially argumentum ad hominem. According to Johnstone, the person's argument attacked may comprise an entire philosophical world-system. Hence it can only be attacked internally if the attack is to be successful. Johnstone is clearly using the term ad hominem in the Lockean tradition, and thereby re-poses the question: How do we get to the notion that argumentum ad hominem is a fallacy?

We saw in the previous section that the approach of formal dialectic answers the question. The fallacy lies in the general assumption that the inconsistency of a proposition with some dialectic participant's concessions implies the falsity of that proposition (apart from this participant's position). In this monograph, we will defend that answer as being basically right. The problem is that the traditional account of the ad hominem fallacy developed subsequently to Locke, as we will see later in our study of Richard Whately and Augustus DeMorgan's treatments, tends to move in a different and broader direction. As a result, ad hominem has survived in modern logic texts in a way that deviates in at least two major respects from the dialectical analysis of Barth and Martens. To be adequate to the modern conceptions of the fallacy, therefore, the dialectical analysis must be enriched, particularly in two directions.

The modern texts standardly distinguish between the circumstantial ad hominem and the abusive variety. In the

abusive <u>ad</u> <u>hominem</u>, the arguer's character is attacked
by "character assassination." Whatever sort of fallacy
this is, it is an argument from the inconsistency of
the attackee's concessions. We will argue later that
this species of <u>ad</u> <u>hominem</u> is really a variant of the
<u>ad</u> <u>verecundiam</u>, or illegitimate appeal to authority.

The circumstantial <u>ad</u> <u>hominem</u> fits the dialectical
analysis somewhat better, except that in the modern
tradition the inconsistency alleged is usually between
an arguer's proposition he advanced and some action
that he brought about. The accusation is that the
arguer does not practice what he preaches. The inconsistency involved, if there is one, is pragmatic, or at
any rate not purely logical. The following case will
illustrate the type of argument very often typified in
textbook accounts of the <u>ad</u> <u>hominem</u>.

A driving instructor tells you not to drink and drive
because it leads to accidents. Upon inquiry, you dis-
cover that he himself has recently had an automobile
accident as a result of drunken driving. You say that
his argument is worthless because he himself is guilty
of the very act he counsels against. Is your <u>ad</u> <u>hominem</u>
refutation too hasty? Yes, because the instructor's
claim that drunken driving is dangerous is in itself not
unreasonable. True, there is a circumstantial inconsistency, but that need not imply that his argument per se
is a bad one.

So far, the analysis seems similar to that of Barth and
Martens. However, the difference is that the circumstantial inconsistency refers not just to the driving
instructor's concessions (propositions), but to his past
behavior or actions.

Therefore, in evaluating this allegation of the <u>ad</u>
<u>hominem</u> fallacy, an additional query must be raised.
Does this individual's evident inability to follow his
own advice impugn his credibility as an advocate of this
particular thesis? The answer is not necessarily.
Indeed, he may well have profited from his unfortunate
experience in a way that, if anything, somewhat adds to
his credibility. He himself has had the relevant experience, and can say with some authority that driving while
intoxicated is indeed dangerous.

The situation is changed, however, if you notice his

concealed flask as he stumbles into the car reeking of gin. Then you can have serious doubts whether he knows what he is talking about. Yet, here again, it is not his argument that drunken driving is dangerous that is shown to be incorrect per se. It is rather that his own sincere and serious advocacy of it is in doubt. If the fault is not in the argument itself, however, how can this particular sort of ad hominem be a logical fallacy? If it is appropriate to call it an ad hominem allegation, how can it be evaluated one way or the other? If this sort of case is to be dealt with, a pragmatic dimension has entered the picture.

What does it mean to say that in committing a circumstantial ad hominem inconsistency, one's advocacy of the argument is impugned? Does it mean that the argument is logically invalid or merely that one's credibility is lessened? If the former, then the argument is certainly incorrect. But if the latter, does the error amount to any more than a psychological failure to convince a target audience? This lapse could be a purely psychological or perhaps sociological or rhetorical matter, and would not as such represent a fallacy in the sense of a logical error or incorrect argument. Is it therefore really a criticism of the correctness of someone's argument to say that it is circumstantially inconsistent, or could it just be a psychological evaluation that the arguer has used an unpersuasive rhetorical strategy for a particular audience?

Neither of these alternatives is very satisfactory. There is nothing inconsistent, as far as purely formal logic--let us say classical logic--goes, about maintaining p as a proposition and at the same time deliberately acting so as to bring it about that the proposition not-p is made true. On the other hand, however, if you do so deliberately act and maintain, for me to point out your circumstantial inconsistency amounts to a very serious criticism of your argument. It has become in some sense an argument worthy of careful criticism for its failure. But precisely what is the failure? That is the difficult but relevant question. It must be confronted, however, if the formal dialectical model of argument is to be applicable to the sorts of ad hominem allegations that are nowadays taken to be standard examples of that fallacy in textbooks of logic.

There is the suspicion that with this sort of example we

are dealing with the ethics of argument as well as its
logic. The question posed is how to judge hypocrisy.

The word hypocrisy stems from the Greek word hypokrines-
thai (to play a part, pretend), made up from the words
hypo (under) and krinesthai (to contend, dispute). In
English it means roughly a feigning to be what one is
not, especially in regard to morals--a kind of deception.
Thus a hypocrite is a dissembler, one who assumes the
appearance of virtue when he or she is in fact destitute
of virtue. Luke XII:1 warns us: "Beware of the leaven
of the Pharisees which is hypocrisy."

If the circumstantial ad hominem involves hypocrisy then
it is certainly a moral turpitude to be caught in, but
is it a logical fallacy? If a reporter does something
unethical in order to ferret out an unethical practice
she reports on, she is surely being hypocritical if she
commits the very turpitude she rails against. On the
other hand, her argument discrediting the subject of her
report may be a sound argument. If the reporter is to
be criticized it may be more for her ethics than for her
logic. Is the circumstantial ad hominem more a moral
failure than a logical fallacy? The modern conception
of the ad hominem requires a resolution of this question.
How far can we extend formal dialectic to the pragmatic
realities of ad hominem disputations?

The second way in which current characterizations depart
from the Lockean model is in their insistence that the
ad hominem, like the ad baculum, ad populum, and ad
misericordiam, is somehow a failure of relevance by means
of emotional distraction. The appropriate model of argument here would seem to be more in the area of relevance
logic than formal dialectic.

A FALLACY OF RELEVANCE?

The ad hominem fallacy is often, and perhaps even characteristically, treated by logic texts as a failure of
relevance. Copi (1972) cites the following argument as
an instance of the abusive ad hominem: Bacon was removed
from his chancellorship for dishonesty, therefore Bacon's
philosophy is untrustworthy. According to Copi, "This
argument is fallacious, because the personal character of
a person is logically irrelevant to the truth or falsehood of what the person says, or the correctness or

incorrectness of that person's argument" (p. 75). Copi
nowhere tells us, however, precisely what is meant by
saying that one proposition is irrelevant to another.
In this he is quite representative of the standard treatment of the ad hominem in textbooks. However, he does
make some general remarks about relevance that apply to
a number of fallacies he classifies under the heading of
"fallacies of relevance" including the ad baculum, ad
misericordiam, and ad populum.

Copi writes that fallacies of relevance are fallacious
because their premisses are logically irrelevant to, and
therefore incapable of, establishing their conclusion
(p. 74). He adds that psychological relevance can be
confused with logical relevance, and that the former is
connected with emotions like fear, pity, enthusiasm,
hostility, or awe that may cause the acceptance of a
conclusion without supplying grounds for its truth.

According to Copi, the circumstantial ad hominem, like
the abusive, can also be a failure of logical relevance
(p. 75). For example, he cites as the "classic example"
of the circumstantial ad hominem the sportsman's rejoinder (see Chapter 3, first part) when accused by a critic
of sacrificing innocent hares or trout for his amusement:
"Why do you feed on the flesh of harmless cattle?"
According to Copi's explanation, the sportsman commits
an ad hominem because he does not try to prove that it
is right to sacrifice animals for his amusement, but
rather dwells on the critic's own circumstantial inconsistency posed by the fact that the critic is not a
vegetarian. Thus, according to Copi, the fallacy is
really a failure of relevance: "Arguments such as these
are not really to the point; they do not present good
grounds for the truth of their conclusions but are
intended only to win assent to the conclusion from one's
opponent because of the opponent's special circumstances"
(p. 76). Once again, however, Copi does not tell us what
is meant by saying that an argument is "to the point."

Let us note here that Copi's remarks are of special
interest in one particular regard. He links the notion
of an argument being "to the point" with the notion of
an argument's providing good grounds." This suggests
that he may be proposing that a premiss is logically
relevant to a conclusion if, and only if, that premiss
provides good grounds for that conclusion. In the context of deductive arguments, what this would appear to

amount to is the claim that an argument is deductively
valid if, and only if, the premises are logically
relevant to the conclusion. However, in the earlier
remarks on page 75, Copi had written more as though
logical relevance could be a necessary, but not necessarily sufficient, condition for the validity of an
argument. There he had remarked that in fallacies of
relevance, the premisses are logically irrelevant to,
and therefore incapable of, establishing their conclusion. Here then is a question to be noted: Is logical
relevance--at any rate, in the context of deductive
arguments--just the same thing as validity, or is it
something at least partially different?

Copi's treatment of the ad hominem leaves us with this
puzzle, but since he does not venture to define relevance, we are really left to our own devices to think
about it. Iseminger (1980) raises the question of
whether various formal relevance logics can be applicable to fallacies like the ad hominem and ad baculum,
but is inclined to be skeptical. In Walton (1979) there
is the suggestion that relatedness logics may be applicable to studying ignoratio elenchi.

Perhaps some extension to the ad hominem, and other fallacies evidently having to do with failures of relevance,
could vindicate the modern view of these fallacies. Here,
then, is a direction that the modern tradition suggests
as an enrichment of the dialectical analysis of the ad
hominem. Some modern examples will serve to indicate
that notions of relevance are built into a dialectical
question-and-answer approach to the fallacy.

An interesting specimen of the ad hominem argument is
given by Woods and Walton (1982b) in the context of contemporary arguments about the abortion issue. A common
rejoinder is the "You can't help being opposed because
you are a man" argument. As is pointed out in Woods and
Walton, however, a suitable counter to this rejoinder is
available in the following form: "You can't help being
in favor because you are a woman, someone who is in a
position to experience unwanted pregnancy, and consequently is unable to resist favoring abortion on demand."
The rejoinder creates a stalemate situation because it
implies that neither side can help taking their particular position, and that consequently there is no point in
continuing the argument.

This situation illustrates a noteworthy aspect of the ad
hominem--as a move in argument it is often designed to
stop or at least has the effect of stopping, the argument
by undermining the opponent's position (in the above
case, both positions) so badly that further argument is
made pointless or ineffective. Perhaps for this reason,
some forms of ad hominem have been called "poisoning the
well." This term was evidently coined by Cardinal Newman
who protested to Charles Kingsley's accusation that
Newman, as a Catholic priest, did not place the highest
value on the truth. Cardinal Newman replied that this
accusation created a presumption that made it impossible
for him, or any other Catholic, to state his case and
make his arguments. How could he prove, in light of
this accusation, that he did have regard for the truth?
And if he could not prove that, any argument whatever
that was henceforth propounded by him would be automatically suspect, covered by the same cloud of doubt and
suspicion. Hence the term "poisoning the well" is particularly appropriate--once the source of the argument
is impugned, any argument that subsequently proceeds
from that source, no matter how soundly it is backed up
by careful evidence, is not likely to overcome the
obstacle of the original accusation.

Both the above illustrations of ad hominem ploys show
that sometimes the merest allegation of the ad hominem
is so powerful that it stops the argument in midstream,
prevents the arguer from continuing, and possibly even
shuts him or her up altogether. After all, how can one
credibly respond if, whatever one says, all one's arguments are declared worthless in advance? So one point
is clear. One accused of the ad hominem must be given
fair opportunity to reply to the charge, in any fair
dialectical exchange.

Sometimes, however, as in the abortion example, the train
of argument is derailed so effectively that it seems
scarcely possible for it to continue at all. What has
happened is that the issue has been changed.

In the abortion example, the point is made that the
opponent happens to be a man. This fact is true, and
may therefore appear unchallengeable. But it may be
overlooked that the issue has been not so subtly changed.
The true fact brought forward is not really relevant to
establishing whether or not abortion is morally right.
Similarly, in the other case, we are brought up abruptly

to the question of whether Cardinal Newman may be said to
have regard for the truth, and in the excitement of such
a challenge, we forget what the particular issue was in
the first place, and whether Newman's specific arguments
for it were evidently sound.

So once again we come round to the idea that one thing
that has gone wrong in the successful and unfair use of
the ad hominem accusation is that some sort of perpetra-
tion of irrelevance has transpired. In some way, the
topic or issue has been forcefully changed or rerouted
so that the original argument is cut off or spoiled,
leaving the arguer no option but to attempt to respond
to the ad hominem allegation and at least temporarily
drop his line of argument, to come back to it later if
he can. It is a disruption of the argument by switching
it onto a different track, very often a threatening and
upsetting one for the original arguer to find himself on.
Once the accusation is made, it is very difficult and
hazardous for the arguer not to respond to it. But if
he does respond, he loses track of his original case.
It tempts one to think that in fair argument there are
times when such an allegation should not be allowed at
all, even to be initiated.

Given that an ad hominem is such an aggressive attack
that virtually forces its victim to reply to it and thus
change the subject, or risk sacrificing credibility
entirely, it is a moot point just what sorts of responses
to it are legitimate and fair. In the abortion example,
the man replied, tu quoque, that a parallel point disqualified his attacker to the same extent as her intended
victim. This is a strategy that seems not unfair, and
can certainly be effective in nicely turning the tables
on the attacker. However, in other arguments, shifting
the burden of proof by replying to one ad hominem with
another is not above criticism.

R. H. Johnson and J. A. Blair (1977, p. 42) criticize
one such reply as fallacious. They cite a speech of a
Quebec politician who levelled some heavy charges at the
press, including "conducting hate campaigns," "destroying
careers and reputations," conducting inquisitorially
directed campaigns designed to destroy certain men and
institutions, and so forth. In reply, the Windsor Star,
which reported the speech and then commented on it,
reported a number of alleged findings about this politician's past conduct that strongly suggested that he was

a "shady operator." Johnson and Blair comment that, in
so replying, the Star attacked this individual personally
instead of confronting the arguments alleged against the
press, instead of challenging their attacker to back his
argument up with specifics, instead of replying that his
allegations were "vastly overstated" (p. 42). Here, it
would seem that Johnson and Blair are suggesting that
the Star's "tit for tat" reply was not appropriate or
reasonable. Instead of turning the tables on this politician by replying in kind, Johnson and Blair appear to
be suggesting, the Star should have replied directly to
their attacker's ad hominem criticisms of the press and
tried to rebut them.

The problem is that it is hard to know here why it is
thought incorrect for the one party to reply ad hominem
to another's ad hominem. Perhaps all Johnson and Blair
are saying is that the first argument was bad enough--it
is no commendable move to reply with one just about as
bad. And Johnson and Blair go on to argue that the
Star's argument is in itself open to criticism on the
ground that it presupposes a very weak, missing premiss
to the effect that a person of bad character cannot hold
any true views.

It should be noted, however, that one could have said
much the same thing about the criticized politician's
original arguments. Neither argument is free from
blemish, although one cannot resist puckishly adding
that the Star's argument is more compelling and punchy
than the vague, somewhat ineffectual accusations of the
politician's original argument. Still, the really interesting question is, even granted that neither argument is
above criticism, Why is the second not a reasonable or
fair response to the first?

I take it that the answer suggested by Johnson and Blair
is that the Star should have dismantled the politician's
arguments themselves, by criticisms directed to those
arguments, rather than by the admittedly effective
expedient of resorting to the handily available skeletons
in this vulnerable politician's closet.

The notion evidently presupposed is that a response by a
participant in a dialectical interchange to an opponent's
proposition may be fairly ruled irrelevant if it changes
the topic or issue. In particular, if it veers off the
opponent's previous response and onto irrelevant personal

characteristics it can be evaluated as an illegitimate
ad hominem response. Still, we are no closer to knowing
what "irrelevant" means in the context of dialectical
challenge and reply.

Our major goals in the remainder of this monograph will
be to attempt to enrich further the dialectical analysis
of what we take to be the modern conception of the ad
hominem fallacy by extending it in two directions. First,
we want to analyze detailed case studies of the ad hominem
to bring out its pragmatic character, and to provide an
analysis of these cases. Second, we want to pursue this
notion of relevance a little further, to see if there is
anything in it.

NOTES

     1. I would like to thank Siew Khim Soon for drawing
this example of parliamentary debate to my attention.

3

Pragmatic Inconsistency

The last chapter took up the theme that, in the modern
tradition, many allegations that form the basis of an
ad hominem argument concern not logical inconsistencies
between concessions of an arguer, but what we might call
pragmatic inconsistencies. These are contradictions
between a proposition advanced by a disputant and another
proposition that describes some action attributed to that
very disputant.

One contested circumstantial ad hominem of this sort was
remarked on by Whately and then studied further by
DeMorgan. This particular example survives in many a
current text, and the treatments of it by Whately and
DeMorgan are worth detailed analysis.

THE SPORTSMAN'S REJOINDER

A specimen of ad hominem argumentation that is both historically and conceptually interesting in the development
of doctrines of this fallacy is one that might be called
the sportsman's rejoinder. The sportsman, accused of
barbarity in his sacrifice of hares or trout for his
amusement, retorts: "Why do you feed on the flesh of
animals?" Archbishop Whately was, to my knowledge, the
first to identify this argument as a species of ad hominem.

According to Whately's own evaluation of it, the argument
is a justifiable response--it is a correct or at any rate
nonfallacious move in argument for the sportsman to have
so queried in reply to his critic. How was Whately led
to arrive at that evaluation?

Whately reckoned that there is a class of arguments,
including the ad hominem, that is only fallacious when
used unfairly. Thus for Whately it is possible that an
ad hominem argument can sometimes be correct, or at any
rate used correctly (not unfairly). According to Whately,
in the correct use of the ad hominem, the conclusion
established is relative to the particular circumstances
of this man: "in the argumentum ad hominem the conclusion
which actually is established, is not the absolute and
general one in question, but relative and particular;
viz. not that 'such and such is the fact,' but that this
man is bound to admit it, in conformity to his principles

of Reasoning, or in consistency with his own conduct,
situation, &c." (1836, p. 196). According to Whately,
how the fallacy occurs lies in the attempt to substitute
this partial and relative conclusion for the more general one that the proposition is established universally.
In other words, the fallacy occurs when you show that
some proposition espoused by your opponent is inconsistent with your opponent's circumstances, and then conclude quite unjustifiably that the proposition must in
itself be false.

Thus Whately believed that the ad hominem is sometimes
quite a reasonable move to make in argument, and he
believed that the sportsman, in querying his critic's
circumstantial consistency, was on safe grounds. It was
Whately's view that the ad hominem was sometimes a fair
and even salutary type of argument, that it could have
the beneficial effect of fairly shifting the burden of
proof back onto one's critic. The details of Whately's
own evaluation of the particulars of the sportsman's
rejoinder are worth careful scrutiny (p. 196).

> "The argumentum ad hominem" will often have
> the effect of shifting the burden of proof,
> not unjustly, to the adversary. A common
> instance is the defence, certainly the
> readiest and most concise, frequently urged
> by the Sportsman, when accused of barbarity
> in sacrificing unoffending hares or trout to
> his amusement: he replies, as he may safely
> do, to most of his assailants, "why do you
> feed on the flesh of animals?" and that this
> answer presses hard, is manifested by its
> being usually opposed by a palpable false-
> hood; viz. that the animals which are killed
> for food are sacrificed to our necessities;
> though not only men can, but a large propor-
> tion (probably a great majority) of the
> human race actually do, subsist in health
> and vigor without flesh-diet; and the earth
> would support a much greater human population
> were such a practice universal. When shamed
> out of this argument they sometimes urge that
> the brute creation would overrun the earth,
> if we did not kill them for food; an argument,
> which, if it were valid at all, would not
> justify their feeding on fish; though, if
> fairly followed up, it would justify Swift's

> proposal for keeping down the excessive
> population of Ireland. The true reason,
> <u>viz</u>. that they eat flesh for the gratifi-
> cation of the palate, and have a taste for
> the pleasures of the table, though not for
> the sports of the field, is one which they
> do not like to assign.

Whately remarks that the sportsman's reply has scored a
good point, and this is evidenced by the fact that the
critic in reply will usually be pressed to resorting to
a palpable falsehood, namely that it is necessary for
people to eat meat in order to survive.

What should be said about Whately's analysis? For one
thing, there is the important insight that the <u>ad hominem</u>
can be sometimes used correctly as a dialectical rejoinder
that can fairly shift the burden of proof. And his analysis of the fallacy as a shift from the particular or
circumstantial refutation to the universal conclusion of
falsehood is, as we have seen, seminal.

But there are two questionable aspects. First, Whately's
conclusion that "the fallaciousness depends on the <u>deceit</u>
or attempt to deceive" (p. 197) suggests an unnecessary
psychologism, and adds nothing helpful to the analysis.
But second, Whately may have overlooked an absolutely
essential point, and in effect sponsored a kind of <u>ad
hominem</u> himself, by overlooking a certain fact nicely
brought out by DeMorgan's commentary on the sportsman's
rejoinder. DeMorgan questioned whether the meat eating
critic was really and truly being inconsistent in condemning the sportsman's hunting of game. Could Whately
have been unclear in identifying the propositions that
allegedly make up the inconsistency cited by the sportsman's rejoinder?

A further variation on the circumstantial <u>ad hominem</u> can
arise when the very premises advanced in argument are
misdescribed or confused. The error here is a failure to
locate and identify the argument in the first place, even
before steps are taken to evaluate its soundness. What
can happen is that a third proposition that resembles one
of the original pair is illicitly substituted for one of
that pair. What results is the mere appearance of inconsistency where it does not in fact obtain. As DeMorgan
(1847) put it, "it is not absolutely the same argument
which is turned against the proposer, but one which is

asserted to be like it, or parallel to it" (p. 265). But, as DeMorgan warned, parallel cases may also be divergent in some respects.

According to DeMorgan there is no strict inconsistency, as Whately had alleged, in the position of the critic who is accused of inconsistency by the sportsman. There is merely the superficial appearance of inconsistency (p. 265). "A celebrated writer on logic asserts, that no one who eats meat ought to object to the occupation of a sportsman on the ground of cruelty. The parallel will not exist until, for the person who eats meat, we substitute one who turns butcher for amusement." Here Whately is neatly caught out in not specifying more clearly just how the alleged inconsistency is to be established. DeMorgan is surely right to caution that great care is needed in examining alleged inconsistencies on the basis of parallel propositions-- parallel, that is, in some respects.

On the other hand, Whately was not claiming that there was a logical inconsistency to be established, but rather only a circumstantial inconsistency. But it is not even clear yet that a circumstantial inconsistency can be pinned down. Let us analyze the sportsman's rejoinder a bit further.

The point to be stressed is that whether or not there really is an inconsistency is highly dependent on how the actions at issue are specifically described. Consider the following pair of propositions: (1) x asserts that hunting should not be brought about; (2) x brings it about that meat eating obtains. These are not logically inconsistent. Surely also DeMorgan is right; the following pair is not logically inconsistent either: (3) x asserts that nobody should take pleasure in killing animals for amusement; (4) x brings it about personally that x eats meat. But let us go on to ask, Are (1) and (2) pragmatically inconsistent?

The initial answer seems to be no. It is clear that obtaining meat for human consumption can be brought about by ways other than hunting. Hence there is not a tight conflict, even of the action-theoretic or pragmatic sort between (1) and (2). On the other hand, there is also a connection, if of a looser sort, between hunting and meat eating. If the critic is really condemning not just hunting but the killing of animals, and if he is willing to admit that meat eating is causally connected to the killing of animals, he could be on much shakier ground if the

sportsman is clever enough to reformulate his argument
somewhat. What the sportsman could point out is that
the practice of eating the flesh of animals is a main
economic factor in making the slaughtering of animals a
profitable activity. Meat eating, as it were, is a way
of sponsoring or contributing to the extent of the practice of the killing of animals by humans.

Let it be noted, however, that whether or not such a
connection can be made is very much dependent on how the
actions at issue are described. Moreover, the pragmatic
inconsistency between (5) x condemns the killing of
animals and (6) x eats meat is not of a direct sort.
By eating meat, x is not himself directly killing animals.
Rather, x is indirectly contributing to the slaughter of
animals. He is, we might say, making this practice possible, or providing some incentive for others to engage
in it. By this means, however, he is indirectly sponsoring the killing of animals. Hence his assertion that
animals should not be killed runs counter, even if not
directly, to his own practice. But is this close enough
of a contradiction to matter? Some would argue so, and
clearly there is some basis of justification for so
arguing.

So who really committed the ad hominem fallacy, the
sportsman or the critic? The answer is that it all
depends on how you describe the propositions that go
together to make up the alleged inconsistency. Described
one way, the sportsman comes out right, described another,
the propositions make the critic's argument come out
right. What you have to do in order to untangle the disputation to see who committed the alleged ad hominem is
to formulate precisely the propositions by means of fixing
to one act-description relative to one allegation of
fallaciousness. If that act-description is altered, even
though the participants are still talking about the same
action, it is a reformulation of the argument and consequently needs to be evaluated again, perhaps quite differently.

A major lesson is that it is better initially to concentrate on the set of propositions that make up the argument rather than on the actions, intentions, or individual circumstances of the participants. This result
augurs well for thinking of the argument as being at least
a set of propositions. Whether or not an ad hominem allegation can be justified or shown to be fallacious depends

on whether a certain pair of propositions are inconsistent. Of course, participants in argument can reformulate their positions and change how they want the actions being disputed to be described. But then there is a different argument being advanced.

The sportsman's initial argument was fallacious because the inconsistency he alleged--the way he described it--did not really obtain. In effect, therefore, the sportsman simply selected the wrong premisses. His error was that his premisses were misdescribed or confused. He had what looked upon superficial perusal to be a logical inconsistency. But upon analysis of those propositions, the allegation of inconsistency could not be justified. The sportsman's attempt to mount an ad hominem was not successful. In the end, it is best to say that he really committed the fallacy himself in doing such a clumsy and misleading job of attempting to make the charge stick.

Is this an ad hominem fallacy itself, the failure to justify an allegation of inconsistency by shifting act-descriptions? Woods and Walton (1977b) argue that it is, and I would still support this view of the matter.

According to this view, there is a certain symmetry to the ad hominem. Once the propositions are shown to be inconsistent, the accused, who has maintained these propositions jointly, has committed the ad hominem. However, if the propositions can be shown not to be inconsistent then it is the accuser himself who has committed the fallacy. Perhaps this failure is a different fallacy: the fallacy of incorrectly mounting an ad hominem allegation. It could be called the attacker's ad hominem fallacy.

The key thing to remember is that an ad hominem argument has two sides; it is a double-edged weapon in argument and it can also damage the case of its exponent or user if not employed carefully. The allegation may be justified or not, depending on an analysis of the propositions that occur in it. If not justified, it is the attacker who is at fault and must either formulate his position or concede that he himself is refuted, not his opponent.

The two propositions alleged to be incompatible by the sportsman, and also, according to him, alleged to be held by the critic, are not logically incompatible as they stand. There is, at best, a causal relationship between

two act-descriptions. But we have already observed that
a common allegation, typical of the ad hominem, is that
there is some action-theoretic inconsistency being
attributed to an opponent in argument. And often this
inconsistency is not an outright or direct logical contradiction.

The sportsman's rejoinder shows how careful we have to
be in sorting out an ad hominem disputation in order to
clarify the actual inconsistent set of propositions
within the accusation. And then we have to determine
whether the contradiction is of a logical or merely
pragmatic sort.

We have to be particularly careful with pragmatic inconsistencies because it is by no means clear how they are
to be analyzed in general. In fact, some readers will
no doubt be very skeptical that it is useful or coherent
even to talk about inconsistencies that are not strictly
logical inconsistencies. However, there is some preced-
ent for concern about self-refuting propositions other
than strictly logical inconsistencies. In some cases
that have been remarked upon, the self-refuting nature
of the proposition seems to be tied in with speech acts
or other action-theoretic factors.

In the case of the sportsman's rejoinder, the pragmatic
inconsistency, if one was committed, was of a deontic as
well as action-theoretic sort. If I say "One should
never eat meat" while eating a steak dinner, my action
runs counter to what I say ought to be done. My prescription conflicts with my own action. However, there
is a narrower class of pragmatically inconsistent propositions like "I am not writing anything" that can be
purely action-theoretic in the nature of their own self-
refutation. Let us examine these.

SELF-REFUTING SENTENCES

Self-referential sentences like "This sentence is false"
have been thoroughly analyzed by philosophers. There is
a sense in which it is correct to say that such sentences
are self-refuting. Indeed, the sentence in quotation
marks leads to inconsistency. If it is true, then what
it says is not true, and hence it is false. If it is
false, then what it says is true, and hence it is true.
Hence it is true if and only if it is not true, and that

is inconsistent. We assume that "true" is the opposite
of "false" and that every sentence is either true or
false. Alfred Tarski's analysis of this type of self-
refuting sentence turns on the presumption that the
language in which the quoted sentence is expressed is
semantically closed--that is, the object language in
which the sentence is expressed is not differentiated
from the meta-language in which conditions for the truth
of the sentences in the object language are formulated.

Another type of expression that is also self-refuting,
and has from time to time come to the attention of the
philosophical community, occurs when someone says "I am
not saying anything." Here, however, it is not the sentence in quotes that is in itself inconsistent. Rather,
it is the act of saying that sentence that leads to its
own self-refutation.

An analysis of J. L. Mackie (1964) brings out how different forms of self-refuting propositions work. The first
form of self-refutation is called absolute self-refutation
and applies to self-refuting sentences like "It can be
proved that nothing can be proved." This sentence can be
shown to refute itself as follows. If it can be proved
that nothing can be proved, then something can be proved
(namely, that nothing can be proved). However, if it can
be proved that nothing can be proved, it follows (by virtue of the truth entailing nature of the operator 'It can
be proved that p') that nothing can be proved. Hence,
from the sentence we began with, "It can be proved that
nothing can be proved," a proposition and its negation
both follow. Consequently, the sentence we began with is
logically inconsistent.

Some modal operators like 'It is possible that p' are not
truth entailing, in the sense that it is not the case that
the truth of p is implied by 'It is possible that p.'
However, the possibility operator is, as Mackie says,
prefixable in the sense that 'It is possible that p' is
implied by p (p. 195). A self-refuting sentence of this
type would be "Nothing is possible." This sentence can
be shown to be self-refuting as follows. If nothing is
possible then at least one thing is possible, namely that
nothing is possible. Why? Because the statement "Nothing
is possible" is prefixable. On the other hand, if nothing
is possible, it is not the case that even one thing is
possible. By virtue of this contradiction, the sentence
"Nothing is possible" is shown to be logically inconsistent.

Another class of sentences like "I say that I am not saying anything" is shown by Mackie to be, as he says, pragmatically self-refuting, even though the operator 'It is
said to be true that p' is neither prefixable nor truth
entailing. Here, only one of the pair of implications
that led to logical contradiction in the previous two
types of self-refuting sentences is applicable. Thus we
can reason that at least this is true: if I say that I
am not saying anything then I am saying something. However, we cannot reason as before that if I say I am not
saying anything, I am not saying anything (because the
operator 'It is not said that p' is not truth entailing).
Nor can we reason from "I am not saying anything" to "I
say I am not saying anything" because 'It is not said
that p' is not prefixable. So we cannot get a logical
contradiction the way we did with absolutely self-refuting statements. The best we can say is that the contained
noun clause in "I am saying that I am not saying anything"
is false. We cannot show that the whole sentence in
quotes is logically inconsistent. It is only self-refuting in the lesser sense that the operation or action of
saying refutes the content of what it operates upon. A
formal theory of this class of self-defeating sentences
is given by Daniel Vanderveken (1980).

There is an additional reason, not mentioned by Mackie,
why my saying "I am not saying anything" might legitimately be thought to be self-refuting. Mackie says that
in pragmatic self-refutation it is not the proposition in
quotes above that should be called self-refuting, but
rather the actual operation it describes. However, he
elucidates that the question is self-refuting only in the
sense that the sentence in quotes is false (p. 194). If
I say that I am not saying anything then I am saying something. Therefore it is false that I am not saying anything.

Mackie makes it clear that he thinks my saying that I am
not saying anything is not self-refuting in the sense
that it is logically inconsistent or in the sense that it
cannot be true, by contrast with the other cases he cites
of absolute self-refutation. Indeed, he points out that
there is "no bar to the occurrence of the actual operation" (p. 194). I can actually come out and say "I am
not saying anything," and according to Mackie the proposition "I am saying that I am not saying anything" will
be true.

But can that proposition really be true? If I say that

I am not saying anything, then, if what I say is true, I am not saying anything. But if I say that I am not say- ing anything, then I am saying something. It is a law of logic, though, that any proposition that implies both another proposition together with the negation of that other proposition must itself be logically impossible. Hence the proposition "I am saying that I am not saying anything" is logically impossible.

What is shown here, however, is quite consistent with Mackie's account. What we have shown in the paragraph above is that I cannot _truly_ say that I am not saying anything, not that I cannot say that I am not saying any- thing. If I say "I am not saying anything," then, as Mackie points out, the sentence "I just said that I was not saying anything" is true, as a report of what just transpired. On the other hand, although the report is true, it is the report of a saying that could never be true. For if it were true, as I said, that I was not saying anything, then I really was not saying anything, so I could not have said what I said.

In Mackie's terms, what is shown here is that the oper- ator 'It is truly said that p' is truth entailing. Hence the sentence "I truly say that I am not saying anything" is logically inconsistent and absolutely self-refuting.

What Mackie has shown is that there are two kinds of self- refuting propositions. In both cases the self-refutation has to with the speech-act of how the proposition is asserted. One kind is a class of logically inconsistent propositions, the other is pragmatically inconsistent, but not strictly logically inconsistent. In the latter class of cases, the action, if actually carried out, is incon- sistent with the very proposition that is produced by this action. If I truly say "I am not saying anything," there is an inconsistency between what I say and what I do. Is this phenomenon not the same thing as the circumstantial ad hominem--a clash between the action and assertion of the same person?

The answer is yes, in essence. For the circumstantial ad hominem is at bottom just this very sort of inconsistency. However, as we saw in the sportsman's rejoinder, the inconsistency is not simply of a purely praxeological type like those studied by Mackie--a conflict between action and assertion. Rather, the inconsistency is more complex. Following Woods and Walton (1977b), it is called a deonto-praxeological inconsistency--a conflict between what the agent actually does and what she says ought to be done. Here, the deontic notion of universal prescription also enters into the conflict between act and assertion.

Moreover, as the preceding analysis of the sportsman's rejoinder showed, sometimes the relationship between the act-descriptions attributed to the person who is alleged to be pragmatically inconsistent is neither praxeological nor deonto-praxeological, at least directly. At best, it is reducible to one of these by a process of redescribing the actions attributed to the arguer accused of committing the ad hominem. The connection is more causal than logical. As we saw in the sportsman's rejoinder, it is hard to know how to evaluate this class of ad hominem allegations because it is not clear how the actions may be fairly redescribed in attributing them to an opponent in argument.

Nonetheless, at least we are now getting a better grasp of the core structure of the circumstantial ad hominem. We can see that two types of pragmatic inconsistency, the purely praxeological and the deonto-praxeological, can be reduced to logical inconsistency. However, as we have seen, such reductions do not always settle the dispute over whether or not an ad hominem has been committed. Another case study will make this clearer.

THE ARMS EXPORTER

A student accuses an arms exporter of selling weapons to nations that use arms for unjust wars and the persecution of innocent persons. The arms exporter replies by pointing out what appears to be a contradiction: the student's university has invested funds in corporations that manufacture arms. The student appears to be caught in an embarrassing inconsistency. However, if he is clever he might argue that the arms exporter has committed an attacker ad hominem fallacy because there is no inconsistency in condemning weapon sales and studying at a university. Who is in the right? I will argue that both parties are in the wrong--at least to some extent--but that each of them also has raised a criticism that is valid up to a point.

The student accuses the arms exporter of contributing to

a morally reprehensible outcome of providing arms to those
who use them for wrongful acts. Now if the student were
himself found to be implicated in the arms export business
to customers of an equally dubious moral stature, he would
indeed be open to a fair accusation of circumstantial
inconsistency. But such, we presume, is not the case.
Rather, the student is implicated with a university that
manufactures arms. So the first point is this--there is a
difference between manufacturing arms and distributing them
to known killers or perpetrators of unjust and violent acts
who use these arms as their means. There is enough of a
difference to justify the point that there is no outright
circumstantial contradiction between manufacturing arms and
censuring the selling or distribution of these arms to
known felons. So far the student is in the right, and has
a good point.

But on the other hand the arms exporter might reasonably
query: Is not manufacturing arms also a contribution, a
necessary link in the chain that culminates eventually in
wrongful acts of homicide and persecution, just as the act
of selling is also a contribution to the same acts? Manufacturing may not be the same act as selling, but there is
definitely a connection between the two, and an outcome in
question that is sufficiently parallel to raise questions
of practical inconsistency. Thus in replying that there
is no contradiction between condemning weapon sales and
studying at a university, the student is being ingenuous.
There is no contradiction between these actions, so
described. But if the acts are described more fully,
there would seem to be a connection between them of some
sort.

It is a question of act-descriptions. Consider the following act-descriptions.

    (a)   a sells weapons to nations that use the arms for
          unjust wars and the persecution of innocent per-
          sons.

    (b)   a attends a university that has invested funds
          in corporations that manufacture arms.

    (c)   a studies at a university.

    (d)   a manufactures arms.

    (e)   a sells weapons.

    (f)   a condemns weapon sales.

    (g)   a condemns unjust wars and the persecution of
          the innocent.

    (h)   a manufactures weapons that are later used by
          nations that use them for illegal or immoral
          purposes.

(i)   a manufactures weapons that he plans to sell to
       persons whom he knows plan to sell them to
       nations that use the arms for unjust wars and
       the persecution of innocent persons.

Practical inconsistencies can be found between certain
pairs of these propositions but not between other pairs.
As the student has claimed, there is no inconsistency
between (f) and (c). There is, however, a practical
inconsistency between (e) and (f), and certainly also a
practical inconsistency between (g) and (i). Why is the
latter pair inconsistent? They are not directly inconsistent, as in the practical inconsistency of an arguer
who argues that some proposition p should not be made
true yet at the same time makes it true that p. Rather,
it is a question of means and ends.

The person who acts as stated by (g) and at the same time
also acts as stated by (i) is condemning a certain type
of outcome of certain possible lines of action and yet at
the same time is undertaking the very line of action he
fully knows and plans to result in that very outcome he
condemns. His line of action and its planned upshot is
the very thing he condemns. This person is practically
inconsistent.

What of the arms exporter's allegation that the student
is practically inconsistent in acting as stated by (b)
and the same time acting as stated here by (j): a condemns the selling of weapons to nations that use them for
unjust wars and the persecution of innocent persons? The
link between (b) and (j) is an indirect one. The exporter
reminds us that the student has condemned the selling of
weapons to nations that use these arms for unjust wars
and the persecution of the innocent. Presumably, the
student is thereby committed to (g), the condemnation of
unjust wars and the persecution of the innocent. Yet at
the same time, so maintains the exporter, the student
attends a university that has invested funds in corporations that manufacture arms. True, the student does not
directly himself bring about the very outcome he deplores.
Yet he does indirectly contribute to such an outcome. He
sponsors or allows the manufacture of arms, or at any rate
he is connected to an institution that is in turn connected
to arms manufacture in a supportive way. By attending that
university, he supports and contributes to the institution.
Therefore, indirectly, the student contributes to, supports,
and is connected to the manufacturing of arms. The

manufacture of arms is in turn connected to and supportive of the utilization of arms for the persecution of
the innocent. Hence, according to the claim of the
exporter, the connecting links are there to be established. The student acts so as to promote the very end
he condemns the exporter for promoting, by the latter's
action of selling arms to perpetrators of unjust acts.

But notice the differences in the two cases. In the
case of the connections in the student's act-sequence,
the linkages are more indirect between (b) and (j). It
may be that the arms manufactured by the corporations
invested in by the university are not those sold to the
nations complained about by the student as persecuting
the innocent. What the student condemns is the selling
of arms to the specific type of user. It is not clear
that he himself has committed this specific type of act.
At best, he may have contributed to such an act indirectly through a number of contingent linkages. There
is a difference.

Still, the student may be not altogether innocent. By
indirectly making possible a certain outcome of a type
he specifically condemns, the student may still be
enmeshed in a partial form of practical inconsistency.
He condemns a certain outcome as a form of action to
produce, then he indirectly makes this very outcome possible by the connections and affiliations he himself
maintains. He has not directly brought about this type
of outcome by his own hand, to be sure, but he has failed
to prevent it from occurring, and even indirectly sponsored it by the institutions and corporation he has supported through his affiliations. His hands may not be
quite as dirty as those of the arms exporter, but they
are not spotlessly clean either.

ADJUDICATING ON THE CIRCUMSTANTIAL
AD HOMINEM

The foregoing case studies show that sorting out the
rights and wrongs of the dispute in any moderately realistic specimen of argumentation where there is an ad
hominem accusation is a subtle matter. Just because
there is a pragmatic inconsistency, it does not always
follow that there is also a logical inconsistency to be
derived. In this situation an error can arise either
way. The defender, showing that there is no logical

inconsistency, may declare the attacker guilty of a vicious
ad hominem. However, he could be wrong if there is a
serious pragmatic inconsistency in his own argument. The
attacker, seizing on the pragmatic inconsistency, may find
that quite a sufficient basis for an accusation of ad
hominem fallacy, logical inconsistency or no. And perhaps
he cculd have a good case.

Thus a circumstantial inconsistency between the arguer's
argument and his own circumstances may, but then again it
may not, constitute an illegitimate argument. As the first
step of analysis the argument must be evaluated, not just
by its circumstances of its particular advocacy by this
particular advocate, but by its own merits as an argument
per se. Having first established that evaluation, then
one can go on and try to determine whether or not there
is a circumstantial inconsistency, how serious the inconsistency is, and whether it should detract from this
arguer's practical advocacy of this argument.

Take the classical smoking example, where the parent cites
medical evidence for the conclusion that smoking is harmful, and is a bad habit. The child replies, "What about
you? You smoke, don't you? You're not being consistent!"
By way of sober analysis, the evaluator should proceed in
steps. The child first of all should evaluate the argument on the basis of the scientific evidence correlating
smoking with various disorders, if that is the premissary
basis put forward by the parent. However, the fallacy,
the faulty step of reasoning, can occur when the child
rejects the argument per se because of the circumstantial
inconsistency occasioned by the fact that the very advocate of the argument is himself a smoker. This is indeed
a serious circumstantial inconsistency to be wondered at
and explored, perhaps even to be deplored. It is grounds
for questioning the parent's sincerity, and the circumstantial squaring of his own argument with his advocacy
of it. But the point should not be obscured that, in
itself, the argument may be a good one. The child may be
doing a disservice to himself and others by hastily
rejecting it on grounds of inconsistency.

How serious is a pragmatic inconsistency? We know that
a logical inconsistency in a person's position means that
the position as a whole must contain falsehood. With a
pragmatic inconsistency, the seriousness of the error
depends on the extent to which the contravening practice
of the arguer is a deliberate and resolute action that by

its commission reflects his own convictions. Insofar as
the act-description reflects a commitment of the actor,
it points toward a proposition he may be committed to,
and in pragmatic inconsistency this proposition is logically inconsistent with another commitment of the actor.
Thus pragmatic inconsistency increases in seriousness as
it approaches logical inconsistencies in an arguer's
propositions he has actually conceded. However, the link
between the two types of inconsistency is not a tight one.
The would-be self-contradictor's adversary has to show by
filling in the gaps through questioning that the one
leads to the other.

Suppose Reverend Smith preaches on Sunday that one should
not lie, but a member of the congregation remembers the
time the minister told a fib in order to spare someone's
feelings. Could a circumstantial ad hominem be made out
of this? The answer is that, at our present state of
knowledge, an allegation could be made of pragmatic
inconsistency, but the seriousness of the allegation can
only be weighed by further dialogue. Reverend Smith could
be asked to explain the apparent contradiction. Was his
action at that time a reflection of any conviction that
there are some circumstances in which lying is permissible?
Or was it merely a lapse on his part as he now views it?
A moral lapse of the latter sort may be serious enough as
a moral failure, but it does not reflect a logical failure
in Reverend Smith's moral philosophy as a coherent position to be argued for and advocated to others. An ethical
position may be hard to live up to, but that does not make
it wrong.

On the other hand, if the minister's action expressed a
conviction that lying is not an absolute prohibition then,
given his universalistic pronouncement, there is some
question whether his moral position is confused and indeed
contradictory. As an error or failing of correct argument,
this situation is more serious, for logical inconsistency
requires that at least one proposition be false among
those forming his position.

Suppose a drunk medical practitioner advises a patient to
stop drinking because alcohol can lead to malfunctioning
of the liver. The patient might retort, ad hominem, that
the doctor's advice is not consistent with the doctor's
own practice. However, suppose that the doctor has given
good medical evidence, clinical findings that support the
harmful effects of alcohol usage on liver function in

patients.   Is the patient's ad hominem criticism fallacious or reasonable?

One point that can be made by this example is that the
patient's retort is fallacious to the extent that it is
meant or taken to be a refutation of the general propo-
sition--as argued for by the doctor--that there is a link
between alcohol usage and liver problems.   It is as if
the patient were to reason as follows: "Liquor can have
no effect on the liver, for the doctor who made this claim
was himself inebriated."   Clearly there is something
badly wrong with this sort of refutation.   What is wrong?
It appears to be a confusion between the doctor's argument
per se and the doctor's argument in relation to his own
personal conduct.

When the patient makes this sort of reply, he is confusing
the subjective and objective aspects of the doctor's argument, it seems.   The patient seems to argue ad verecundiam:
"This man is a doctor.   I should take what he does serious,
as an expression of his expert conviction.   He drinks.
Therefore, liquor must be medically harmless."   Needless
to say, such an argument is weak in the extreme, given
that the doctor's act of imbibing may not express any
serious commitment to drinking alcohol as a medically
indicated practice.

In this chapter we have more perspicuously raised, but
still not answered, the question of how to respond to an
ad hominem allegation.   We have seen how to sort out
various factors, and put them in an order.   But the disputes in the case studies of this chapter, as enlightening
as they have been, have not been fully resolved.   What
stands out is that it remains very difficult to prove,
beyond question, that one party is in the right.   We have
even seen that one ad hominem can be replied to with
another.

There is the possibility of tu quoque to a tu quoque, of
building one ad hominem onto another.   For example, suppose a reporter accuses a politician of preaching the
virtues of honesty while at the same time lying to cover
up his own questionable activities.   The allegation is
one of circumstantial inconsistency.   Further suppose that
a critic accuses the reporter of decrying this inconsistency while at the same time indulging in a similar circumstantial inconsistency himself--for example arguing
that there should be conflict-of-interest guidelines for

the professions while at the same time attempting to
exempt his own professional activities from such guidelines by lobbying for removal of ethical standards for
reporting practices. This is a particularly telling
form of rejoinder to the tu quoque, because the original
victim of such an embarrassing allegation can turn the
tables on his tormentor and say "What about you? You
preach practicing what you preach, but you don't practice it yourself. For shame!"

The effect is that of a double rejoinder. Not only is
the reporter shown to be guilty of circumstantial inconsistency, but since he was the one who, by his allegation,
upheld the value of circumstantial consistency in the
first place, he is being again circumstantially inconsistent by his failure to live up to that standard. One
must be careful not to overreact, however, because, despite being hoisted by his own petard, the reporter's
initial fusillade might have been quite accurate. What
is needed is a more systematic approach to sorting out
these complex disputes.

One problem with the circumstantial ad hominem is that it
may discredit someone to such a great extent, in advance
of his even beginning to argue, that his arguments are
such to be ignored or dismissed out of hand. Yet any
person, no matter what his particular circumstances,
should at least have the right to present an argument.
Although the circumstances may dictate a climate of reser-
vation concerning this person's sincerity, that should
not mean that the argument is to be categorically ignored
no matter what form it might take. An allegation of circumstantial ad hominem should not be regarded as such a
conclusive refutation of a person's argument that there
is no room for rejoinder or further discussion. It is
more like a warning than a conclusive refutation.

On the other hand, the same thing could be said concerning logical inconsistency. Anyone who has upheld both
one proposition and another proposition that entails the
negation of the first has committed himself to falsehood.
But he still should have the right to argue that he has
changed his mind, or wants to make certain qualifications
or retractions that will dissolve the contradiction.

The case study approach has shown that ruling fairly on
realistic ad hominem disputation has many facets of complex interplay between the various possible moves and

countermoves. How could the methodology of dialectical
games help to resolve such adjudications?

CONTINUING THE DIALECTIC

One way to handle pragmatic consistencies in dialectical
games is to attempt to reduce the pragmatic inconsistency
to a logical inconsistency between propositions actually
conceded by one's opponent. The way to do this is to
continue the questioning process to fill in the gaps. For
example, in the smoker example, this method would require
the child to proceed by asking the parent some Socratic
questions along the lines indicated by the following
dialogue.

Move	Child	Parent
1.	You claim that smoking is unhealthy?	Correct.
2.	But you yourself smoke.	Correct.
3.	So you think it's all right to smoke?	Well, yes, I suppose.
4.	Do you agree that health is a good thing?	Of course.
5.	So you agree that any activity injurious to health is wrong.	Yes.
6.	It follows from your concessions at 5 and 1 that smoking is wrong. Yet you conceded at 3 that it is all right, i.e., not wrong to smoke. You're inconsistent!	Well, just a minute. I don't think smoking is always all right. But I'm a lot older than you, and anyway I've tried to quit but haven't succeeded yet.

At moves 1 and 2, the child has already obtained sufficient concessions for his argument to go forward. Assuming, as conceded at 4 and 5, that the parent is willing to

concede that smoking ought to be carried out as an activity, then by 2 the child has clinched the pragmatic inconsistency. What is required to reduce that pragmatic inconsistency to a logical inconsistency is the move from 2 to 3. If the parent will concede that his activity of smoking implies that in his opinion it is right to smoke, then the parent is caught in logical inconsistency. If so, the child has succeeded in his Socratic task.

But the point to note is that the parent may or may not be willing to make this concession. In an alternative dialogue to the one above, the parent might reply at 3, "Well, yes, I do smoke. But that doesn't mean I think it's all right. In fact, I have tried to quit many times. But that's the insiduous thing about smoking. Once you start, it becomes a habit, and you can't stop even if you think it would be prudent to stop. True, I do smoke. But I still feel it is a harmful and morally wrong activity." The parent here is pragmatically inconsistent. He admits his own failure to carry out what he admits is the right course of action. But he is not logically inconsistent.

At step 2, we know the parent is pragmatically inconsistent, but only after the intervening moves from 3 onward do we acquire further information to determine whether or not the parent's position is also logically inconsistent. The latter is not determined by the former.

The point is that, in fairness, the respondent should have the opportunity to clarify his position further, once he is accused of pragmatic inconsistency. In the dialogue above, it has been shown by 6 that the parent's position is logically inconsistent, and at this move he somewhat feebly tries to cope with the contradiction. However, in the alternative dialogue, he admits pragmatic inconsistency, but is unwilling to be led into logical inconsistency.

Hence a best option and strategy for the opponent, having found the respondent in pragmatic inconsistency, is to pursue the dialogue further in order to determine whether the respondent's position is also logically inconsistent.

There is quite a difference in the two results. If the respondent's position is logically inconsistent, then it must be false. However, if his position is pragmatically inconsistent, that does not mean it is false. It may only

mean that his own admitted actions do not square with
what he advocates. However, his actions may or may not
fairly reflect his position. He may be guilty of weakness of will, and may even be excused for it, but that
is quite different from his advocating or conceding
inconsistent propositions. The first may or may not be
some evidence of the second. Only further questioning
can lead from one to the other. In short, it may be
quite unfair to infer the one inconsistency from the
other, if the respondent has been given no chance to
deny the inference, based on his own admissions.

We now have some idea of what sort of problem is at stake
in attempting to analyze the circumstantial ad hominem.
We have some grasp of the target explicandum, we have
some conception of the methodology needed to analyze this
target data, and we can see how to apply that methodology.
The use of analytical case studies of realistic disputations has revealed the ad hominem in its dialectical
subtlety to a degree beyond the inklings given by the
Standard Treatment of the textbooks.

We now need to develop the hints we gave in chapter 1 concerning methodologies available to help sort out the problems created by these cases. As our solution to the problem of adjudicating ad hominem disputes develops in subsequent chapters, we will see that the method advocated
adopts a model of argument called practical reasoning.
This method involves linking the actions or other personal
circumstances of an arguer into a statement of that
arguer's position. The method is highly relative to a
particular case. For what an arguer takes to be necessary
or sufficient to implement his position is a matter that
is highly relative to the particular situation as the
arguer sees it. It will follow that the logic of ad
hominem criticisms is very much a practical logic--truly
a matter of pragmatics or practical reasoning--and each
case must be judged on its own merits. We do give general
guidelines for adjudicating on ad hominem disputes in the
sequel, but these guidelines can only be applied to real-
life disputes by making certain judgments about background
information as the arguer may plausibly be taken to be
aware of it. In short, judging ad hominem disputes in
real cases is, to some significant extent, a practical
matter of judgment in how to apply dialectical guidelines
to a specific argument.

To stress this practical aspect, we will close this chapter

by mentioning a case brought to the author's attention by
Krister Segerberg. As this case was related to me, its
outline is essentially as follows. A woman in Scandinavia
owned an apartment building that was assessed for taxes
under a certain law. This woman had also gone on record
as being an advocate of a tax reform bill that would alter
the tax laws applying to certain buildings. She had
argued against a certain loophole that would enable land-
lords to avoid paying a higher tax rate on their buildings.
As it turned out, she herself was taking advantage of this
loophole to pay a reduced tax rate on the apartment building she owned. As things turned out, the tax reform was
not passed through the legislature, and this woman continued to pay the lower rate of taxes on her apartment
building by taking advantage of the loophole.

This woman, according to the story, was criticized for
being inconsistent. She argued, however, that she was not
inconsistent at all. Prima facie, it might seem that a
case can be made out for defending her against the charge
of inconsistency. She argued that if the new law had been
passed, she would have conformed to it. But in the
absence of the law, she felt free morally to take advantage of the same shelter that other owners of such dwellings
were also eligible for. Though she felt that the new law
was a good one, since it was not now law, she felt free to
follow the law and, consistently with others in her position, take advantage of the benefits it permitted her.

Was she being inconsistent or not? One hint is to be aware
of the potential equivocation implicit in "morally obliged"
versus "legally obliged" as discussed by Hamblin (1970a,
p. 292). But beyond that, could her argument for her own
consistency of practice be defended in this particular
case? I leave this case as a problem to the reader. This
chapter, of course, suggests that such a particular case
may best be resolved by continuing the dialogue between
the disputants. If the participants are not around to
attack or defend the case themselves, such continuance can
take place hypothetically--under certain restraints--
through the procedure of dialectic. Subsequent chapters
will show better how it is done, but further analysis of
this particular case will be left as an open problem.

4

Formal Models of
Ad Hominem Argument

We now have some grasp of how to approach the circumstantial ad hominem where the circumstances at issue are the
arguer's previous concessions or actions. But in many
common illustrations of ad hominem offered by current
texts, personal circumstances appear to range over more
than just these two types. As we saw in chapter 1, the
abusive ad hominem brings in personal circumstances that
may be other than actions or concessions of the person
attacked.

A common type of argument standardly characterized as ad
hominem occurs where, instead of evaluating the evidence
relating to his opponent's claim, an attacker simply
vilifies the character of the opponent. Such an attack
may be vituperative, slanderous, highly emotional, and,
above all, intensely and unfairly personal in what it
alleges about the person of its victim.

An argument of this type may have many faults. Just to
call it an ad hominem and leave it at that could be a
dangerous oversimplification. For one thing, as we saw
in chapter 1, an emotional outpouring may not even
strictly be an argument.

The fact is that a large part of what seems to be wrong
is that argument of any sort has been foregone in favor
of a direct and quite successful appeal to powerful
emotions and attitudes. Where are the premisses and conclusions in such an appeal?

ABUSIVE AD HOMINEM AS A FALLACY OF
SUBJECT-MATTER DISJOINTEDNESS

Yet it may be felt that the fallacy consists in the
evasion itself. What is wrong is that the emotional
appeal is somehow irrelevant, a deception by distraction.
Indeed, many textbooks propose that what is fallacious
about the ad populum, ad hominem, and other fallacies
associated with emotional appeals is that the emotional
appeal is irrelevant to the conclusion of the argument.
What remains to be seen, however, is how the requisite
notion of failure of relevance interacts with the existence of an argument, and what sort of relevance is
involved. What we are being told is that in effect the

ad hominem is a species of ignoratio elenchi, or misconception of refutation.

The problem is that until we know what "relevance" means, we have no clear guidelines for showing clearly what really is fallacious about these arguments that seem to be wrong by being "irrelevant."

Formal logic of the classical sort does not seem to be any help in resolving the problem. It is well known that classical logic has theorems like p ⊃ (q ⊃ p) and ¬p ⊃ (p ⊃ q), which suggests that classical logic is simply neutral on the issue of whether p and q are in any way topically related to each other. The classical material 'If . . . then' or ⊃, only assures us that p ⊃ q never takes us from a true p to a false q, never mind whether p and q are connected in any way.

The branch of formal logic called relevance logic is specifically designed to deal with fallacies of relevance like the two classical tautologies above. But the problem with it, as shown by Iseminger (1980), is that although a variety of formal logics based on the idea of relevance are offered, somehow--at least so far--we have not been provided with a clear basic idea of what "Your argument is irrelevant!" means in one or more of these formal logics. We need a concept of relevance that can be applied to fallacies like the ad baculum and ad verecundiam so that we can see specifically how these arguments are, at least sometimes, dramatic failures of a proposition to be relevant to a given argument or conclusion--Relevant, that is, in a sense which shows us why such arguments can correctly be said to be fallacious. The problem is that the pragmatic task of showing the relevance of relevance logics or other formal logics to the major fallacies of relevance remains unsolved, or perhaps even unaddressed. It is by no means clear that "relevance" in the technical sense of relevance logic is even related to the concept of relevance that is meant when we say that the ad hominem is a fallacy of relevance.

The suggestion may be that we should be working in a relatedness logic. It has been shown in Walton (1979) how relatedness logic is applicable to the ignoratio elenchi, so let us look to treating ad hominem in a similar way. P implies Q in relatedness logic if, and only if, it is not the case that P is true and Q is false, and there is subject matter overlap between P and Q. To

determine if there is subject matter overlap, take a set
T of the most specific possible topics. Then assign to
P and Q the subject matters p and q respectively, where
each subject matter is a subset of T. P is said to be
related to Q in this sense if there is at least one topic
in T that is in both p and q.

True conditionals in classical PC like 'The moon is made
of green cheese, therefore 3 is the square root of 9'
fail to come out true in relatedness logic provided the
two putative implicationally related propositions fail to
admit of common subject matters. 'Not-p implies p-
implies-q' is not a theorem and therefore is a formal
fallacy, from the viewpoint of relatedness implication,
when connectedness of subject matters is thought to be a
part of the argument. Of course there is nothing wrong
with this theorem if connectedness of subject matters is
not at issue. In that case, classical logic is perfectly
applicable. Indeed, we may say that classical logic
represents the philosophical view that all propositions
really are connected by subject matter overlap, and therefore in classical logic matters of connectedness in topics
need not be specified or taken into account. On the
classical approach, 'Not-p implies p-implies-q' is acceptable because the assumption is that p and q really are
related in some fashion.

If topic sensitivity is required, and the requirement of
implication is that there be subject matter overlap between
implicans and implicandum, then relatedness logic is
clearly more applicable than classical logic or other
alternatives. Thus, if the failure of argument is one of
topic relevance, the use of relatedness logic as developed
by Epstein (1979), would seem to be a primary candidate
for analysis of the model of correct argument concerned.

I suggest that there is considerable promise in this line
of approach to the ad hominem, provided a relatedness
logic is brought into play in order to define clearly the
semantics of subject matters in implications. But it is
an approach that needs to be pursued with some circum-
spection. There are several grounds for caution.

First, it is clear that failure of relatedness is at best
a necessary condition of the ad hominem because one's
premises may be unrelated to one's conclusion without
there being any element of personal attack characteristic
of the ad hominem. That is, ad hominem may be one species

of _ignoratio elenchi_, but the question remains unanswered
of how it can be identified as that species.

Second, it is not clear that failure of relatedness is
even a necessary condition of the _ad hominem_ because in
the most outrageous _ad hominem_ there might be considerable
subject matter overlap between the conclusion and the
statements that form the basis of the emotional appeal.

As Jacques Ellul (1972, p. 84) points out, genuine information can often be mixed in with propaganda in order to
heighten the overall effect of the propaganda. In adver-
tisements for automobiles or electical appliances there
are often legitimate facts about technical specifications
or proved performances mixed in with personal appeals to
feelings and passions. Thus, even in an argument that is
an _ad hominem_ there might be considerable subject matter
overlap between the conclusion and some premises.

If subject matter overlap occurs, still the _ad hominem_
may fail as a relatedness implication because it is not
true that the premises imply the conclusion in virtue of
the truth-values. In other words, sometimes an _ad hominem_
may be thought to be an irrelevant appeal simply because
the conclusion can be false even if the premises are true.
This may explain why sometimes an _ad hominem_ or other
fallacy of failure of relevance may seem to have occurred
even if relatedness exists in the argument.

To sum up, relatedness implication is at best a necessary
condition for the analysis of the _ad hominem_ and, even so,
still does not define the fallacy or differentiate it from
the _ad populum_, _ignoratio elenchi_, or other fallacies that
arise through failure of relatedness.

The proposal is that in certain instances of arguments
standardly characterized as fallacious because they are
ad hominem--especially those of the abusive sort--part of
the explanation of what has gone wrong is that the attacker
is so far off topic that subject matter relatedness fails.
Clearly, however, not all abusive _ad hominem_ fallacies are
of this sort.

OBVERSE OF THE _AD VERECUNDIAM_

Many instances of _ad hominem_ criticisms we have cited in
this monograph constitute, to a significant extent, attempts

to undermine or damage someone's credibility or reliabil-
ity as a source of information or reasonable argument.
The allegation is in effect this: "Because of your personal circumstances or qualities, you are not qualified
or in a position to be trusted to pronounce correctly
upon the topic at issue. In fact, in virtue of your personal aberrations, you are positively disqualified on this
subject, and for this reason, we have grounds for thinking
that your opinions will tend to be incorrect." For
example, in the illustration concerning the abortion dispute, one implication of the accuser is that the man will
always tend to be biased to one side in his thinking on
this issue, and therefore his opinions will tend to be
incorrect because they must always cleave simplistically
to the one side of a complex issue. Moreover, the implication is that the man cannot be in a position to know
first-hand certain facts about motherhood, and is therefore positively disqualified to pronounce on the subject
of abortion.

The same point is being alleged on abusive ad hominem.
The allegation is that the accused is so deficient in
knowledge, methodology, expertise, or requirements for
rational thinking that he or she is not only not worth
paying attention to, but is likely to be misleading or
off the mark in any pronouncements on the subject at
issue.

So it is that one form of the ad hominem is characterized
by Wesley Salmon (1963) and Woods and Walton (1981) as a
kind of inverse ad verecundiam. While the ad verecundiam
argument is an attempt to increase the credibility of the
sayso of some source of authority or expertise on a topic,
the ad hominem can be a parallel but inverse attempt to
discredit some arguer's pronouncements as biased or dis-
oriented, and therefore to debase that proposition's
credibility. According to Salmon, "In the argument from
authority, the fact that a certain person asserts p is
taken as evidence that p is true. In the argument against
the man, the fact that a certain person asserts p is taken
as evidence that p is false (p. 67). The assumption here
is that just as the ad verecundiam can be correct or
incorrect as a type of argument, depending on whether the
appeal to expertise is legitimate or fails in certain
ways, so too the abusive sort of ad hominem can sometimes
be legitimate yet other times fallacious.

In the case of the ad verecundiam, it has been argued in

Woods and Walton (1974) that rational criteria do exist
for the adjudication of appeals to expertise, and that
some appeals to authority are legitimate arguments. It
is also argued there that arguments for the credibility
of a proposition on the basis of appeal to the sayso of
an expert are best viewed as neither deductive nor
inductive in nature--where access to inductive evidence
or to deductive argument is available, the appeal to
expertise may lose its usefulness and relevance. In
general, deductive or inductive justification is to be
preferred, if it is available. Still, appeals to expertise can still be rational arguments under imperfect
evidential conditions, if better evidence is not available and there is a need to decide or act.

If this line of approach is acceptable, the question is
thereby raised: What type of argument is an appeal to
expertise--whether positive or negative--if it is not
deductive or inductive? Hamblin (1970a, p. 218) suggests
that we could at least begin with the deductively valid
form of argument: everything x says is true, and x says
that p, therefore p. By itself, however, this scheme is
not much help. True, x may have said that p. But some
other expert y, who also has always said only what is
true, may now say that not-p. Are we to conclude that p
and not-p? We cannot, of course, unless we want to
accept a conclusion we know to be false. But deductive
logic does not rule out a conflicting situation of this
sort arising. So deductive logic by itself is not helpful.

Salmon (1963, p. 64) proposes an inductive model of the
correct argument from authority. The vast majority of
statements made by x concerning subject S are true, and
p is a statement made by x concerning S; therefore p is
true. This proposal meets the same abrupt fate, however.
Perhaps y is also an authority whose pronouncements are
very likely to be true, and y asserts not-p. According
to the probability calculus, the probability of not-p
must equal unity minus the probability of p. Hence p and
not-p cannot both be at the same time highly probable.
If p is high, not-p must be low, or vice versa. The
pluralism of probabilistically veracious sources (a not
uncommon situation--experts do disagree) must, by Salmon's
analysis, land us in contradiction. Consequently, we know
that an inductive model of the correctness of the appeal
to expertise cannot provide a realistic analysis of many
legitimate appeals to backing an argument by expertise of

an authority.

Deductive and inductive logic do not guide us well enough when dealing with inconsistent givens, and are therefore not by themselves much help when confronting the real-life ad verecundiam or ad hominem. For this reason, we turn to a third model of argument, the notion of plausible argument developed by Rescher (1976).

PLAUSIBLE ARGUMENT

The task of plausibility theory, as Rescher sees it, is to help us carry on an orderly process of reasoning in the face of inconsistent data. In the interest of consistency, some information must be "given up." Neither the probability calculus nor classical deductive logic are very helpful in telling us how to proceed when confronted with inconsistency. In classical deductive logic, given an inconsistency you can derive any statement you like. In the probability calculus we have it that:

$$pr(q \text{ given } p) = \frac{pr(p \wedge q)}{pr(p)}$$

So if p is inconsistent, $pr(p) = 0$, and $pr(q \text{ given } p)$ cannot be defined. We cannot determine probabilities relative to an inconsistent given. Yet cognitive dissonance is a familiar enough phenomenon in the psychology of ratiocination when a reasoner is confronted with inconsistency. How then are we to proceed?

The central methodology of plausibility evaluation is essentially given by six rules which tell us how to obtain what is called a plausibility indexing. The rules are quite simple. They are, as Rescher says, more designed for comparing rather than calculating. This simplicity is appropriate, however, for a level of analysis that is more basic or even more primitive than, say, probability theory, we are told. We start with a set

$$S = \{P_1, P_2, \ldots P_n\}$$

of propositions that represents a set of theses we are inclined to accept. These data for plausibility theory are taken to be propositions that are vouched for by "sources," for example, experts, eyewitnesses, historical sources, conjecture, or even principles such as simplicity

or uniformity.   Degrees of plausibility are indicated on
a scale

$$1, \frac{m-1}{m}, \frac{m-2}{m}, \ldots \frac{1}{m}$$

where 1 represents a maximal plausibility and $\frac{1}{m}$ represents
minimal plausibility for m > 0.   The plausibility indexing
is a value |P| such that 0 < |P| ≤ 1.   The key idea of
plausibility theory is that a conclusion cannot be less
plausible than the least plausible premiss of a deductively
valid argument.

The question of deductive closure of S is especially interesting.   Since plausibility evaluations are designed to
deal with an inconsistent p-set S, inferential closure
would make the enterprise absurd.   However, in the special
case where S is consistent, Rescher extends the plausibility indexing to cover its deductive closure S_C (set S plus
all its deductive consequences).   The rule of thumb here
to determine the plausibility of some proposition P in S_C
amounts essentially to this: take all the sets of S propositions that entail P, determine a plausibility indexing
for each set based on the least-plausible premiss rule,
then pick the maximum of these values.   Rescher calls this
case the special (artificial) source of reasonable inference, X*.   Practically speaking, in connection with evaluating the pronouncements of authorities, this feature can
be quite important for, as DeMorgan (1847, pp. 281-285)
observed, authorities are not always quoted directly so
that in practice we are often confronted with what is
taken to be an inference from the original pronouncement.
What often happens may begin something like this.   Authority a asserts p and then individual b infers that q.
Next, c credits a with q.   And so forth.   We need not go
too far in order to see how it can be dangerous indeed to
confuse what a source is thought actually to have said
with what is thought to be inferable from what was said.

Plausibility theory, as Rescher sees it, provides a method
for the evaluation of the reasonableness of claims made
by various sources of the sayso of authorities: experts,
historical sources, traditional wisdom, commonly held
beliefs, witness observation and memory, and conjectures
or assumptions based on simplicity and uniformity of hypotheses.   For our purposes here, the interest of the
plausible model of argument lies in its applicability to
arguments on the basis of the authority of expertise.

One particularly relevant application of this sort is given in Woods and Walton (1981, chapter 5) where Rescher's technique of plausibility evaluation is applied to the case where a group of suitably qualified experts collectively disagree on a question. In this instance, we must start with an inconsistent given set of propositions. We then array all the maximum consistent subsets of that set, and proceed to choose one or more of these consistent sets as the appropriate one to represent the best advice of this group of experts.

Suppose, for example, that we have three experts and we can rate them comparatively on a scale from 1 to 10 as follows: X (value of 8), Y (value of 5), Z (value of 2). Suppose that X asserts $p \supset r$ and $\lnot r$, Y asserts $p \lor q$, and Z asserts $q \supset r$. Collectively this set of propositions is inconsistent. However, by scanning a truth-table, we can see that there are four maximal consistent subsets:

(1) $\{p \lor q, p \supset r, q \supset r\}$

(2) $\{p \lor q, p \supset r, \lnot r\}$

(3) $\{p \lor q, q \supset r, \lnot r\}$

(4) $\{p \supset r, q \supset r, \lnot r\}$

We notice that (1) rejects $\lnot r$, which is a highly plausible proposition (value of 9); (3) rejects $p \supset r$, which is also highly plausible (value of 8). The policy accepted by Rescher is to maximize overall plausibility. That is, the policy is to reject sets of propositions that exclude propositions of greater plausibility. Accordingly, we reject (4) and accept (2), for (4) rejects $p \lor q$, a proposition of plausibility value 5, whereas (2) rejects only $q \supset r$, which has the lesser value of 2 . In this example then, the rational way to proceed in the face of conflicting pronouncements is to accept the maximal consistent subset (2). This policy allows us to accept as much highly plausible information as we can, without accepting inconsistency.

So the method of plausible reasoning is quite different in its goals and procedures from either deductive or inductive models of reasoning. It can tell us how to proceed in the event of inconsistency. It shows us how the ad verecundiam argument from expert sources can sometimes be a correct type of argument, namely plausible argument--hence its

applicability to the ad hominem as well. For as we saw,
the ad hominem, especially the abusive sort, is often an
obverse of the ad verecundiam--an argument to lower or
degrade the plausibility of a putative source of reliable
testimony. In addition, however, plausibility theory is
also a useful model of argument for the circumstantial ad
hominem because of course the latter is based on the
allegation of inconsistency. Thus one rational way to
proceed in the face of inconsistency is to reduce one's
commitments to a maximally consistent highly plausible
subset of the original inconsistent set.

Once plausibility enters the picture, it becomes possible
to formulate the problem of understanding ad hominem
criticisms. To say that a proposition is plausible is to
say less than the claim that the proposition is true,
known to be true, or is even probably true. It is only
to say that the proposition may be presumed to be true
provisionally, in the absence of refutation. Plausibility
is an essentially subjective presumption based on testimony, appeal to expert testimony, or other subjective
sayso. Plausibility is a matter of burden of proof. To
say that a proposition is plausible is only to claim that
the burden of proof is on the critic to give an argument
for rejecting it. But this very same subjectivity of
source is equally characteristic of ad hominem as a form
of argument. Indeed, some textbooks are given to treating
the ad hominem argument as always being a fallacious move
precisely because of its inherent subjectivity. They
adopt the idea that personalistic, subjective judgment is
always wrong, either as a basis for supporting or attacking an argument. But this way of treating ad hominem is
a big mistake, according to our viewpoint, because it
fails to take plausible reasoning into account as a form
of argument that can sometimes be reasonable and defensible.

The question that remains--what are the appropriate rules
for plausible reasoning in games of dialogue where ad
hominem criticisms are advanced? Rescher's key idea for
plausibility theory is a good place to start. However,
as has recently been suggested in Walton (1984), there
are alternative sets of rules for plausible reasoning
that may be appropriate for various contexts of reasonable dialogue where fallacies are to be modelled.

The various rules for plausible inference in games of
dialogue correspond to different kinds of answers that

can be given to a why-question in a Hamblin type of game.
Hamblin rules that the answer to 'Why A?' should be
restricted to a limited set of replies like 'No commitment A' or 'B, and B implies A,' for some set of premisses, B. However, in the games of dialogue appropriate
to study ad hominem criticisms, there are some restrictions that should be applied to the set of premisses B
supplied by an answerer. One approach is to require that
each of the premisses in B should be more plausible than
A. Rescher's rule amounts to the requirement that the
least plausible member of B must be less than or equal to
the plausibility-value of A. Different approaches are
possible here. To explore the matter further, we must
look to the properties of games of dialogue in a more
general way.

DIALECTICAL THEORY AND FORMAL MODELS

In chapter 1 we saw, following Barth and Martens, how the
ad hominem can be located as a formal fallacy in a certain
class of formal dialectical games. In chapter 2, we saw
how this conception of the ad hominem needed to be extended
to take into account pragmatic inconsistencies. The most
common type of pragmatic inconsistency involved in ad
hominem arguments is a deonto-praxeological sort, where
the attack is of the form: "You (my opponent) claim that
everyone ought to do x, but you yourself fail to act so
as to do x." Ultimately, a formal model adequate to study
such arguments would be a deontic logic. In the present
chapter, we saw how relatedness logic and plausible inference also play a role in helping us to study the formal
structure of some ad hominem arguments. Is this plurality
of formal models capable of being unified in one single
theory?

The ultimate answer, I suggest, lies in viewing games of
dialectic as the outer context of argument, and conducting
further studies to see how these other models can be
absorbed within dialectic.

The problem of how to deal with the ad hominem in games
of dialectic is closely tied to problems of the regulation
of commitment-stores in these games. When one participant
in a game of dialectic accuses another of inconsistency,
the problem is how the inconsistency is to be resolved.
This is to presume that there may be different types of
inconsistency--pragmatic as well as logical varieties--and

that an inconsistency among the set of commitments of one
participant has been <u>correctly</u> identified by the other.

If so, the problem is what to do about it. Does being
found in inconsistency among one's commitments mean that
a participant should lose the game? Or should he have a
chance to remedy the inconsistency, let us say, by
retracting one or more of his commitments and thereby
restoring his position to consistency? The answer is
that it depends on the type of dialectical game one is
engaged in. In fact, some games of dialectic, like the
obligation game, the Lorenzen games for intuitionistic
logic, and some of the Hamblin games, do not admit of
retraction of commitments.

Moreover, in the obligation game, a win-strategy has been
carried out if one's opponent has been led into a self-
contradiction, and that is the end of the game. Here
there is no possibility of retraction of one's commitments
at all. In effect, therefore, a successful prosecution
of <u>ad hominem</u> is the deadliest form of attack, at least
if there is a logical contradiction determined upon one's
opponent's commitments, where commitments refer to propositions actually advanced by the opponent.

In the Hamblin games there are rules that allow for the
retraction of commitments by participants in the game.
An <u>ad hominem</u> attack in these games is not always a win-
strategy if the opponent can remove the contradiction by
retraction of a commitment.

Different dialogical games offer different ways of handling contradictions in commitments. Barth and Martens
(1977, p. 88) rule, following Lorenzen, that any participant who shows verbal inconsistency in his line of attack
loses that attack. They define verbal inconsistency not
as uttering two contradictory propositions one after the
other, but as both uttering and challenging the same
proposition by a participant within the same line of
attack. For example, if the proponent has already conceded ⌐p, but then at some later point challenges ?p to
the opponent, then the opponent wins that line of attack.

Hamblin (1970a, p. 271) proposes another way of handling
verbal inconsistency by formulating a rule requiring that
'Why p?' may not be asked unless p is a commitment of the
hearer and not of the speaker. This ruling means that
verbal inconsistency can never arise in the game at all,

provided the speaker's commitment-store is consistent.
If the speaker is committed to ¬p, then if his commitments are consistent, he cannot be committed to p. Hence
he can never, according to rule, ask 'Why p?' However,
if commitment-stores are allowed to contain inconsistencies, then the rule allows asking 'Why p?' even if one
is committed to ¬p. For the speaker is then allowed to
be committed to ¬p even if he is also committed to p.
Since Hamblin generally allows inconsistent commitment-
stores, verbal inconsistency would be allowed in Hamblin
games.

The above two facts about the Lorenzen games utilized by
Barth and Martens raise the question of why this particular set of games was chosen. Could it not also be possible or desirable to have some degree of closure or
retraction of commitments in these games if natural moves
in argumentation are to be formalized? As Frank Van Dun
(1972) points out, one in effect sets up certain criteria
of "reasonableness" in setting up a formal game of this
sort. Could not other games be set up that are equally
"reasonable"? Thus the general question of the appro-
priateness of formalizations of natural dialogues is
raised.

Of course, one very good way to provide motivation for
these formal dialogical games, and to reduce the possibility of arbitrary variation of the rules, is to
study these games in relation to the pragmatic dimension
of case studies of the fallacies, like the ad hominem
fallacy. According to Barth and Martens, one form of
the ad hominem fallacy occurs when the respondent in a
Lorenzen game argues to the refutation of a defense
relative to any opponent on the basis of the refutation
of a defense relative only to one particular opponent.
However Van Dun notes that Lorenzen seems to restrict
his conception of a win-strategy to two-person games
(p. 125). Thus in order to model the notion of a win-
strategy against every conceivable opposition, Van Dun,
following a suggestion of Professor Apostel, allows for
coalition partners by generalizing the structure to an
n-person game. By this suggestion, the notation Lp, for
any proposition p put forward by the proponent, indicates
that he wishes to strengthen his claim by inviting the
opponent to call in the help of any co-player he wishes.
If the proponent prefixes his claim with the M-operator,
this means he is only willing to defend it against a
co-player of the opponent that he, the proponent, is

allowed to select. Then Van Dun goes on to show how
standard modal logics can be constructed to model different classes of games, using the relation 'a is a co-
player of b,' for participants a and b, as an accessi-
bility relation.

These developments suggest that dialectical games are
somewhat flexible and variable as models of the outer
procedural structure of criticisms and fallacies. The
precise rules that are appropriate to the context of
realistic dialogues may be in many instances vague or
indeterminate, and should be agreed upon or clarified
by the parties to the dispute. The rules will also partially depend upon the objectives and nature of the
particular dispute. Further research might extend the
study of various rules for these games to include the
various formal models studied in this chapter. Our goal
in this monograph, however, is not a purely formal
study. The question for us, rather, is how these formal
models help us to organize evaluations of case studies
of actual arguments like the ones we have examined. We
propose the following more practical analysis of ad
hominem argumentation.

ANALYSIS OF THE AD HOMINEM

In evaluating any argument where the ad hominem is
alleged or suspected to have been committed, it is
necessary to follow a checklist of questions to pursue
the analysis of the fallacy. First, one must judge
whether the ad hominem is abusive or circumstantial.
The abusive ad hominem involves the rejection of the
argument because of the lack of plausibility of the
source of that argument as an authority or witness. The
circumstantial ad hominem consists in the allegation of
inconsistency in the position of one's opponent, very
often a pragmatic inconsistency.

> Abusive Ad Hominem: Steps to Check
>
> 1. Is what is advanced really an argument? Can
>   there be identified a specific set of proposi-
>   tions making up a set of premises and a con-
>   clusion?
> 2. Is the allegation of the personal property
>   brought forward by the attacker relevant to the
>   conclusion at issue?

3. If relevant, does the premiss constitute a deduc-
    tively (or perhaps inductively) correct argument?
4. If 2 does not apply, is the argument plausible?

Circumstantial Ad Hominem: Steps to Check

1. What are the propositions that are alleged to be
    inconsistent?
2. Who advanced the allegation of inconsistency?
3. Who is alleged to have committed the inconsis-
    tency? Is it an individual, a group, part of a
    group of individuals, or some class of individuals
    (the press, the clergy, middle-class white males)?
    Is this class clearly and consistently specified
    throughout the argument?
4. What type of inconsistency is involved? Is it a
    logical inconsistency or a pragmatic inconsis-
    tency? If the latter is the inconsistency action-
    theoretic, or deontic action-theoretic (the
    arguer says something should be done but then
    himself does not do it)?
5. Once the type of inconsistency has been specified,
    as in 4, can it be proven that the propositions
    identified in 1 really are inconsistent?
6. If the inconsistency among the identified set of
    propositions cannot be demonstrated, has a substi-
    tution been made? Is it the case, as DeMorgan
    warns, that there is merely a near parallel but
    no real inconsistency?
7. If there is no direct logical or action-theoretic
    inconsistency between the propositions identified,
    is there an action-theoretic linkage between the
    given act-descriptions that make up the proposi-
    tions?
8. If there is no inconsistency at all, as in 5 or 7,
    but merely a near parallel as in 6, is the accuser
    himself guilty of committing an ad hominem? That
    is, has he claimed the existence of an inconsis-
    tency whereas in fact it can be shown that there
    is none, as the propositions in question have
    been stated?
9. If there is a pragmatic inconsistency, how bad is
    it? Is it a serious flaw in the arguer's posi-
    tion or merely a trivial slip that can be remedied
    by retraction of some commitments?
10. Does the accused have a chance to respond to the
    allegation of inconsistency?
11. Has the accuser committed the fallacy that Barth

and Martens warn about, of finding an inconsistency in the opponent's position or commitments
and then concluding that his conclusion must be
false (no matter who might try to defend it,
even with different commitments)?

A key to understanding the circumstantial ad hominem
fallacy as a fallacy is that it can be quite a legitimate
move in argument to find an inconsistency, whether logical or pragmatic, in an opponent's argument. Sometimes
an ad hominem type of argument is not fallacious. But
in making this type of move, the refutation may be carried
out badly. Indeed, the attacker may commit at least four
different types of fallacy, depending on how he tries to
refute the defender's position. It is important to distinguish these fallacies.

1. The attacker finds merely the appearance of
    inconsistency, but does not prove there is really
    an inconsistency of any sort (DeMorgan's point).
    Nevertheless, he rejects the argument.
2. The attacker finds a logical (or perhaps) prag-
    matic inconsistency, and then rejects the
    defender's conclusion per se, not merely his
    internal position (Barth and Martens's point).
3. The attacker finds a pragmatic inconsistency,
    but then rejects the defender's argument as
    logically inconsistent (without proving the
    inconsistency).
4. The attacker finds some connection between two
    or more act-descriptions attributed to the
    defender, but fails to show why the actions in
    question may be redescribed fairly so as to
    establish the existence of a pragmatic inconsis-
    tency on the part of the defender. Instead, the
    attacker simply concludes that the defender is
    inconsistent, and therefore his argument is
    incorrect.

As an exercise, the reader can now go back and apply this
analysis to the cases of chapters 1 and 2. We now propose
even more strenuous tests of it in the subsequent chapters. In the next chapter, we proceed to the most detailed
case study yet given.

5

A Case Study of the Circumstantial *Ad Hominem*

In this chapter we will give a detailed analysis of an actual
specimen of circumstantial ad hominem argumentation. In a
magazine article, an author, Gerald L. McAuliffe, mounted an
ingenious and unusual series of arguments on the topic of
ethical guidelines for the news media (see Appendix 1). In
this article, entitled "Just How Ethical Are the News Media?"
which appeared in Quest in 1980, McAuliffe utilizes an
extended version of the circumstantial ad hominem argument.
He argues that members of the news media engage in the very
same unethical practices, such as conflict of interest, as
the politicians they criticize for unethical practices. The
news media are pragmatically inconsistent, he says, in that
their own actions conflict with their condemnation of certain practices.

McAuliffe's whole article consists of one prolonged, carefully reasoned circumstantial ad hominem attack. It is
therefore a uniquely valuable specimen for our analysis. We
will analyze it with the purpose of attempting to determine,
or at least evaluate, whether or not it is a correct or
fallacious use of the argumentum ad hominem, utilizing the
analysis given in previous chapters.

The article is reprinted in this monograph as an appendix.
There are, we postulate, five basic allegations of pragmatic
inconsistency in the overall argument. We begin by stating
and commenting on these five arguments. Our major preoccupation in the first section will be with step 1 of analysis,
isolating the propositions alleged to be inconsistent.

THE FIVE ALLEGATIONS OF INCONSISTENCY

Argument 1, mounting a circumstantial ad hominem allegation,
runs as follows in the form of two propositions. (1) When
the common-law wife of a cabinet minister was given a free
ride on an airline, it was considered front-page news by the
press. (2) But at the same time, many persons working for
the press think there is nothing wrong with taking free
benefits while doing their best to cover up these free
benefits. Here it is alleged that there is a conflict.
First "the press" (the collective noun used in the first
proposition) thinks it worthwhile to expose the free benefits received by politicians. But second, "many publishers,
editors, news directors and reporters" (this time it is

many of these persons working for the press who are cited)
do exactly the same thing themselves, but they try to
cover it up when they do it. But what specifically does
the conflict between (1) and (2) consist of?

Probably the first suggestion is this: the press does
something, but then they criticize someone else, a politician, for doing the very same thing. Is this not inconsistency, or at any rate hypocrisy? Intuitively, there
seems to be some inconsistency in this pair of actions,
but one has to be careful. What may be sauce for the
goose may not always be sauce for the gander--undertaking
brain surgery may be commendable for you, a neurosurgeon,
but morally culpable for me, a person who does not happen
to be qualified for that activity. We cannot automatically assume that what is culpable behavior in a cabinet
minister must always be equally culpable behavior when
undertaken by a reporter. In short, (1) and (2) are not
inconsistent--certainly not logically inconsistent, nor
has it been shown that they are pragmatically inconsistent.

What needs to be shown in order to justify the allegation
that (1) and (2) are somehow in conflict is that the members of the press cited are on the same footing in relation to the actions alleged as the cabinet minister they
criticized. Presumably, the action of the press in criticizing the action of this minister is being taken to
suggest that the press is committed to maintaining a general
principle to the effect that every person of such-and-such
description who takes free benefits is doing something
wrong and may be publicly criticized for it. What remains
open, however, is precisely how the such-and-such description blank is to be filled in. Clearly step 3 of the
analysis of the circumstantial ad hominem will have to be
handled with care.

Thus we should say that McAuliffe has suggested what could
be a nice inconsistency between (1) and (2), but has not
established yet that the inconsistency actually exists.
The press stands fairly accused, but not yet fairly
indicted of committing the circumstantial ad hominem fallacy.

Argument 2, following immediately upon the previous one,
points out that cabinet ministers are barred from holding
stocks and other interests in private corporations except
in blind trusts. The editors and reporters who lobbied
for such regulations themselves are not covered by

regulations forbidding them from holding financial interests in companies they report on. This is the first part
of the alleged conflict. Then a second pair of propositions is put forward. Reporters would publicize for breach
of conduct any cabinet minister who spoke in parliamentary
sessions about a company he had a financial interest in.
However, reporters receive award money from private industries, and their editors see nothing wrong with that.

In this new allegation, the case for a pragmatic inconsistency is on somewhat better justified footing than the
previous one, because it is clear that journalists and
cabinet ministers both have potential for illicit gain by
using their positions to manipulate public opinion to
promote private interests. Still, however, there is no
flat inconsistency demonstrated. Cabinet ministers are
elected, and paid by taxpayers, unlike most journalists.
Cabinet ministers have access to privileged and secret
information, to a much greater extent than do most
reporters or editors. Why must what is appropriate
behavior for one group always be appropriate for the
other? If not always, then no inconsistency is shown.
Once again, at step 3 we will have to proceed with caution.

Still, some case for the parallelism has been made. Both
groups have the potential to earn money illicitly for
doing favors for private interests. Both are open to
conflict of interest. Thus is it not inconsistent for
the one group to criticize the other for doing things it
does itself and does not think it should be censured for,
when both groups are on the footing with respect to the
action in question. The missing such-and-such description
of argument is now closer to being filled in. We know it
has something to do with conflict of interest in relation
to some sort of obligation to the public. But this still
needs to be spelled out further before the alleged inconsistency is tightened up enough to really pin down a
charge of ad hominem circumstantial inconsistency.

Argument 3, the next few paragraphs, postulates another
parallelism. Doctors, lawyers, politicians, and other
professionals have strict and precisely formulated codes
of discipline or ethics. Yet the press often argues that
it is beyond such rules, and at best has very weakly formulated rules that are not enforced or taken seriously by
journalists. Once again, a circumstantial inconsistency
is alleged: the press supports and even demands such
rules for others, but not for themselves. Then the article

goes on to detail the financing of newspaper awards and
other media benefits by private industries, and to cite
the many close affinities and personal links between
journalists and politicians.

Then a fourth allegation of circumstantial inconsistency
is levelled. First, it is stated that a cabinet minister,
upon retirement from the government, cannot act for a
firm in dealings with the government for two years.
Second, it is stated that many journalists float back and
forth between jobs in government and the press. Moreover,
we are reminded that reporters get numerous government
benefits like free offices, phone services, and convention facilities. Here then, the same sort of allegation
of inconsistency is once again levelled--the same potential for conflict of interest is there--but the rules are
different for reporters versus cabinet ministers.

The fifth argument is more specific than the other four
in its allegation and in the group it targets. First, it
is stated that the Hamilton Spectator exposed in a front-
page story that Mayor Jack MacDonald had gone on a free
fishing trip courtesy of Nordair. Then it is stated that
the travel writer of this very same newspaper had "roamed
the world on free airline passes" for years. Moreover,
when a complaint was made, the Spectator's publisher
insisted on holding the hearing behind closed doors, and
blocked testimony of an expert on press ethics. This
allegation is somewhat similar to the previous ones, but
much more specific. Instead of "the press" or "many
journalists" being the target, it is narrowed down to one
newspaper, and one specific pair of events is paralleled.

In allegation 5, the inconsistency is between the following two propositions: (a) A cabinet minister who returns
to private life cannot--by virtue of government rule--be
on the board of, or act on behalf of, a firm that deals
with government for a period of two years; (b) Many journalists float between press and government jobs, and there
is no acknowledgment of conflict of interest, either by
these reporters or their editors.

In this allegation of practical inconsistency, we should
point out by way of commentary that there are some noteworthy nonparallels. In (a), we are not talking about
any politician, but a cabinet minister, a man who carries
a great weight of influence and may have access to privileged information through his former position. This

person is likely to have a powerful potential to use his
influence for a firm's interests. However, in (b), the
journalist who floats between jobs may not even be an
elected official, and may even be in a government job
that is of little influence or power. The journalist
may be biased in favor of the party that employed him,
and this could be reflected in his writing. But in many
cases that would not be nearly as worrisome as the case
of the exminister. Most of us have political biases
anyway, and it may be well known that this particular
reporter or editor is inclined towards some political
persuasion.

The point is that in (a) and (b) it is not the same kind
of conflict of interest that is involved. There is
nothing flatly inconsistent in advocating regulations
for a former cabinet minister who acts for a private
firm, and at the same time stating that we do not need
government regulations for other government employees who
take up jobs in the field of journalism. Thus the inconsistency between (a) and (b) is not established. There
is certainly no logical inconsistency, and because of the
way the actions are described, there is no pragmatic
inconsistency either. All government employees who go
into the private sector may not be alike in regard to the
need to regulate their subsequent actions. Claim (b) is
about many journalists, and does not cover all former
government employees. Hence as (a) and (b) stand, there
is no inconsistency between them.

Thus it is dubious whether this ad hominem allegation has
been mounted in an adequate way. More argument is
required in order to tell us why the "many journalists"
of (b) must or should fall under the class of persons
regulated in (a). True, some journalists could be in a
position similar to (a), and require regulations in like
fashion. But McAuliffe's argument, as far as it goes,
really leaves the issue open. The journalists and
editors opposed to such regulation can still maintain
that (a) and (b) are significantly different, and that
journalists do not need to be regulated in the same way
as former cabinet ministers. Thus the charge of inconsistency fails here, and it is McAuliffe himself who is
open to the charge of having committed the ad hominem,
in the absence of further argument to build up his case.

Although many of our remarks in this section pertain to
step 1 of the analysis, obviously we have made several

preliminary evaluations concerning subsequent steps of
the analysis as well. Step 2 is trivial. We carry on
to an analysis of step 3, a major consideration in this
case.

WHO COMMITTED THE INCONSISTENCIES?

We do have to be careful in assessing McAuliffe's arguments 1, 2, and 3. He is open to a charge that he is
misrepresenting the media position by postulating a
universal position among all members of the press. In
these arguments, he uses the expression "the press" with
the definite article, and this may well be taken to mean
"the press universally" or "all members of the press."
If the press really is univocally saying that it is wrong
for politicians to accept gifts from their affiliated
companies, but not wrong for the press to do the same
thing, McAuliffe's argument is close enough to establishing a powerful ad hominem to become very compelling. One
might support it by querying: Why would people employed
by the media be any more immune to the influence of such
benefits and affiliations than politicians?

We are getting so close to establishing the inconsistency
here that the burden of proof falls heavily on the opponents of McAuliffe's argument to rebut the charge of
inconsistency. For, after all, it is a widely accepted
presumption that politicians should not accept gifts from
or publicly promote companies that they have been affiliated with. This would be agreed to by the general public,
presumably including the press themselves. So far so
good. But here is the rub. Is the press collectively or
universally stating that it is not wrong for they themselves to be involved in similar sorts of activities?

Perhaps some members of the press have made such denials,
but how many of the press would agree? Perhaps some
reporters have taken these sorts of benefits, but that is
not the same thing as the media as a whole saying it is
acceptable to do so.

Any critical analysis of McAuliffe's argument must study
the step 3 question: Precisely by whom is the circumstantial inconsistency claimed to have been committed?
Is it the press collectively, is it identifiable corporations or groups of members of the press, or is it really
certain specific individuals against whom the allegation

is directed?

No one simple answer to this question in the present case
is entirely satisfactory. It would be a dubious claim,
nor is it what McAuliffe in fact claims, that <u>all</u> persons
of the media accept gifts or other benefits from those on
whom they report. Nor would it be correct to say that
every media person would be opposed to ethical guidelines
of the sort advocated. And, once again, McAuliffe is not
making that claim. So the allegation of practical inconsistency is not levelled at the media as a whole, nor
should it be if the argument is to be plausible.

The claim made is only that <u>many</u> publishers, editors, news
directors, and reporters feel there is nothing wrong with
taking the free benefits cited, yet do their best to cover
up these practices from public view. But when clinching
the inconsistency, McAuliffe writes that "the press" (meaning collectively or generally we presume) considers it
publishable news when a politician takes advantage of some
free benefit like an airline ride. In argument 1, therefore, the subjects paired in the alleged inconsistency are
respectively "many media persons" and "the press."

In argument 2, journalists, editors, and reporters are
cited--that is, not specific ones, but this class of persons generally, or at any rate some of them. In example 3,
"the press" is the subject of the alleged inconsistencies.
In short, there is a certain vagueness and also a certain
shifting going on as the argument builds up. Sometimes
the argument is directed towards "the press" as a kind of
collective entity. Sometimes the argument is directed
towards "many members of the press," thus presumably
excluding some, or even perhaps quite a few.

Perhaps what McAuliffe really wants and needs to claim,
to make his argument plausible, is that in some instances
editors who lobby for regulations on politicians are the
very same persons who have reporters working for them who
commit the same or very similar breaches of conduct as
those towards which ethical regulations on politicians
are directed. That is, McAuliffe can be taken as talking
about some specific persons here. But this class of persons is representative enough of what reasonably seems to
be the general practice of enough editors and media persons that it constitutes a problem of significant propor-
tions. Thus in example 4 he writes once again of the
practices of "many journalists."

On the other hand, in order to make his arguments well
supported by empirical evidence, he needs to, and in fact
does, cite commendably specific instances of practical
inconsistencies by particular individuals and organizations.

It is interesting to note that in example 5 it is an
institution that appears to be accused of a circumstantial
inconsistency, or at any rate certain individuals whose
practices are being said to be collectively inconsistent,
where these individuals belong to a certain institution.
It is said that the Spectator ran a number of stories
that advocated opening to public scrutiny debates con-
ducted by those in a position of public trust. Presumably
these stories may have been written by a number of different reporters or authors. Then we are told that a front-
page story in the Spectator revealed Mayor MacDonald's
free fishing trip courtesy of an airline. This story,
for all we are told, may well have been written by someone other than the previous group of writers. Then we
are informed that, ironically, the Spectator's travel
writer, who may be none of the above mentioned authors,
travelled the world on free airline passes. Finally, it
was the Spectator's publisher who insisted that hearings
on this last issue be held behind closed doors.

Notice that if each of the persons mentioned in these
individual allegations is different from the others, no
one person has committed a circumstantial inconsistency.
However, the Spectator, as a corporate group of affiliated individuals may be said, as it were, to have collectively committed a circumstantial ad hominem. This raises
a nice question. Can groups of individuals collectively
commit this fallacy? Or is it more correct to say that a
number of individuals each committed it through their
connection with the Spectator? We are reminded here of
the arms exporter case study of chapter 2, where insti-
tutional affiliation provided the link between the alleged
sets of circumstances.

One way McAuliffe puts his argument is particularly relevant to the question of how many of the press he is talking about, or how many he at any rate needs to make his
claims about in order to mount a reasonable circumstantial
ad hominem. At one point he remarks that press owners are,
as he puts it, "at the public trough in a style and degree
the media would find unacceptable in any other industry."
It is clear here that we are talking matters of degree,

and moreover that the claim is a counterfactual one.
McAuliffe's first claim is that there is a certain level
of a certain kind of activity going on, sponsored by a
certain number of media persons. Now if we were to
transfer this level of activity to another industry,
then the second claim is that the media themselves--but
note, once again, a <u>certain</u> <u>number</u> of them must be
meant--would find thi̅s level of activity objectionable.
In other words, there is a certain number, <u>n</u>, of media
persons engaged in some activity such that i̅f <u>n</u> persons
in some other industry were doing the same thing then a
significant number of media persons (again presumably <u>n</u>
media persons) would object.

McAuliffe's argument is vague; he is not telling us how
large <u>n</u> is, or has to be. Still, that is no objection
per se̲, if he can convince us by specific instances that
<u>n</u> is large enough to worry about. To be sure, there is
room for some criticism. Would those who would (counter-
factually) object to conflict-of-interest activity in
some other industry be the same members of the press who
indulge in it in their own industry? If the answer could
be no, then McAuliffe's <u>ad</u> <u>hominem</u> must be weakened.
There is nothing inconsistent in Mr. X objecting to
practice Y in some other industry, where at the same time
Mr. Z indulges himself in or condones practice Y in
industry U, which it so happens is the industry that both
he and X are employed in. As long as X and Z are separate
individuals, they may contradict each other, but nobody
contradicts himself. In short, McAuliffe may be presup-
posing a certain sameness of individuals in two classes
he cites in his claim. This presupposition may or may
not be justified. In some cases, such as the <u>Spectator</u>
argument 5, he has drawn the two classes closely enough
together to mount a good <u>ad</u> <u>hominem</u>. But whether he has
established that the degree of participation by the media
in the activities he questions is great enough to warrant
a collective, large-scale, practical inconsistency on the
part of some clearly identifiable group of media persons
remains an open question.

In grappling with the question of who precisely is alleged
to have committed the circumstantial inconsistency, one
wonders whether McAuliffe needs or wants to make a statistical claim about the degree of unethical conduct of the
sort that is cited among journalists. McAuliffe makes
claims that "many journalists" commit these practical
inconsistencies. One way to attempt to criticize his

argument is to query "How many?" or alternatively to try
to rebut the premiss by arguing that, in actual fact,
many journalists do not preach one way and act another
in regard to the practices cited by McAuliffe.

One might attempt to argue, for example, that many journalists conduct themselves ethically, while only a few do
not. Just as we cannot judge all members of parliament
by a few conflict-of-interest cases, or all doctors by a
few malpractice suits, it is not fair to conclude that
journalists do not practice what they preach because
there are problems about how some members of the press
conduct themselves.

But McAuliffe is not arguing that we should judge all
journalists by these cases, or that we should judge all
doctors by a few malpractice suits. He is arguing, however, that the two professions are similar in that both
need ethical guidelines. He really does not need to show
that all or even a majority of journalists have committed
specific ethical breaches. He does need to show that
such practices are widespread enough, or at least worrisome enough, to call for ethical guidelines.

All that said, however, McAuliffe's argument is in danger
when, in allegation 3 particularly, he uses the abstract
noun "the press," seeming to make a universal claim about
all journalists. But there is one interesting way his
argument can be defended. Perhaps he does not need to
make a statistical claim about the extent of media male-
factors. Rather he is making a dialectical counterargu-
ment against what we might call the received opinion of
the press, in this case in Canada (and possibly elsewhere
as well, especially in democratic countries), that freedom of the press from censorship means that there should
not be strict codes or rules governing investigation,
reporting, and writing by the media. We refer here to
the so-called freedom of the press doctrine, often taken
by its opponents to imply that the press must have certain freedoms unique to its own profession, thus requiring
freedom from the interference of codes of conduct like
those applicable to other professions, such as medicine
or law.

Now the point may be not how many media persons believe
this doctrine--it is rather that it represents enough of
a well-entrenched doctrine for use in arguments about
ethics in the media to be worth analysis and criticism.

It is not a straw man. Moreover, McAuliffe shows that
the lack of a clear and useful code of media ethics in
Canada can be linked by argument to the freedom of the
press doctrine. That doctrine can be and is used as an
argument basis for concluding that there should be no
ethical codes, or at least not very strict ones, for the
media, unlike other professions. Here, then, is a position worth refuting, or at any rate criticizing. And
McAuliffe does just that by criticizing the pragmatic
consistency of those who held such a view.

What we are suggesting is that McAuliffe's argument is
not an inductive or statistical one at all. It is therefore most charitably viewed as a dialectical argument and
a plausible argument. It is a refutation of a certain
given or received argument. And he uses the circumstantial ad hominem to question the coherence of that argument.

PERSONAL CIRCUMSTANCES

Where is the borderline between the circumstantial ad
hominem and the abusive ad hominem? McAuliffe's article
points out several circumstantial inconsistencies. One
reaction, particularly by those so indicted, could be a
countercharge that the press is being collectively vili-
fied in an unfairly abusive way. McAuliffe concludes
that the press may tend to lose credibility with the
public by their inconsistencies of practice, but one
might be tempted to think that what he really concludes
is that the press should not be given credence as objective news reporters. Does not his own attack not very
effectively undermine press credibility?

I think here that one must be very careful not to read in
conclusions that are not really there. One may come away
from reading the article thinking that the press is not
always as purely objective as one, as a somewhat naive
layperson, may have generally tended to think. But
McAuliffe nowhere states that reporters, in general,
should not be believed or trusted. In fact, he nowhere
concludes that the findings of conflict of interest in
political affairs by the press is in itself incorrect,
false, or unbelievable. True, he argues that existing
practices are less than perfect, and that this state of
affairs could be ameliorated by some ethical guidelines,
but that is a far cry from an abusive ad hominem, that

the press is so misguided that one should seldom or never take their reports seriously as accurate information.

Moreover, although McAuliffe does mention certain members of the press by name, he nowhere vilifies anyone by excessive use of emotional language--possibly except the paragraph where he writes about "pack journalism"--or vilifies any particular individual or group as being a source of low or worthless credibility. He does come close to this--for example, by citing travel reporters who take free rides on airlines, who therefore might possibly be expected to be biased in their reports. But he adds that this practice is now being discouraged and is tending to disappear. And he nowhere makes claims to the effect that some particular reporter distorts facts or reports falsehoods for his covert corporate employer. It is fair to say, then, that muckraking is not his objective. The conclusion that the press as a group is not a credible source of information is just not there to be found, as I see it. Moreover, although it would have been easy for McAuliffe to fine some classic cases of inaccurate or unfair news stories reported by nondis-interested members of the press or other media, none of these are to be found in the article. Such inclusions would surely have simply confused matters and distracted from the thrust of the argument. I think it is greatly to McAuliffe's credit that he, for the most part and almost altogether, avoids the temptation to mount abusive ad hominem attacks on his colleagues.

McAuliffe's basic strategy of circumstantial inconsistency postulates a parallel between the activities of reporters and their reports on public figures. A serious objection is that the parallel breaks down because it is the right of the public to be informed about public figures. Politicians are public figures, whereas reporters generally are not. Moreover, personal and private facts about personal and private lives should not be reported in the media, especially if for example they pertain to the private life of a reporter or writer who is not a public figure.

This objection raises an interesting point. There are personal and private facts about a person's actions or life that are not relevant to whatever issue concerning that person that a reporter or writer has a legitimate right or even obligation to report. Certain periodicals--the National Enquirer is a famous one--virtually hold their

subscribers by a policy of not staying within the limits
of relevancy to issues of public affairs interests in
reporting on private lives or practices. People magazine
is another periodical that has less topical interest in
informing the public of news stories and issues than in
frankly getting down to intimate details of personal life
concerning individuals in whom their readers appear likely
to be interested.

However, in a serious public affairs news periodical or
even nonprint medium, clearly there are limits beyond
which the reporting of personal or private facts or practices concerning the individual included in the news
account of the issue becomes irrelevant, scurrilous,
pointlessly distracting, or even verges into the abusive
ad hominem. But where is the line to be drawn?

So, admittedly a valid point is raised by this objection.
But the objection mistakenly presumes that politicians,
as public figures, always are open game for reporting of
any personal details or practices, while reporters as
private figures are not at all open to personal reportage
themselves. The distinction between a public figure and
a private figure is not all that easy to draw. At what
point does one legitimately become a public figure, by
these lights? Even if the line could ethically and correctly be drawn here, the point remains that if a reporter
takes funds from businesses whose services he is supposedly
reporting objectively on and evaluating for the consuming
public, that reporter is at fault. The public has a right
to know that he is a biased source, not an objective
evaluator of the services he allegedly reports on, especially if he writes in a periodical or medium that advances
itself to its readers as a serious source of authoritative
news, not merely a partisan advertiser or promoter of certain products. The distinction between public and private
lives is not clear or strong enough to justify protection
of secrecy to the reporter or writer who does not wish to
reveal his acceptance of funds from a business whose product ostensibly has been evaluated objectively by that
reporter.

Conversely, too, there may be personal facts about politicians that, even though they are public figures in some
sense, do not merit publication by serious reporting media
if only because publication might be pointlessly embarrassing and the personal detail in question might be clearly
irrelevant to any serious political issue of real public

interest. Here, the abusive <u>ad</u> <u>hominem</u> could be indulged
in, for no good reason.

There could be a significant difference between the ethical obligations of the press and those of politicians who
are elected officials or government-paid employees. Individuals in public life or government employ are in a position of public trust. Therefore, their opinions, debates,
deliberations, and personal actions should be open to
public scrutiny. However, those of the press not employed
by the government are working for companies that must
survive in the competitive marketplace. True, the press
has the duty to enlighten, and not knowingly to mislead
the public on matters of national or international importance. But still, because they are paid by the private
sector, their actions and pronouncements are not always
accountable in precisely the same way as those of government officials. The illicit use of taxpayer's funds for
nongovernmental purposes is a specific wrong that the
reporter's use of his employer's funds for his own selfish
purposes does not fall under.

Still, there are important parallels. Both politician and
reporter have an obligation to inform the public, and to
forgo the use of any funds to subvert or undermine that
obligation. Both the obligation to avoid lying or other
deceitful practices, including cover-up of their own
questionable practices in the pursuit of their own jobs.
Perhaps, for somewhat differing reasons, both have a
special obligation to be honest and open in making information available to the public.

In allegation 5, one might argue that it is the travel
writer's job to travel, whereas it is not likely that it
was part of Mayor MacDonald's job to go on the fishing
trip. That may be true, but on the other hand it hardly
detracts in any significant way from the irony of the
facts that the Spectator publicized the politician's
practice widely while at the same time they made great
efforts to prevent public exposure of their own similar
practice. It may have been the reporter's job to travel,
but the point is that he should have taken his travel
funds from his employer, not the airlines. His being in
debt to the airlines could constitute every bit as much
a conflict of interest in objective reporting as Mayor
MacDonald's indebtedness to Nordair could constitute a
conflict of interest in possible future political decision making.

RELEVANCE AND INNUENDO

The ad hominem is similar to other fallacies of relevance
most particularly in that, circumstantial or not, the
basic purpose of it may be to evade the argument proposed.
In such an instance, the alleged fact about one's opponent
in disputation, if true and well known to be true, may be
mistakenly taken by observers to be a telling thrust of
argument, even if it is so far off topic to be beside the
point at issue. One of the most abusive uses of the ad
hominem fallacy occurs where, even though the truth is
told, it is intensely personal and at the same time irrelevant to the line of reasoning in the development of the
argument. The arguer's integrity may be discredited, but
unfairly.

Although McAuliffe's article consists in the main of the
mounting of an extended, coherent, and well-connected
sequence of arguments consisting of a number of nicely
mounted ad hominem allegations that are by and large
sound and reasonable, at one particular point he leans
towards the fallacious use of the ad hominem. After discussing the relationships between the press and industry,
he goes on to argue that the close "kinship" between many
members of the press and politicians is good supportive
evidence that there is a prevailing lack of ethics among
individuals of the press. The premissary evidence presented includes canoe trips, card games, and banquets
where politicians and press socialize together. However,
I think we should question here how good a foundation
these circumstances are to support the implication that
this relationship is unethical or corrupt. It is asserted
that reporters or their workers are churning out copy
"like working in a sausage factory" and do "pack journalism." They are really "part of the system," not adversarial critics as they often like to portray themselves
on the news.

These are serious charges against the press, but even if
they are true--and they are couched in such provocative
and metaphorical terms that they could be impossible to
verify--it is not clear that the kind of close relationship cited really represents an unethical practice that
needs to be corrected by the application of code or principle, or is in some way a "vested interest" or unfair
collusion. What is called "cross-pollination" between
politicians and the press need not in itself be bad. Why
then mention these social relationships? The innuendo

would seem to be that if two parties are that close there
must be some funny business going on. However, no specific transgressions are specifically cited. Rather, it
appears that the subject has been subtly changed. These
personal references about social relations that, for all
the reader knows, are true, are nonetheless not an adequate
basis for arguing that the press is ethically deficient in
a way that they themselves accuse politicians of being.
It is really beside the point.

On the other hand, it is reasonable to point out that
McAuliffe's argument does raise a good issue that is per-
tinent to the overall argument. If a reporter had to do a
story on a very close friend who is a politician, it could
be very difficult to report objectively, particularly if
the friend stood accused of some moral turpitude. Clearly
this is a situation fraught with difficulties, and McAuliffe
is not entirely off the topic to raise it. On the other
hand, it is quite possible that many a newsperson has
handled this difficult sort of situation very well. It is
not impossible, in such a situation, to give a fair and
accurate report or to ask to be relieved of the assignment
because of conflict of interest.

However, the problem is that McAuliffe gives no actual
examples of ethical violations of the sort he suggests
here. Moreover, perhaps we might speculate that he did
not because making allegations of this sort would not
really advance his argument very much. Camaraderie between
reporters and politicians is not in itself a bad thing, it
is probably impossible to prohibit or to regulate it anyway, and while it may lead to problems, it is not in itself
unethical.

So the fairest evaluation here would be to conclude that
McAuliffe has not established that there are widespread
examples of ethically serious collusions here--he has only
suggested it--and consequently his argument is an innuendo.
As innuendo, it may be effective, but should be evaluated
with care if serious criticism is the object. It could be
a relevant issue, but the argument as presented has not
established that.

ANALYSIS OF THE INCONSISTENCIES

One way to analyze McAuliffe's reasoning is to construct
a set of premisses that are logically inconsistent. One

could extrapolate from his arguments that the media are
maintaining both of the following propositions. (1) All
persons in public life hold a position of public trust
and should therefore have their private dealings open to
public scrutiny. (2) The private dealings of news media
professionals should not be open to public scrutiny.
Given these two propositions as established to have been
asserted by some media representatives, we can then turn
the screws tight enough to yield an inconsistent set by
adding a third proposition, an enthymeme or tacitly presupposed premiss to the set, namely: (3) News media
professionals are persons in public life. From (1), (2),
and (3) it follows that all persons in public life should
have their private dealings open to public scrutiny, but
that some should not. And this is of course a logical
inconsistency.

But does this represent what is in fact McAuliffe's argument? It does seem to come close to it, in argument 5 and
perhaps also in argument 3. Let us spare the reader
speculations about what McAuliffe might have really meant
to argue. The most interesting question is how what he in
fact put forward as an argument can stand up to critical
analysis. The biggest loophole is the enthymeme. Those
McAuliffe criticizes cannot, at least here, be posed the
question of whether or not they accept this enthymeme.
The dialectic is closed, as far as we go here. Would
serious opponents of McAuliffe's argument, say these media
professionals who are thereby criticized, really be very
likely to accept (3) as an indisputable part of their
position on the issue? True enough, McAuliffe has shown
that (1) and (2) are propositions that are central to the
position he wants to criticize. But what about (3)?

Surely the astute critic is going to question (3) severely.
What is meant by the phrase "in public life"? Are politicians "in public life" in the same way that reporters are?
It would seem not. Politicians are paid by the taxpaying
public; reporters, very often at least, are not employed
by the government or elected to public office. They are
"in public life" in a very different sense--they report
to the public on events that are of interest to the public.
Surely, then, the opponent of McAuliffe's argument would
spot in (3) a glaring equivocation. He would deny that
reporters or other media professionals are "in public life"
in any sense which makes (1) true or justifiable.

It is this reasoning which makes me think that the better

and more charitable way to analyze McAuliffe's argument is
not as an allegation of logical inconsistency, but as an
allegation of pragmatic inconsistency, as in the analysis
given in the first part of this chapter. Not that the
above allegation of logical inconsistency is not to be
found in what could pass for McAuliffe's reasoning in
several passages, and not that such an argument is entirely
implausible or worthless. Indeed, with further dialectical
filling in of arguments, it is quite possible that a case
could fairly be made of it. But as far as it goes, so outlined above, it is not as powerful as the argument McAuliffe
gives for pragmatic inconsistency of the media. The enthymeme is too large a loophole of plausibility to enable us
to tighten the argument into a successful demonstration of
logical inconsistency.

We have seen that in the ad hominem, one form of the
attacker's fallacy is to utilize the pragmatic inconsistency in order to reject the opponent's argument per se.
The person mounting an ad hominem allegation must be careful not to fall into the delusion or deception of thinking
that because his opponent's advocacy of their position is
impugned by circumstantial inconsistency, there must be
sufficient evidence to refute the opponent's thesis as a
proposition in itself, apart from the opponent's personal
advocacy of it.

However, an even more aggressive type of criticism may be
levelled against the person who mounts an ad hominem argument. This counterattack takes the form of replying that
the attacker is not evaluating one's own argument on its
own merits, but rather is dwelling unfairly or irrelevantly
on apparent inconsistencies. The reply, in essence, is
this: "You're not sticking to the question of the objective merits of my argument. Instead of studying the independent evidence for or against my thesis, you're quibbling
about my own personal circumstances. That is not the
point. Ergo, you're guilty of the ad hominem fallacy yourself." This is answering tu quoque to a tu quoque--tit
for tat.

For example, one might allege with reference to our case
study that McAuliffe evaluates the media not on the basis
of their argument, but only on the personal inconsistencies
of their position.

Is this a legitimate form of counterattack? The answer is
that it can be justifiable or not, depending on how the

reply is supported. But where it is not justified it can
be disastrously fallacious. It could be vexatious and
unfair to dwell oppressively on the internal dialectics
of one's opponent's pragmatic inconsistencies if the
opponent has in fact advanced arguments and evidences for
his thesis that are quite independent of the question of
whether his own actions are consistent with his advocacy
of that thesis. On the other hand, providing--as we have
tried to show--that pointing out and establishing the
existence of pragmatic circumstantial inconsistencies in
someone's argument is sometimes legitimate criticism,
such a counterattack could be unfair. Perhaps independent,
circumstance-free evidence has not been offered at all by
the counterattacker, or perhaps such evidence has been
fairly dealt with by the attacker, or is not at issue at
this juncture of the argument.

The dispute here is one of relevance. Circumstantial
counterargumentation may be irrelevant in some instances,
but need not always be simply a ploy to distract an
audience from whatever evidence that opponent may have
marshalled for his position. Moreover, if the exercise
is one of criticizing somebody's stated position, as we
have done here with McAuliffe's arguments for example,
the issue concerns the internal coherency of the stated
arguments. It is not at issue whether additional premisses may be brought in, either for or against the theses
being evaluated.

To return to our case study, is McAuliffe guilty of committing an ad hominem by dwelling on these internal inconsistencies of their advocacy of their thesis, rather than
looking at the merits of their arguments per se? I think
McAuliffe's argument can be defended from this charge as
follows. His job, as he evidently sees it and carries it
out, is to criticize the stated or widely accepted position of the press that they should not more rigorously
formulate ethical guidelines as do other professions, on
the grounds of freedom of the press. The doctrine of
freedom of the press is, we may reasonably presume, a
widely enough accepted and advocated position in some form
or other that it is open to dialectical challenge and
criticism. It does not appear to be McAuliffe's own per-
ception of what he sets out to do in this article to look
into all the good arguments and reasons that might be given
for the thesis of the freedom of the press, including the
extents of that freedom. Presumably the press themselves
have plenty of good arguments for this--it is certainly

one of their favorite theses--and presumably also arguments against it have been offered that may be reasonable
or not. However, all McAuliffe queries is whether the
press's own practice in their daily activities of pursuing
their work is consistent with their own advocacy of their
position on the extent of their professed freedom of conduct and inquiry. He argues to establish certain circumstantial inconsistencies therein. Is he therefore at
fault for not going back to look at the press's other
arguments and evaluating these on their own merits?

While I do not want to acquiesce too quickly into a dog-
matic stance of firm refusal here, I think McAuliffe may
be excused from going into these other matters, unless he
is challenged to do so, say, by the press. Then, in all
fairness, he should reply squarely. But otherwise, surely
he may be excused, even commended perhaps, for limiting
his article to internal dialectical criticisms. One can
always demand more of any treatment of any topic, particularly one as interesting as this, but it would be unreasonable to expect a too-encyclopedic coverage, given
McAuliffe's evident objectives. He makes his point, and
it is open to those he has criticized to reply. What more
should one ask of a participant in dialectic?

I can appreciate the press saying: "Yes, he made his
point, but it is all one sided. He does not really deal
with our main arguments." This is a good reminder: those
criticized should have a right to fair reply. But that
does not mean, in this instance, that McAuliffe should
take on the task of doing their job for them. He should
have the right to criticize the internal coherency of his
opponents' advocacy of their position. It may be hard for
the press to live up to this kind of criticism. But that
is the price of those who would profess ethical standards
and ideals--like the freedom of the press doctrine--and
act as moral critics of others, as the press does daily.

So here is yet another variant on the ad hominem fallacy:
obscuring independent evidence for a thesis by changing
the subject to allegations of circumstantial inconsistencies. These allegations may be very entertaining indeed,
and thus provide quite good material for sophistical
topic changes, just as the abusive ad hominem often works.
However, whether such an allegation has become fallacious
is a question that can be answered affirmatively or negatively, for engaging in the dialectic of establishing
pragmatic inconsistencies in an opponent's position can

be a reasonable form of argument.

It is important to get McAuliffe's argument right. He is
not claiming that the news reports are false, or that
they cannot or should not be believed. He is only claiming that the press is being circumstantially inconsistent--
this does not imply that what they say must be false. But
he is pointing out that the press will lose credibility in
the public eye if they continue to be circumstantially
inconsistent. He is not arguing that what they say is
false, only that what they say and do is inconsistent.
Thus apart from our several reservations stated above, we
conclude that McAuliffe's argument is by and large a
correct use of the circumstantial <u>argumentum</u> <u>ad</u> <u>hominem</u>.

6

The Logical Form of
Action Propositions

We have now clearly established that the full traditional
conception of the circumstantial ad hominem fallacy very
much depends on an understanding of how different act-
descriptions (propositions) are made true by, or at least
connected to, individual agents who are participants in
argument. A good deal of ethics, or causal analysis of
responsibility for actions, would appear to be involved
in these matters. We are therefore confronted by the
question, Is the ad hominem a logical fallacy, or is it
an ethical breach of conduct? This question has considerable force even though, especially in the area of deontic
logic, there is good reason to believe that logic and
ethics need not be mutually exclusive. Still the question
remains: Is there a formal logic that can elucidate the
interconnections among act-descriptions in such a way that
we can say that the fallacious circumstantial ad hominem
of the action-theoretic sort fails to be a correct argument as opposed to being merely a culpable act, a breach
of morality?

The presumption of this question is that a logical fallacy
should be an incorrect argument and not merely a breach
of ethics, manners, or civil conduct. And in order to be
a logical fallacy, it should be a set of propositions,
and this set may be shown to exhibit a failure to be valid
in some logical structure. By "logical structure," we do
not necessarily mean classical logic. But some clear
semantic structure should be given so that we can decide
in a precise manner which forms of argument are deemed to
be correct and incorrect. In short, whether the ad hominem
is a logical fallacy, or an ethical breach of conduct
exclusively, depends on whether there is a logical form
for action sentences.

Any modern logic is based on propositional calculus, and
so pursuing the study of the logical form of action sentences ultimately will come down to the question of what
sort of propositional calculus if any is applicable when
one evaluates inferences that have to do with actions. So
that is the direction our study will now take.

It is highly disputable at present whether there is a
logic of actions. However, by evaluating the propositional
foundations of arguments about actions, we hope to convince
the reader that certain interconnections among act-

descriptions do display a basic logical form in propositional logic, although it will not be a classical logic.
Insofar as our arguments are justified on this score, it
follows that the circumstantial ad hominem of the act-
theoretic variety does legitimately have a place in the
study of the logic of argument. It is not merely, or at
any rate exclusively, a moral deceit or rhetorical failure. First, let us examine some current theories of the
logical form of action sentences.

LOGIC AND ACTIONS: CURRENT THEORIES

Davidson's theory of the logical form of action sentences
makes an action a species of event, where an event is
represented as an extra variable in classical quantifica-
tion logic. Thus 'John took a walk by the river' is
parsed out as (∃x) (x is a walk and x is taken by John
and x is by the river). The advantage of this theory is
that inferences like the one below come out valid.

John took a walk by the river.
_____

John took a walk.

Validity is upheld because the parsing given above implies,
in classical logic, (∃x) (x is a walk and x is taken by
John). So this theory works acceptably for conjunctions.

But Davidson's theory runs into heavier weather as an
account of the logical form of conditional action sentences, for it makes inferences like this one come out
valid.

John took a walk.
_____

If bananas are yellow then John took a walk.

Moreover, ⌐(∃x) Fx implies (∀x) (Fx ⊃ Gx) in classical
logic, with the questionable result that by Davidson's
account, the following is a valid inference.

John did not take a walk.
_____

Every walk John took was a walk on the water.

Disjunctions are about as questionable as conditionals on
this approach, since the following sorts of inferences

also come out as generally valid.

John mailed the letter.
_____
John mailed the letter or John burned the letter.

This consequence is not particularly helpful when we
come to add a deontic operator to the classical logic of
action sentences. If we attach the 'It is obligatory
that . . .' operator to the premiss, we have to attach
it to the conclusion as well, on the presumption that if
Op, and p implies q, then Oq. Such an approach has
seemed paradoxical however. If John is obliged to mail
the letter, it does not seem to follow at all that he
can perform his obligation by burning it. For deontic
logic, it would be better to have a propositional calculus for action sentences that does not have the unrestricted inference from p to infer p ∨ q.

We are not saying, however, that Davidson's approach is
incorrect. Rather, Davidson's theory represents the
view that complex action-sentences must be truth-functions
of atomic action sentences, and the presumption that
action sentences are not related to each other except by
their truth-functionality. In Davidson's approach,
relatedness of action propositions does not matter. We
could say that, as far as it goes, Davidson's theory is
acceptable; it models the notion that all action propositions are connectible. Hence the correct logic of
action propositions for this model is the classical propositional calculus.

Where Davidson's theory may be criticized is for its simplicity. By not taking relatedness of action propositions
into account, it produces a logic of action sentence that
is too coarse to capture the basic idea that action propositions are related to each other in ways other than by
their truth-functionality.

The theory of action presented by Pörn (1977, p. 5) is
"causal" in the sense that the principal construction
employed, 'a brings it about that p,' is an agent-causal
notion. But Pörn's approach to this notion proceeds by
first defining the preliminary concept 'it is necessary
for something which a does that p.' The latter is defined
by considering all those possible situations (worlds) u'
in which the agent does at least as much as he does in a
given situation u. The condition is: p is necessary for

something a does in u if, and only if, every situation u'
contains the state of affairs that p. The relation of
relative possibility that characterizes the set of possible worlds Pörn has in mind is reflexive and transitive.
So in other words, 'p is necessary for something a does,'
written as D_ap, comes out to be the 'necessity' operator
in S4. Thus the following theorems obtain, by way of
syntactic illustration.

R1 If p implies q, then D_ap implies D_aq.

R2 If p ≡ q is a theorem then, D_ap ≡ D_aq is a theorem.

F1 $D_ap ⊃ p$

F2 $D_ap ⊃ ¬D_a ¬p$

F3 $D_a(p ⊃ q) ⊃ (D_ap ⊃ D_aq)$

F4 $D_ap ⊃ D_a(p ∨ q)$

F5 $D_a ¬p ⊃ D_a(p ⊃ q)$

As in Davidson's theory, the classical base logic raises
some questions about conditionals. For example, F5 has
the following as an instance: if it is necessary for
something Socrates does that the cup is not on the table,
then it is necessary for something Socrates does that if
the cup is on the table the earth collides with the sun.
This may seem a bit peculiar, but it is possible to look
at it as simply one ramification of the way Pörn uses
'it is necessary for something which a does that p.' On
the other hand, it is possible to look at it as one
worthwhile reason for moving to an appropriate departure
from classical logic.

Having defined D_ap, Pörn moves on towards 'bringing it
about that' as follows. First, an operator D'_ap, read as
'but for a's action it would not be the case that p' is
characterized by the following condition: all hypotheti-
cal situations u' must be such that the opposite of everything that a does in u is the case in u'. Next, C'_ap,
read as 'but for a's activity, it might not be the case
that p' is defined as $¬D'_a ¬p$. Then E_ap, read as 'a
brings it about that p' is defined as $D_ap ∧ C'_ap$. Thus
for Pörn, what it means to say that an agent a brings p
about is that p is necessary for something a does and but
for what a does it might not be that p.

This definition seems a bit elusive somehow. True, it
may be necessary for something I do, writing this review,
that I am awake. And it may be true that if it were not
for writing this review I might be asleep in the deck
chair in the garden, but it hardly seems to follow that
I bring it about that I am awake at this moment. But
then perhaps there is some sense in which I do bring it
about that I am awake at this moment, even though I had
not really thought of being awake as an action of mine.
And then, too, according to Pörn, just because I bring it
about that p, it doesn't follow that p is an action of
mine according to the definition of an act-predicate that
constitutes the very essence of Pörn's theory. Let us
see how Pörn was led to this definition.

Perhaps the most fundamental problem for an enterprise
like that attempted by Pörn is to take some commonplace
action expressions like 'Smith kicked the table' or
'Robinson removed Smith's appendix' and show how their
logical form can be enlighteningly displayed in the
structure being recommended. In Pörn's case, the problem
is not as simple as it might initially seem. 'Smith
brought it about that Smith kicked the table' need not be
the same statement as 'Smith kicked the table.' For
example, perhaps Smith kicked the table accidentally so
that it is false that he brought it about that he kicked
the table. Nonetheless, it might be true that he kicked
the table. Variants like 'Something Smith did was necessary for the table's being kicked' seem even further from
the mark, for this could be true if Smith moved the table
in front of Jones's foot, making it ready for the kicking
by Jones.

As Davidson (1966) observed, a statement like 'Robinson
brought it about that Jones no longer has an appendix'
could be true if Robinson ran down Smith in his Lincoln
Continental, but that would not make 'Robinson removed
Smith's appendix' true.

So it's not hard to see the problem. Since no exact
match in a set of truth-conditions for these commonplace
action expressions seems to be forthcoming, how do you
relate the commonplace analysandum to the theory, with its
technically well-defined and ostensibly actionlike operators and other symbolic elements? Unless some relationship is given, it remains unclear whether or how the theory
can be applicable to actions as we know them. Pörn
approaches the problem by formulating the concept of an

act-property. This concept marks off acts from nonacts.

According to Pörn (p. 11), the most obvious intuitive
difference between the relations of kicking and being
taller than is that, in the first but not the second case,
whether or not a pair of elements satisfies the relation
is a fact that is brought about by an agent. In other
words, whether or not 'a kicks b' is satisfied by a pair
(a,b) is something that is brought about or not by a,
whereas the same is not true of 'a is taller than b.'   In
the latter case, the relation is independent of what a and
b do. Thus Pörn rules that p, an n-place relation (n ≥ 1)
is an act-relation only if $\forall x1 \forall x2$ . . . $\forall x_n(p \supset Ex_i p)$ is
true for some i from 1 to n. Since $Ex_i p \supset p$ is true for
any i as a theorem in Pörn's system, the definiens may
equivalently be rewritten as follows: $\forall x1 \forall x2$ . . . $\forall x_n$
$(p \equiv Ex_i p)$. This definition is presumed to work in virtue
of the falsehood of $(\forall x)((x$ is growing old$) \equiv Ex(x$ is growing old$))$, which contrasts with the truth of, say, $(\forall x)$
$((x$ kicks the table$) \equiv Ex(x$ kicks the table$))$. The basic
idea is that if what one does is really an act, it may be
said that one brings it about that one does it.

So far the definition seems simple, but Pörn notices that
there is a fly in the ointment, occasioned by the fact
that in his system all tautologies and no inconsistencies
are brought about by an agent. The problem is that $(\forall x)$
$(\lnot(x = x) \equiv Ex \lnot(x = x))$ is therefore true, which would
imply that the relation of not being self-identical is an
act-relation.

The remedy suggested by Pörn is to require that the pred-
icate $Ex_i p$ of the definiens can apply to or be true of
some agent. Accordingly, the revised definition reads as
follows: p, an n-place relation (n ≥ 1), is an act-
relation if, and only if,

$$\forall x_1 \forall x_2 \text{ . . . } \forall x_n \ (p \equiv Ex_i p) \land M(\exists x_1 \exists x_2 \text{ . . . } \exists x_n Ex_i p)$$

is true for some i from 1 to n. This is Pörn's full-fledged
definition (Df 9). He defends it against the expected
charge of circularity (p. 13) and argues for its usefulness
as a device that exhibits principles of our reasoning concerning agency, as a helpful bit of logic for understanding
Ross's paradox.

Pörn evidently has some second thoughts about (Df 9), however, because he considers modifying it by adding an

N-operator (it is unavoidable that . . .) to the left
conjunct. By what he calls (Df 11), p is an act-relation
if, and only if,

$$N[\forall x_1 \forall x_2 \ldots \forall x_n (p \equiv Ex_ip)] \land M(\exists x_1 \exists x_2 \ldots \exists x_np).$$

But he rejects (Df 11) because its acceptance would imply
that nobody can bring about the equivalence that is characteristic of act relations. This undesirable consequence
tags along because N_ap implies $\neg E_ap$ in Pörn's system.

My own view is that (Df 9) is somewhat less felicitous
than Pörn thinks, and that he is therefore on the right
track to consider an alternative. But, for the reason he
gives, (Df 11) is clearly not an acceptable alternative.
Let us evaluate (Df 9) more closely to see what could be
problematic.

The serious intuitive bug I find in the ointment is that
by (Df 9),   any property that happens to be falsely
predicated to any agent you choose, but could possibly
apply to some agent, must be ruled an act-property. Consider the property 'x is older than k years' where k is
any number of years greater than the number of years anyone has lived. This property satisfies the first require-
ment of the definition that $\forall x_1 \forall x_2 \ldots \forall x_n(p \supset Ex_ip)$ be
true for some i from 1 to n. And it seems, uncontrover-
sially enough, to satisfy the second property.

Thus according to (Df 9), any relation you care to choose
that fails to apply to every element of its domain but
that could apply to one element, turns out to be an act-
relation. Take as another example the property of having
one's appendix removed by Sir Alfred Ayer. We may presume
that nobody is having his appendix removed by Sir Alfred,
and moreover that it could be true of some individual, as
unlikely as it seems, that his appendix is being removed
by Sir Alfred. It follows, by Pörn's definition, that the
property of having one's appendix removed by Sir Alfred
is an act-relation. However, this consequence seems quite
contrary to the intent of the definition. Having my
appendix removed by Sir Alfred Ayer is not a type of action
that I perform at all--it is something that I suffer
rather than do; something I undergo, not something I perform.

This problem is occasioned by the fact that a universal
generalization like $(\forall x)(Fx \supset Gx)$ must come out true in

classical logic if the open sentence of the antecedent--
in this case Fx--is not true of any individual in the
domain being considered. Pörn's definition can be fulfilled if the relation p is false for every individual
x_1 . . . x_n you put in it. All that is additionally
required is that p can be true of some agent. Clearly,
therefore, this definition is too easily satisfied to be
intuitively adequate in the way Pörn wants.

Ultimately, I think the only fully satisfactory way
around this sort of problem may be to take a base logic
other than classical logic, as proposed below, but that
route is quite understandably not one Pörn wishes to consider at this point. So what can he do? (Df 11) is not
acceptable, as he has shown, but neither is (Df 9), as I
have shown.

The best way to proceed, I suggest, is to construct a
third alternative by putting in an operator, 'it is logically (analytically) necessary that . . .' in front of
the first conjunct of (Df 9) instead of the N-operator
used by Pörn in (Df 11). But that is not the only modi-
fication that would help.

There seems to be another problem introduced by basing
the definition on propositional functions. In the definition, p is an n-place relation, or propositional function, like 'x is moving his finger.' Any definition of
the sort being considered should leave it open for some
of these functions whether they conform to the definition
or not, in a specific instance. For example, we want to
leave open the possibility that sometimes when I move my
finger, I bring it about that I move my finger. But we
also want to allow for the possibility that sometimes
even though I move my finger, I do not bring it about
that I move my finger. In the latter sort of case, someone else might bring it about that I move my finger. The
way Pörn's definition works, 'x is moving his finger' is
either an act-relation or not. There is no room for possible variation in the instances of this function.

Consequently, it is preferable to approach the characterization problem for actions by way of specific instances
rather than generalized properties. Thus, to ameliorate
both Pörn's problems, a definition of the following sort
is needed. For some designated individual, a, $\jmath$ is an
action proposition if, and only if,

$$L(p \equiv E_a p) \land M(\exists x)Exp$$

where L and M are logical necessity and possibility
respectively.

Now we can utilize the framework of bringing about to
bear on commonplace action sentences. Consider the
quotidien statement 'Jones coughed.' What did Jones
bring about? A 'cough-state'? But what is that? And
so on--as Davidson has ably shown, the obvious candidates are highly problematic. But now we have a better
answer. We can say that 'Jones coughed' is a pure
action proposition if, and only if, necessarily, Jones
coughed if and only if Jones brought it about that Jones
coughed, and possibly, someone brought it about that
Jones coughed. This solution is highly favorable
because 'Jones coughed' can be brought into the language
intact, without having to produce a truncated description
for the outcome-state.

Despite the immense promise of Pörn's theory, ultimately
it must be limited--as the problem of Sir Alfred and the
appendix indicates--by its classical propositional base
logic. Perhaps, then, our investigation should turn to
the root of the problem: propositional logic.

RELATIONS ON ACT-DESCRIPTIONS

The beginning point for any discussion of the logic of
action propositions involves a realization that a model
for the appropriate logic must involve more than a simple
assignment of truth-values to all the propositions on the
basis of the truth-values of the simple (noncomplex)
propositions. For example, we cannot say that generally
for every pair of propositions p, q, that 'If p then q'
is true simply because q by itself is true or p by itself
is false. Just because q is brought about by some agent,
it should not always follow that 'If p then q' must also
be brought about by what that agent did. In order to
determine the truth-value of 'If p then q' or 'p or q,'
we must take into account the relationship between p and
q as well as their truth-values.

But what sort of relationship is involved, when p and q
represent act-descriptions that are outcomes of something
done by an agent? There are many kinds of relationships
that have been discussed between pairs of action propositions, but two of these are especially relevant on a
certain view of what action propositions are about.

According to this view, each proposition that is brought
about by an action has a historical genesis, a sequence
of points or so-called world line that runs through a
point at which that proposition was made true. In fact,
each proposition has a set of world lines that represents
the different ways it could have been made true. To say
that p and q are connectible, meaning that there is a
world line segment shared between the world line of the
one proposition and the other, is to say that there is a
way that p could have been made true that is also a way
that q could have been made true. In other words, what
brought about the one could have brought about the other.
To say that p and q are related (connectible) is to say
only that they can be connected by action, not that what
brought about the one actually brought about the other.

However, we must distinguish between direct and indirect
connectibility. To say that two propositions are in a
relationship such that whatever could have made one true
could also have directly made the other true is to say
that the two propositions are on the same world line and
that the one is approximately spatiotemporally coincident
with the other. In this sense, 'My fingers are moved'
and 'This knob is turned' may be approximately spatio-
temporally coincident. What can make the one true can
also directly make the other true. The relation of
approximate spatiotemporal coincidence is reflexive and
symmetrical, but not transitive.

The notion of indirect connectibility of propositions
made true on a world line, however, is finitely transitive, and may be defined by transitive closure as follows.
P_0 is indirectly connectible with p_{n+1} if, and only if,
there is a set of propositions $p_1, p_2, \ldots p_{n-1}, p_n$
such that p_0 is approximately coincident with p_1, p_1 is
approximately coincident with $p_2, \ldots p_{n-1}$ is approximately coincident with p_n, and p_n is approximately coincident with p_{n+1}. This notion of connectibility is modal
and temporally symmetrical--it conveys no information about
the time order of propositions made true, nor does it
tell us whether propositions are actually connected in
the real world.

The relation of connectibility is not the only one that
action propositions may enter into when we look at the
structure of an act-sequence. A second sort of relationship is that of informational inclusion. To say that p
and q are related in this sense means that information
concerning the ways in which p could have been brought
about is included in information concerning the ways in

which q could have been brought about. This relation of
information inclusion is transitive. If information
describing how r could have been brought about is included
in information on how q could have been brought about, and
information on how q could have been brought about is
included in information on how p could have been brought
about, then it follows that the information on how r could
have been brought about is included in the information on
how p could have been brought about.

What we concretely have in mind by a set of world lines
is what Alvin I. Goldman (1970) calls an act-tree or act-
diagram. Act-sequences are linked together by a kind of
relation that Goldman calls level-generation. Four
categories of level-generation are postulated: (1) causal
generation, (2) conventional generation, (3) simple generation, and (4) augmentation generation. The (2) and (3)
are more complex relations, having to do with how rules
and background circumstances enter into act-sequences, so
our concern here will be with the more fundamental relations expressed by (1) and (4).

What Goldman has in mind by (1) is a familiar sequence
like this: by moving his finger, an agent flips a switch,
turns on a light and warns a prowler. We are not concerned
here with what is fully meant by the causal relation or by
the so-called by-relation. Rather we are interested in
the basic propositional structure inherent in a sequence
like this. The sequence can be analyzed as being based
on four propositions: (1) A finger was moved, (2) A
switch was flipped, (3) A light was turned on, (4) A
prowler was warned. The question is how the pairs
{(1),(2)}, {(2),(3)}, and {(3),(4)} are each related by
some binary relation in order to "generate" the sequence.
Surely part of the answer is that (1) is connectible with
(2) in the sense that there is a way that (1) could have
been made true that is also a way that (2) could have been
made true. The same relation of connectibility also
applies to the remaining two pairs of propositions. Of
course that is not all that is expressed by the original
sequence. Also what is expressed is that what brought
about (1) also in fact brought about (2). So we will
have to consider some other aspects of the relation in
what follows.

What Goldman has in mind by (4) is the following sort of
sequence: Smith buttered the toast slowly and deliberately in the bathroom; Smith buttered the toast slowly

and deliberately; Smith buttered the toast slowly; Smith
buttered the toast. In each instance, by our analysis,
there is a proposition that was brought about by Smith:
(1) The toast was buttered slowly and deliberately in the
bathroom, (2) The toast was buttered slowly and deliberately, (3) The toast was buttered slowly, (4) The toast
was buttered. We shall call this sort of sequence an
internal sequence, a contrast with the external sequence
above concerning the prowler. By our analysis of the
internal sequence, (2) is included in (1) in the sense
that the information on how (2) could have been brought
about is included in the information on how (1) could
have been brought about.

COMPLEX PROPOSITIONS

Consider again the external act-sequence: Smith moves
his finger, Smith flips the switch, Smith turns on the
light, Smith warns the prowler. In each step there is a
proposition that is made true by Smith. And each proposition is directly related to the ones it is adjacent to
in the sequence. At step one a finger was moved, and at
step two a switch was flipped. Now, the question is, what
is the relation between these two outcome propositions
such that we can say that by bringing about one, Smith
also brought about the other? There are numerous relations we might have in mind here, not all compatible with
each other. We might mean that the one proposition is
necessary or sufficient (or both) for the other. We might
mean that the one proposition is necessary, or probable,
or possible, given the other. We might mean that some laws
connect the one to the other. We might mean that one is
connected through a plan or purpose in Smith's mind to the
other.

We select from these possibilities one particular kind of
relationship. Let us say that the proposition 'Smith's
finger is moved' is related to 'The switch is flipped' in
the sense that these two propositions are connectible--
what could have brought about one also could have brought
about the other. We mean directly connectible in the
sense that both propositions share a world line segment.
Then we rule that p_0 is <u>indirectly connectible</u> to p_{n+1} if,
and only if, p_0 is directly connectible to p_1, p_1 is
directly connectible to p_2, . . . p_{n-1} is directly connectible to p_n, and p_n is directly connectible to p_{n+1}.
In this sense 'Smith's finger is moved' is indirectly

connectible to 'A prowler is warned.'

As we said at the outset, we are interested in examining
what sort of propositional logic could be appropriate for
a language of actions. That means we shall have to seek
out the meaning of 'not,' 'and,' 'or,' and 'if . . . then.'
What, for instance, could we mean when we say that if Smith
flipped the switch then he made the light go on. In light
of considerations above, the very least we must mean is
that the flipping of the switch and the going on of the
light are connectible. So if we are to work towards a
logic that is as close as possible to classical propositional calculus, we could define a conditional connective
$p \rightarrow q$ as follows: $p \rightarrow q$ is true if, and only if, p is
connectible to q, and it is not the case that p is true and
q is false. This conditional embodies the idea that p is
a sufficient condition for q in the action-theoretic sense
that p and q are connectible in an act-sequence. We read
$p \rightarrow q$ as whatever makes p true also makes q true. Note,
however, that we do not mean to imply that p and q must be
necessarily connected or causally related in the sense that
p actually causes q. All we mean is that p and q are connectible and that the material conditional, $p \supset q$, obtains.

If a logic of action proposition is to be possible, we
have to ask about an agent's bringing about complex propo-
sitions like $\neg p$, $p \wedge q$, $p \rightarrow q$, and so forth. We can say
that Smith brought it about that if the door was opened
the alarm was sounded. So we have to investigate the
conditions under which one proposition p will be said to
be connectible to a complex proposition $q \rightarrow r$. In order
to be connectible to $q \rightarrow r$, does p have to be connectible
to both q and r, or one particular member of the pair, or
is it enough that p be connectible to either q or r? Consider the conditional 'If the door was opened the alarm was
sounded.' Let us say that 'A prowler was warned' is connectible to 'The alarm was sounded.' Then we have to ask,
Is this enough to conclude that the proposition 'A prowler
was warned' is connectible to the whole proposition 'If
the door was opened the alarm was sounded'? It does seem
to be enough, so we will rule generally that p is connectible to $q \rightarrow r$ if, and only if, p is connectible to q or
p is connectible to r.

In discussing negation of action sentences, it is well to
begin by remarking on the distinction between 'Smith did
not make it true that p' and 'Smith made it true that
not-p.' The second is the stronger form of negation, but

the first is what one has in mind by "omission." Of
course, there is the third possibility, 'Smith did not
make it true that not-p.' We are concerned here with
the logic of propositions that are the outcome of agency,
so our primary concern in this section will be with the
second form of statement, where the outcome proposition
itself is negated.

We want to study the relationship between (1) 'A spade
was played' and (2) 'A spade was not played' in the context of both statements being outcomes of something
brought about by some agency. Probably the first hypothesis to occur to one is this: none of the ways in
which (1) could have been brought about are ways in which
(2) could have been brought about. Let $W(p)$ be all the
ways in which p could have been brought about, and $W(q)$
be all the ways in which q could have been brought about.
Then the first candidate for a form of condition on
negation is this: $W(p) \cap W(q) = \emptyset$. However, this condition is not always appropriate, for one of the ways
Smith could make (1) true, by giving orders to Jones,
could also be a way that Smith could make (2) true. Thus
the condition $W(p) \cap W(\neg p)$ is not generally applicable to
negation for action propositions.

A second characterization of negation might be that negation is more general, in the sense that all of the ways
in which p could be made true are included in the ways
in which $\neg p$ could be made true: $W(p) \subseteq W(\neg p)$. By this
conception, (2) could have been made true in any number
of ways, for example, by playing a heart, club, not doing
anything, and so on. Whereas (1) could only have been
made true by a much narrower range of world lines. However, this conception of negation fails for the following
reason. One way in which (1) could have been made true,
such as by moving one's hand in such a way as to take a
spade from the deck and put it on the table, is not a way
in which (2) could have been made true. Thus it is not
entirely correct that $W(p)$ is completely included in
$W(\neg p)$.

Moreover, if $W(p) \subseteq W(\neg p)$ is applicable, it would seem
plausible that $W(\bar{p}) \subseteq W(\neg\neg p)$ is also applicable, and so
forth. But this principle does not seem to obtain. 'It
is not the case that a spade was not played' would not
seem to have all its world lines included in the world
lines of (2). Quite the contrary, this last proposition
would seem to be equivalent to (1), which by hypothesis

is itself included in (2) with respect to how (1) and (2) could have been brought about.

We conclude that there is no strict relationship between W(p) and W(￢p) in general, and that as far as negation is concerned, it does not matter how a proposition could have been brought about.

Having now discussed negation and the conditional, conjunction and disjunction remain. Let us take two outcome propositions that appear to be unrelated as far as the question of how they came about is concerned: (5) Julius Caesar is dead, and (6) John F. Kennedy is dead. None of the ways that (5) could have been made true are ways that (6) could have been made true. The world lines of these two outcomes, let us presume, share no common segment. Still, if something or somebody made (5) true, and something or somebody made (6) true, then something or somebody made both (5) and (6) true. And conversely, if something or somebody made them both true, then something or somebody made (5) true, and something or somebody made (6) true. For p ∧ q to be true, it is enough that p and q are each true. We do not need to require that p and q are connectible.

With disjunction it is a different story. If (5) is brought about by some agent, it does not follow that (5) or (6) is brought about by what that agent did. Whoever killed Caesar did not bring it about that either Caesar or John Kennedy is dead. Reason: how the one death was brought about had nothing to do, at least so we may presume, with how the other death was brought about. Thus we cannot say that 'This letter was mailed' implies 'Either this letter was mailed or this letter was burned,' unless the letter can be mailed by burning it, or burned by mailing it. Unless the two outcomes are connectible, p → (p ∨ q) cannot be held to obtain for act-outcomes generally.

RELATEDNESS LOGIC

The properties of reasoning in external act-sequences given above are enough to determine a semantics for 'not,' 'and,' 'or,' and 'if . . . then.' 'Not' and 'and' are given truth-tables the same as classical logic. The remaining two connectives have the truth-tables below. In the sequel, let p, q, r, . . . stand for simple propositions (ones with no connectives), and let A, B, C, . . . be variables for propositions that can be either simple or complex (wff).

A	B	R(A,B)	A → B		A	B	R(A,B)	A ∨ B
T	T	T	T		T	T	T	T
T	T	F	F		T	T	F	F
T	F	T	F		T	F	T	T
T	F	F	F		F	F	F	F
F	T	T	T		F	T	T	T
F	T	F	F		F	T	F	F
F	F	T	T		F	F	T	F
F	F	F	F		F	F	F	F

Given this set of connectives, we can always decide whether a wff is a tautology or not by means of a truth-table.   We show, for example, that the expression for modus ponens, A → [(A → B) → B] is a relatedness tautology.

A	B	R(A,B)	A	→	[(A → B)	→	B
T	T	T	T	T	T	T	T
T	T	F	T	T	F	T	T
T	F	T	T	T	F	T	F
T	F	F	T	T	F	T	F
F	T	T	F	T	T	T	T
F	T	F	F	T	F	T	T
F	F	T	F	T	T	F	F
F	F	F	F	T	F	T	F

One can see that such truth-tables are similar to those of classical logic except that one has to take into account relatedness (connectibility) of all the propositions, as well as all possible combinations of truth-values.

Since connectibility is, as we saw above, a symmetric relation, the correct axiom system corresponding to our semantical requirements for reasoning about external act-sequences turns out to be the following set, given by Epstein (1979, p. 159).

System $\mathcal{S}$:   Symmetric Relatedness

1.   R(A,A)   reflexiveness

2.   R(A,B) → R(B,A)   symmetry

3.   R(A,B) → R(A, ¬B); R(A, ¬B) → R(A,B) ⎫ properties

4.   R(A,B → C) → (R(A,B) ∨ R(A,C))   ⎬ of

5.   R(A,B) → R(A,B → C); R(A,C) → R(A,B → C) ⎱ related-

6.   (A ∨ B) → (B ∨ A)   ⎭ ness on wffs

7.   A → ¬¬A ; ¬¬A → A   ⎫
                                        ⎬ classical negation
8.   ¬(A ∧ ¬A)   ⎭

9.   A → (B → (R(A,B) → (A → B)))   ⎫ connecting R

10. ¬A → (R(A,B) → (A → B))   ⎬ and → classical

11. (A → B) → R(A,B).   ⎭ properties of ∧

12. A → (¬B → ¬(A → B)   ⎫ classical prop-
                                        ⎬
13. A → ((A → B) → B) detachment   ⎭ erties of →

14. A ∧ (B ∧ C) → (A ∧ B) ∧ C   ⎫ classical

15. A → (¬(B ∧ A) → ¬B)   ⎬ properties

16. ¬(A ∧ B) → (¬(C ∧ ¬B) → ¬(A ∧ C)) ⎭ of ∧

The only rule is <u>modus ponens</u>. The system is shown to be complete by Epstein for the interpretation given to it by the semantical conditions we have laid down above. $\mathcal{S}$ turns out to be a fragment of classical logic. It shares some tautologies with classical logic, like 7, 8, and 12 to 16 above, plus some other examples below.

Some Tautologies of System $\mathscr{S}$ of Relatedness Logic

(1)   ㄱB → [(A → B) → ㄱA]   (2)   (A → B) → [(A → ㄱB) → ㄱA]

(3)   ㄱA → [(A ∨ B) → B]   (4)   (A → B) → (ㄱB → ㄱA)

(5)   (A ∧ B) → A   (6)   A → A

(7)   A ∨ ㄱA   (8)   A → (A ∨ ㄱA)

(9)   (A → B) → ㄱ(A ∧ ㄱB)   (10) [(A ∧ ㄱA) → B] → [B → (A → B)]

(11) [(A ∧ ㄱA) → B] → [ㄱA → (A → B)]

(12) (A → B) → [(A ∧ C) → B]

(13) (ㄱA ∨ ㄱB) → ㄱ(A ∧ B)   (14) (ㄱA ∨ B) → (A → B)

(15) (A → B) → (ㄱA ∨ B)   (16) (ㄱA ∧ ㄱB) → ㄱ(A ∨ B)

How we interpret these tautologies as principles of act-
sequences can be illustrated by modus tollens. If the
light is made to be off then if whatever makes the switch
flipped makes the light go on, then the switch is made to
be not flipped. This inference is reasonable, for assume
that the switch is not made to be not flipped. Then it
must follow either that it is not made true that whatever
makes the switch flipped makes the light go on or that it
is not made true that the light is made to be off.

As another example consider contraposition (4). Assume
that whatever makes the switch flipped makes the light go
on. Then whatever makes the light be off also makes the
switch to be not flipped. The reader should check the
remaining tautologies in light of reasoning about external
act-sequences.

Perhaps even more notable are several inferences we would
take not to be applicable to conditionals in act-sequences
must fail on the present interpretation. Consider (1)
from the set given below. Whatever makes A true need not
make it true that whatever makes B true makes A true.
Reasons: B need have nothing to do with what makes A true.
Similarly with (8): Whatever makes A true need not make it
true that A or B.

Some Tautologies of Classical PC That Fail in $\mathcal{S}$

(1)   A → (B → A)   (2)   ⌐A → (A → B)

(3)   ⌐(A → B) → (B → A)   (4)   (A ∧ B) → (A → B)

(5)   ⌐(A → B) → (A ∧ ⌐B)   (6)   A → (B ∨ ⌐B)

(7)   (A ∧ ⌐A) → B   (8)   A → (A ∨ B)

(9)   ⌐B → [⌐A → (A → B)]

(10) [(B ∧ C) → A] → [(B → A) ∨ (C → A)]

(11) [A → (B → C)] → [B → (A → C)]

(12) [(A ∧ B) → C] → [A → (B → C)]

(13) [A → (B → C)] → [(A ∧ B) → C]

(14) ⌐(A ∨ B) → (⌐A ∧ ⌐B)

(15) (A → B) → [(C → A) → (C → B)]

(16) (A ∧ ⌐B) → ⌐(A → B)

(17) [A → (B ∧ C)] → [(A → B) ∧ (A → C)]

(18) (A → B) → [(B → C) → (A → C)]

(19) (A → B) → [A → (C → B)]

(20) ⌐(A ∧ B) → (⌐A ∨ ⌐B)

Failure of transitivity, indicated by (18), has already been noted as a characteristic for the present analysis of extrinsic act-sequences. If the first pair of conditionals below is made true, then is the third thereby made true?

(K)   If the switch is flipped, the light is turned on.

(L)   If the light is turned on, the prowler is warned.

(M)   If the switch is flipped, the prowler is warned.

Our reasoning here is that the third conditional need not be true in the sense that making it true that the switch is

flipped is directly related to making it true that the
prowler is warned. Still, the latter pair of propositions is indirectly related, and thus in that limited
sense of →, (M) does follow (indirectly) from (K).

But it is worth nothing that we cannot allow unrestricted
transitivity on complex propositions generally. Reason:
since A is related to A → B, and A → B is related to B,
by transitivity of →, A is related to B. In short, transitivity of → put us in classical logic, where all propositions are related to each other.

Although transitivity does not generally obtain, a close
analogy to it is a tautology in $\mathcal{S}$.

(T)   [(A → B) ∧ (B → C) ∧ A] → C

This expression is a tautology because A does not have to
be connectible to C in order for (T) to be true, unlike
the case of (18) above. One can see why (T) is a tautology as follows. Assume, contrary to what we hope to prove,
that (T) is false. That means that A → B, B → C, and A
are all made true, and that C is made false. However,
assuming that A is true, the only way A → B can be made
true is if B is true as well. Similarly, if B is made
true, the only way B → C can be made true is if C is true.
But C, by previous hypothesis, must be made false in order
to falsify (T). Therefore, the hypothesis that C is false
leads to contradition.

If the reader goes through the tautologies of classical
logic that fail in $\mathcal{S}$, the difference between the present
approach and the classically based theories of Davidson
and Pörn can be appreciated. Consider (1) as an example.
The following sort of instance is rejected as being
universally true: (T1) whatever makes it true that Smith
is dead makes it true that if this chalk is dropped then
Smith is dead. Of course, if Smith's being dead is connectible to the dropping of the chalk, then (T1) has to
be true. But since we may assume that these two outcomes
may be unrelated in any way, we cannot assume that (T1)
is true. We conclude that (T1) is not generally true
(tautologous) for the interpretation intended here.

Any classically based approach to the logical form of
action sentences has to contend not only with the more
familiar problems posed by A ⊃ (B ⊃ A), ¬A ⊃ (A ⊃ B), and
the like. It is also a fact to be reckoned with that

[(B ∧ C) ⊃ A] ⊃ [(B ⊃ A) ∨ (C ⊃ A)] is a tautology in
classical PC. Although not usually remarked upon, this
tautology is somewhat questionable. 'John is taller than
Fred' and 'Fred is taller than Herman' together imply
'John is taller than Herman' but neither of the former
pair each separately implies the third proposition.

However, (10), the counterpart of the above tautology
with ⊃ replaced by →, fails in relatedness logic. In
(10), if C is related to A, and B is false, that is
enough to make (B ∧ C) → A true. But (B → A) ∨ (C → A)
can still come out false with these values, that is, if
B is not related to A and C is true and A is false.

Looking at examples of (10), the best we can say is that
it is good that it fails for act-sequences, but it is
questionable why it fails. Simply because B and C
together are sufficient to bring about A, it should not
follow that either of B or C is individually sufficient
to make A happen. So far so good. If a gunshot wound
and incorrect medical treatment, taken together, were
sufficient for the death of Smith, we do not want to
imply always that either factor, by itself, is sufficient
for Smith's death.

But why (10) fails is that relatedness and truth-values
can combine together in the antecedent of (10) yet not
in the consequent. Let C = Arnold Palmer swung the club,
and A = The ball swept off the tee. We assume that C is
directly related to A in the act-sequence. Then take
some unrelated proposition that happens to be false, say
B = Caesar crossed the Mississippi. Then B → A is not
true because B and A are unrelated. But C → A could fail
to be true if C is true and A is false. This assignment
makes (B ∧ C) → A true. C is related to A, therefore A
is related to (B ∧ C). And B is false, therefore B ∧ C
is false so (B ∧ C) → A is true. Hence (10) fails as a
tautology.

This reasoning behind the failure of (10) brings out a
limitation of 𝒮. Although ⌐A → (A → B) for any, even
unrelated A and B, fails in 𝒮. Still, [⌐A ∧ (B ∨ ⌐B)] →
(A → B) is a tautology of 𝒮. This means that 'If Socrates
does not run then if Socrates runs Venus explodes' is not
true by virtue of its logical form. However, the following is true as a matter of form: if Socrates does not
run and Venus explodes or not, then if Socrates runs Venus
explodes. The full paradoxicality of Pörn's or Davidson's

approaches is not maintained, but something paradoxical
is still with us. 'Whatever makes A true makes B true'
comes out true if A is not made true and A is directly
related to B. Still, this approach is not as paradoxical as Davidson's or Pörn's because at least it requires
relatedness of A and B for the conditional to be true.

INTERNAL RELATIONS OF EVENTS

Some events are related to other events, as we have put
it, internally. Consider this familiar sequence:
Buttering the toast, Smith's buttering the toast, Smith's
buttering the toast slowly, Smith's buttering the toast
slowly and deliberately, Smith's buttering the toast
slowly and deliberately with a knife, Smith's buttering
the toast slowly and deliberately with a knife in the
bathroom, Smith's buttering the toast slowly and deliberately with a knife in the bathroom at midnight. This
sequence falls naturally into the order in which it is
given above. The rationale of the sequence would seem to
be that as each step in the description of the complex of
events is taken, more information about the development
of what was brought about is given. In each subsequent
case, the development of what was brought about as
described is more specific as an unfolding expansion.
That is, there is a sense in which each stage of the
sequence is included in each other stage that is after it
in the development of the sequence. The relation here is
one of progressive informational inclusion of the action.

We start with the idea that each of the descriptions above
contains some items of information about the way something
was brought about. The first description of what was
brought about contains the information that it was a
buttering and that the toast is what was buttered. The
second description adds to the information in the first
by telling us that the aforesaid toast buttering is by
Smith. It brings forward the previous information, but
at the same time adds a new element. The transformation
from the first to the second step is one of increased
specifity of information. The information contained in
the first step is included in the information contained
in the second one. The converse does not obtain. That
is, information content inclusion in internal event
sequences is not a symmetrical relation. Clearly, however, it is a reflexive relation, as we must say that the
information content in any step of the sequence is

contained in that very step itself.

The third description brings in yet another distinct item of information, namely that the act-description in step two includes the information that it took place slowly. Thus the information content of step three includes that of step two. We have already established that two includes one. Now we can see that informational content inclusion in such a sequence is transitive, and we may conclude that the information in step three also includes that given in step one.

Similar reasoning applies to all seven steps in this sequence. Each subsequent step includes all of its predecessors. The seventh step is therefore related by informational inclusion to every step in the sequence. Thus the relation of informational inclusion effects a linear ordering of the sequence.

As a proposition that contains information about what is included in an act-description, 'Smith buttered the toast slowly' is more specific and contains more information than 'Smith buttered the toast.' "Slowly" adds a new element, and tells more about what happened and how it happened. In this sense of informational containment, we say that 'buttered slowly' contains 'buttered.'

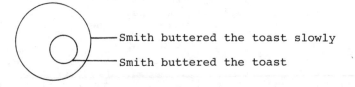

We look at it this way insofar as we regard these two propositions as expressing different degrees of information about the same stage of historical development of an act-sequence.

But there is an ambiguity. If we look at the different possibilities concerning how these two propositions could come to be true, it might seem that the information in 'Smith buttered the toast slowly' is contained in the information in 'Smith buttered the toast' in just this way. It is not the case that every way in which he could possibly butter the toast is a way in which he butters it slowly, for example, he could butter it quickly. Hence,

by these lights, the following is true: all the ways in
which he could possibly butter the toast include the ways
in which he butters it slowly.   In this very different
sense, 'Smith buttered the toast' contains more possibilities about the ways things could have happened than
'Smith buttered the toast slowly.'

But this second notion of containment of possibilities
is not the one that concerns us here.   We are not interested in understanding informativeness as relative great-
ness of different possible ways something could be brought
about.   We understand a proposition as more informative
if it contains more specific content concerning how it
came to be brought about.

Yet a third relation in the above sequence approaches it
from a different perspective, but results in the same
linear order as the first kind of informational containment.   We begin by observing that it is not the case both
that Smith's buttering the toast obtained and that a
buttering of the toast did not obtain.   In other words,
the material conditional 'If Smith's buttering the toast
obtained then a buttering of the toast obtained' is made
true by the sequence.   Similarly, the third step implies
the second, and by transitivity the third also implies
the first, and so forth.   Each subsequent step implies
each of its predecessors in the sequence.

Our main concern in analysis of <u>ad</u> <u>hominem</u> reasoning will
be external rather than internal act-sequences.   Accordingly, we will not develop the notion of information
inclusion much further here, except to contrast it with
the logic of external act-sequences.

First, let us observe that some classical tautologies
will fail to be tautologies in either the relatedness or
information inclusion propositional logics.   For example
$A \rightarrow (B \rightarrow A)$ fails as a tautology for internal act-sequence
propositions because $B \rightarrow A$ could be false if the information in A is not included in the information in B.   For
similar reasons, $\neg A \rightarrow (A \rightarrow B)$ fails to be a tautology in
either type of logic.

Let us go back to schema (10) of the previous section,
namely: $[(A \wedge B) \rightarrow C] \rightarrow [(A \rightarrow C) \vee (B \rightarrow C)]$.   We found
that (10) was not a tautology of relatedness logic.   Would
(10) be a tautology of information inclusion implication?
Consider an example.   Let A = Smith buttered the toast

slowly, B = Smith buttered the toast in the bathroom, and
C = Smith buttered the toast slowly in the bathroom.
Clearly (A ∧ B) → C is true, but (A → C) ∨ (B → C) is
false. To see that the latter is false, we note that it
does not need to be the case that at least one of the
following pair of conditionals is true: (1) If Smith
buttered the toast slowly then Smith buttered the toast
slowly in the bathroom, (2) If Smith buttered the toast
in the bathroom then Smith buttered the toast slowly in
the bathroom. The consequent of (10) does not follow, in
the informational inclusion sense of "implies" from the
antecedent. So (10) is not a tautology for the logic of
information inclusion. In this way, connectibility and
information inclusion act-sequences share some logical
properties at the propositional level.

To contrast the two approaches, however, let us consider
some further schemata. For example, this schema is a
theorem for information content inclusion event sequences:
(1) [A → (B ∧ C)] → [(A → B) ∧ (A → C)] 'If the toast was
buttered slowly at midnight, then the toast was buttered
slowly and the toast was buttered at midnight' implies
'If the toast was buttered slowly at midnight then the
toast was buttered slowly, and if the toast was buttered
slowly at midnight then the toast was buttered at midnight.' The general reasoning is as follows: assume
(i) that it is not the case both that A is made true and
B ∧ C is not made true, and (ii) that the information
content of B ∧ C is included in that of A. Now look at
the consequent of the whole schema. The only ways it can
fail to be true are (iii) if A is made true and one of B
or C fails to be made true, or (iv) if the information in
B is not contained in that of A, or if the information in
C is not contained in that of A. Consider (iii). If A
is made true and one of B or C fails to be made true then
(i) must not be made true. That is, if A is made true
but either B or C is not, then A → (B ∧ C) must be made
false. Now consider (iv). If either B is not informa-
tionally contained in A or C is not contained in A, then
both B ∧ C taken together cannot be contained in A. Hence
(ii) must not obtain. Thus there is no consistent way to
assign truth-values and information content assignments
so that A → (B ∧ C) is made true but (A → B) ∧ (A → C) is
not. So (1) is a theorem for content inclusion of events.

Yet for relatedness of events, (1) fails to be generally
true. To disprove it, suppose A is related to B but not
to C. Then A → C fails to obtain, and hence (A → B) ∧ (A → C)

fails. But A → (B ∧ C) could still obtain. Assume A and
C both fail to obtain. Then A → (B ∧ C) does not obtain,
because A is related to B ∧ C and B and C both fail. Then
A → (B ∧ C) obtains but (A → B) ∧ (A → C) does not. Thus
(1) fails for relatedness of events. For example, let us
assume that my moving my finger is sufficient for the
event of the switch being flipped and the light being on.
It need not follow that my moving my finger is sufficient
for the light being on. That is, it need not follow that
just because I move my finger that by some sort of wizardry
the light must go on.

The failure of (1) in relatedness sequences is clearly
associated with failure of transitivity. If we have A → B
and B → C then the best we can say is that A is indirectly
sufficient for C. That is, A is sufficient for C as
mediated through and conditional upon B. Though the limits
may not be well defined, it is clear that unlimited transitivity cannot be allowed to stretch external event
sequences unrestrictedly and indefinitely. Yet for informational containment conditionals, transitivity must always
characteristically obtain. Here then is a key difference.

What about modus ponens and modus tollens? These schemata
would seem to be true for both kinds of event sequences.
We always have it in either type of sequence that if A → B
is made true and A is made true, then B must be made true.
And if A → B is made true but B is not, then A cannot be
made true either.

What about exportation?

$$[(A ∧ B) → C] → [A → (B → C)]$$

Consider a relatedness sequence first. Suppose it is true
that if I flip this switch, the light will be illuminated.
Then take some unrelated event, say some sand shifting in
the Sahara desert. It would seem to be true that if the
conjunctive proposition 'The sand shifts and the switch is
flipped' is a sufficient condition for the light to be
illuminated. But is the following conditional true? If
the sand shifts then if the switch is flipped the light
will be illuminated? It would seem not, because the
shifting of that bit of sand in the Sahara, we may consistently assume, has nothing to do with whether the light
will be illuminated if the switch is flipped. Similar
examples will indicate failure of exportation for informational inclusion act-sequences.

PRACTICAL REASONING

Above we have sketched out a non-classical theory of the
meaning of → or 'implication' in the context of certain
kinds of inferences about actions. It remains for us to
see how this theory fits into the pragmatic context of
argumentation where act-theoretic inconsistencies are
alleged as a basis of ad hominem criticisms. We do this
by showing how allegations about alleged actions that
take place in disputations fit into a larger network of
action propositions. The vehicle for carrying out this
project is the concept of practical reasoning, most notably
advanced by the works of Anscombe (1957) and von Wright
(1983).

When an action description is alleged to be inconsistent
with some proposition advocated by an arguer whose position is criticized, much background context concerning the
arguer's position (his other actions or commitments) needs
to be filled in. The mechanism for this "filling in" is
practical reasoning.

Practical inference is a kind of argument that concludes
in a directive to action for the one who makes the inference. The study of practical inference is therefore very
interesting to anyone who thinks there could be a logical
structure of reasons for actions. Practical inferences
can be found examined Aristotle, but their introduction
on the modern scene of analytical philosophy appears to
have been given in Elizabeth Anscombe's book Intention
(1957). An up-dated version of one of Aristotle's examples
proposed by Anscombe (1957, p. 60) should give the reader
some idea of what practical inference is like.

> Vitamin X is good for all men over 60.
> Pigs' tripes are full of vitamin X.
> I am a man over 60.
> Here is some pigs' tripes.
> So, I'll have some.

The conclusion of the inference above is an action, or at
least a proposal to undertake an action by the inferer,
but Anscombe has some doubts about the precise form the
conclusion should take. She considers 'So, I'd better have
some' and 'So, it would be a good thing for me to have some'
as possible variants for the conclusion of the inference.

The example chosen by Anscombe is perhaps not meant to be

taken too seriously, but one can immediately sense the importance of this sort of inference is much commonplace reasoning. In making decisions about whether or not to give consent for proposed medical treatment, for example, Anscombe's sort of practical inference could well represent the type of reasoning that is involved. If a patient is looking to his own personal problem of what to do in particular circumstances, he may not have time or resources for maximization (finding the best possible treatment with least side-effects). Rather, he may need to decide on the practical basis of considering a medication that is practically available in relation to the particular circumstances of his problem. Reasoning from a premiss that this medication is good for someone in his situation and will cure his problem, he may conclude by a practical inference that the appropriate conclusion is to take some.

However, many puzzles remain about practical inference. Some of the examples given by Aristotle (De Motu Animalium 701 a 7 - 701 a 25) are so close to deductive (syllogistic) inferences that it is unclear where practical inference is distinctively different from deductive inference.

> Every man should take walks.
> I am a man.
> Therefore, at once, I take a walk.

Moreover, the first premiss of this inference is highly implausible. Taking walks is appropriate for some men in some circumstances, but not for all. Another example is said to have a "breathless" conclusion.

> I should make something good.
> A house is something good.
> At once I make a house.

This example overlooks the possibility that there may be other ways to make something good than by making a house. Perhaps I already have a perfectly acceptable house but I desperately need a barn. Hence the question of whether these practical inferences stand in need of supplementation by the addition of further premisses or qualifications is an open problem.

Chief among those who have investigated such problems is G. H. von Wright. An illustrative sort of example discussed by von Wright comes from his The Varieties of Goodness (1963).

    x wants to reach the train on time.
    Unless x runs he will not reach the train on time.
    Therefore, x must run.

Later revising his claim that this inference is valid,
von Wright (1983) proposed that the demonstration is a
practical not a logical one, and that its premisses do
not logically entail behavior. In his remarks on practical reasoning (1983), von Wright proposed that the conclusion binds the agent within the teleological frame
which he accepts in the premisses. Von Wright evidently
had in mind a binding relationship between premisses and
conclusion weaker than, or at least different from,
deductive validity.

What might von Wright have had in mind here? One suggestion is that practical reasoning pertains to an objective
or intention set by an agent, and to some means of carrying out this objective. So construed, practical reasoning
is a model of a step of deliberation that can be made by
a rational agent in carrying out an action designed to
work towards his stated objective.

One major difference between the conceptions of Anscombe
and von Wright concerns the premiss that states the "means"
being considered by the agent. Anscombe tends to see this
means as stating a sufficient condition in the circumstances for carrying out the agent's objective. Whereas
the cases considered by von Wright focus on a necessary
condition for carrying out the stated objective. To
reflect this dual conception of practical inference
implicit in the literature, two schemata could be given.

    Necessary Condition Schema (n.c.s.)

    My objective is to bring about A.
    Not A unless B, as I see the situation.
    Therefore, I set myself to bring about B.

    Sufficient Condition Schema (s.c.s.)

    My objective is to bring about A.
    If B then A, as I see the situation.
    Therefore, I set myself to bring about B.

The expression 'set oneself,' found in the conclusion of
both schemata here, is due to von Wright's formulation.
As his recent treatment (1983) shows, it is a puzzle to

determine whether the conclusion should best be construed
as an action or as some sort of "should-statement" or
recommendation for an action to be carried out. Hence he
chooses the relatively neutral expression 'set myself'
for the statement of the conclusion.

Another problem is that the formulations above lack certain refinements needed to make them adequately formulated.
Hence von Wright (1971, p. 107) is led to add some temporal
elaborations. $\emptyset$ is a state of affairs and S is an agent.

> From now on S intends to bring about $\emptyset$ at some time t.
> From now on S considers that, unless he does A no
>   later than time t', he cannot bring about $\emptyset$ at
>   time t.
> Therefore, no later than when he thinks time t has
>   arrived, S sets himself to do $\emptyset$, unless he forgets
>   about the time or is prevented.

However, even this more elaborate formulation is open to
certain loopholes which evidently require further qualifications or additional premisses.

One problem is posed by the following type of case. Suppose I intend to do some jogging at the Y.M.C.A. on a certain day, but can't, having forgotten to bring my running
shoes along. However, I see that Smith has left his
running shoes on a bench and that they are my size. In
this situation, the only way I will get in my run at the Y.
is to steal Smith's running shoes. Here, either s.c.s. or
n.c.s., as they stand, could provide a perfectly reasonable inference with the conclusion that I should set myself
to steal Smith's shoes. For I do intend to jog, and that
means is necessary and perhaps also sufficient in the
circumstances.

What this problem suggests is that the premisses of n.c.s.
or s.c.s. do not imply the conclusion <u>simpliciter</u>. Rather,
the action that is necessary (sufficient) must be in itself
acceptable to begin with if the inference is to determine
that action as something I should set myself to do. At
any rate, some qualification of this sort must be included
in the premisses.

Another problem may be a sort of Buridan's ass question.
Suppose I have two pairs of jogging shoes available. I
must put on one or the other pair as a necessary condition
of my jogging at the Y. But practical reasoning does not

tell me which pair to select. I could select either pair,
but perhaps the one pair is better or more suitable. If
so, I should set myself to pick out the more suitable pair.

A third problem is that of known side-effects. I may
intend to cheer uncle up by taking Junior along on my
visit to uncle in hospital. But if Junior has an infec-
tious flu virus, perhaps I should not set myself to take
him along on the visit. For consequences other than
"cheering up" may eventuate as well. At any rate, for
reasons of problems of these sorts, several modifications
of the structure of practical inference are in order.
Some suggestions are included in the modified schemata
given below. E is some state (end) ultimately intended.
$\{A_0, A_1, \ldots, A_n\}$ is a set of possible actions being
considered by the agent.

Necessary Condition Schema

(N1)   I intend to bring about E.

(N2)   I consider that doing at least one of
$\{A_0, A_1, \ldots, A_n\}$ is necessary to bring
about E.

(N3)   I have decided on one member A_i as an acceptable, or as the most acceptable necessary condition for E.

(N4)   Nothing prevents me from doing A_i.

(N5)   Bringing about E is more acceptable to me than
not doing A_i.

Therefore, I set myself to do A_i.

Sufficient Condition Schema

(S1)   I intend to bring about E.

(S2)   I consider that one of $\{A_0, A_1, \ldots, A_n\}$ is
sufficient to bring about E.

(S3)   I have decided on one member A_i as an acceptable, or as the most acceptable sufficient
condition for E.

(S4)   Nothing prevents me from doing A_i.

(S5) Bringing about E is more acceptable to me than
      not doing A_i.

Therefore, I set myself to do A_i.

Perhaps further modifications are still necessary, but I
do not know of any that are needed. If none are needed,
then we should say that the individual who accepts all
the premisses of an argument that has one of these forms
of inferences, but does not set himself to carry out the
action of the conclusion, is pragmatically inconsistent.
Of course, people are sometimes pragmatically inconsistent,
as we have seen. So if someone accepts the premisses, he
still might just not do the act described in the conclusion. Thus action per se is not the conclusion of a
practical inference. The conclusion is that the agent
will or should set himself to carry out the act of the
conclusion if he is acting in a consistent and rational
manner. If he accepts the premisses, then the conclusion
is an acceptable course of action to carry out, relative
to what is accepted in the statements of the premisses.
Here then is the "binding nature" of the practical inference.

The sequence of reasoning characteristic of practical
inferences is often necessary to fill in and thereby
justify (or rebut) ad hominem allegations of inconsistency for the following reasons. Suppose a critic alleges
"You have brought about A, but you claim that everyone
should bring about B. Moreover, bringing about A is
inconsistent with bringing about B. Ergo, you are
refuted." Most often A and B are not directly inconsistent, yet there is some set of linkages or connections
between A and B such that, in the context of those connections, A might be shown to lead through a sequence of
intervening actions to some action description inconsistent with B. But how do we fill in the missing steps?
Answer: we must look over the agent's network of plans,
intentions and actions, and see if the connections that
can be plausibly attributed by the critic to the agent
justify the critic's ad hominem criticism. Our case
studies in the sequel will show how to carry out this
task of analysis for ad hominem allegations.

7

Contradictions in Dialogues

We have now seen that logic and sequences of act-descriptions have enough in common to support the traditional circumstantial ad hominem as a species of correct or incorrect argument. The appropriate account of logical consequence for this application turned out to be relatedness logic--along with a variant propositional calculus based on information inclusion--and thus we have grounded the ad hominem on a formal basis. The appropriate propositional calculus for most instances is a subsystem of classical propositional logic.

What remains is to see how this new approach to propositional logic fits the dialectical framework for ad hominem as suggested by Barth and Martens in our earlier chapters. We begin by looking back to some of our previous case studies and advancing the analysis of them even further. Then we propose some general recommendations based on the case studies. Finally we will raise some philosophical questions about the model of argument we have adopted in pursuing the ad hominem so far.

ANALYSIS OF THE SPORTSMAN'S REJOINDER

Most of the initial moves in the analysis of the sportsman's rejoinder should already be fairly evident to the reader, given the analysis of chapter 4, along with the numerous points already made in the outline of that argument in chapter 1. As we pointed out there, great care must be taken, first of all, to sort out the propositions alleged to be inconsistent. Then, too, we saw that DeMorgan is quite correct to point out that no matter how you describe these propositions in the more-or-less acceptable ways, there is no immediate logical contradiction clinched by the attacker. Thus DeMorgan is quite justified in arguing that the sportsman commits the fallacy of confusing logical inconsistency with something else, evidently some pragmatic inconsistency that is meant to be alleged.

But is there a pragmatic inconsistency to be found? As we saw, much depends on how the actions that are at issue are described. We suggested in Chapter 3 that the sportsman would be on the strongest ground for mounting a charge of pragmatic inconsistency if he were to concentrate on the relationship between meat eating and the killing of animals. Perhaps some legitimate argument can be extracted from what the sportsman says.

The sportsman could be maintaining that eating meat is connectible to the killing of animals. If so, there is some point in what he alleges, but we must ask precisely how these two actions can be connected. It is true that in order for somebody to eat meat then it is quite likely that some animal was killed in order to obtain the meat. However, there is no tight logical connection--it is possible, if unlikely, that the animal in question could have died a natural death. My eating meat is not, in itself, a sufficient condition for an animal to be killed. What then is the connection?

Let us suppose that in subsequent dialectical interchanges to the argument between the hunter and his critic, the hunter manages to get the critic to agree to three propositions.

C1.   Whatever makes it true that meat is eaten makes it true that animals are killed.

C2.   Something the critic did made it true that meat was eaten.

C3.   It is not the case that something the critic did made it true that animals are killed.

This set of propositions is demonstrably and pragmatically inconsistent in System $\mathcal{S}$ of relatedness logic. We have to agree, therefore, that the critic, in accepting C1, C2, and C3 jointly, has committed a circumstantial ad hominem of the action-theoretic sort.

But it must be stressed that the sportsman's rejoinder, as described by Whately and DeMorgan, is by no means identical or equivalent to its dialectical furtherance given in the previous paragraph. The problem for the hunter is that C1 is just not very plausible, and consequently the critic is unlikely to agree to it.

The hunter would be on better grounds to argue a proposition much weaker than C1, namely that meat eating is connectible to the killing of animals. Let us formulate this weaker proposition as follows:

C1a.   Whatever could make it true that meat is eaten could also make it true that animals are killed.

Even here there are grounds for doubt, however, that the
hunter has chosen a proposition he can establish or
plausibly pin on the critic. First, meat eating is not
directly connectible to killing animals. One who eats
a steak need not have just butchered a cow in order to
eat the steak. Rather the world lines between these two
outcomes may be indirectly connectible at best. Probably
what one wants to say is that these two propositions are
indirectly connectible by other factors, such as economic
relationships between consumer demand for meat and the
profitability of farms, slaughterhouses, and other businesses connected with animal processing.

Could such an argument for indirect connectibility be
made? We will not try to do it, but let us concede for
the sake of further argument that such an indirect connectibility could be established. What would it prove?
It would not prove that the critic is inconsistent. C1a,
C2, and C3 together make up a set of the form $\{R(p,q)$, p,
$\neg q\}$, which is consistent in relatedness logic. In order
to prove inconsistency you also have to prove $\neg(p \land \neg q)$.
The best the hunter can say he has proved to the critic
"Be careful, p is connectible to q, and you concede that
p and $\neg q$, so if you concede that p is sufficient for q,
you will be inconsistent." This is a very weak form of
refutation at best. The hunter has accomplished nothing
in the way of successfully refuting the critic. At best
he has offered a warning.

As discussed at the beginning of Chapter 3, Whately
argues that the sportsman's rejoinder may have the effect,
"not unjustly" as he puts it, of shifting the burden of
proof onto the critic. Consequently, according to Whately,
if the critic replies he may do so weakly. It should be
pointed out here by way of analysis, however, that the
critic does not really need to respond at all to the
sportsman's warning, and if he does so weakly, he also
does so needlessly, thus perhaps gratuitously losing the
argument. Rather, the critic should shift the burden of
proof back onto the sportsman by asking him to demonstrate,
if he can, the pragmatic inconsistency alleged to obtain
between meat eating and killing animals.

At any rate, it is clear now what the sportsman's task
consists of if he is to mount a successful ad hominem
attack. He must find a set of propositions that the critic
is committed to where this set collectively generates a contradiction. Let us now turn to constructing a general
framework for this task.

CLOSURE OF COMMITMENTS IN DIALOGUES

According to Hamblin (1970a), the term "contradiction" has a stronger sense in a dialectical context than in its usual one in formal logic. Hamblin asks us to imagine that each participant in a dialogue has a slate on which he chalks statements as he agrees to them, or answers questions that imply them (p. 263). These statements represent the commitment-store of that participant. Commitments may be retracted (wiped off the slate), as well as added on, as the course of a dialogue proceeds. In this context, we can say that participants contradict one another, or that a participant contradicts himself. These are both strong senses of "contradiction."

What is meant when we say that a participant contradicts himself? Hamblin observes that in both senses of the word, "there need be no contradiction between two statements simply on the grounds of their form--if one, for example, is the other's logical negation" (p. 258). What Hamblin means is that A and ⌐A need not jointly constitute a contradiction if A is a commitment of the first participant, but not the second, and ⌐A is a commitment of the second participant, but not the first. No single participant's commitment-store contains the inconsistency A ∧ ⌐A.

In order to deal with problems of retraction and organization of commitments, Hamblin constructs a dialectical game, called a Why-Because-Game with Questions (p. 265ff.). There are two participants, each of whom adds or deletes commitments according to a set of rules that define permissible moves. The language of this game (H) is essentially classical propositional calculus.

When we say that some participant contradicts himself in dialogue, we mean that his slate contains a contradiction. This meaning of "contradiction" is stronger because two statements A and B might be perfectly consistent in themselves, but as members of a commitment-store that also contained 'A implies not-B' they would be contradictory in the sense that the participant contradicts himself when he becomes committed to the entire set.

In order to model dialectical arguments better, Hamblin (1971, p. 144) proposes that in some variations of (H), a weaker nontransitive relation should be substituted for the usual transitive notion of logical consequence (implication). He therefore introduces a relation of immediate

consequence such that whenever there is a consequence
relation between two statements there is a chain of
immediate consequence relations leading from the one to
the other. Parallelling the notion of immediate consequence is that of immediate contrariety.

The general framework given by Hamblin provides a favorable backdrop against which the act-theoretic circumstantial ad hominem can be studied. The problem for the
analysis of ad hominem can be seen as one of organizing
relations among a set of propositions that constitute a
commitment-store of a participant in dialogue who has
been accused of inconsistency. How the problem arises,
as our case studies have indicated, is that one's acknowledged acts (propositions conceded to be made true by an
arguer) may commit one to certain other propositions by
virtue of pragmatic implications in relation to act-
sequences. But these other propositions may be inconsistent with yet other commitments of this participant. Thus
a participant may have conceded A and may admit he has
made B true and is thereby committed to B. But perhaps
his opponent can show by a sequence of steps that by
making B true, this participant has also made it true
that C. And moreover, the opponent may also be able to
show that A and C are inconsistent. If the participant
accused is indeed committed to an inconsistent set, a
successful ad hominem refutation has been carried out.

Now in some cases it does not matter whether the consequence relation utilized in the game is that of immediate
consequence (relatedness implication, in our terms) or
consequence (classical implication). To illustrate by
our previous case studies, if the child accuses the adult
both of smoking (A), and being committed to not smoking
(⌐A), the inconsistency is so direct that it is simply a
case of the familiar A ∧ ⌐A schema, the negation of which
is a tautology both in classical logic and relatedness
logic. But if, as in the sportsman's rejoinder, the
inconsistency alleged to obtain is between the commitment
to eating meat and the commitment to killing animals, the
attacker must demonstrate by a series of steps that there
is some contradiction--in Hamblin's sense that the participant contradicts himself--in the participant's commitment-
store containing these two act-descriptions along with
other commitments of this participant. The basic problem
is really this: Precisely which set of propositions
belongs to this participant's commitment-store at this
point in the dialogue?

Based on the case studies we have examined so far, our
best general solution to this problem is given by this
ruling. A participant is committed to just those propositions (1) he has committed himself to making true
according to the rules of (H), or (2) he has acknowledged
he has made true, or (3) that are immediate consequences
of (1) or (2) by relatedness implication. Moreover, the
participants need not have commitment-stores that are
consistent. Nor do we want commitments to be closed
under transitive classical implication. However, if a
participant's commitments are shown to be inconsistent
by his opponent, a significant stage in the dialogue has
been attained that calls for resolution of the contradiction.

Of course we need to view Hamblin's dialectical game in
two particular directions. First, the particular type
of dialogue we are especially concerned with in connection with the circumstantial ad hominem is that of an
allegation of personal actions by some participant in
dialogue. A quite pointed question in applying dialectical games to this sort of argument situation is When does
an acknowledged act of making some proposition true constitute a commitment to that proposition by the actor?
Suffice it to say that we can treat a proposition as a
commitment if the participant who admits he made it true
has not retracted his commitment when given the opportunity to do so. Second, if this proposition implies
another by relatedness implication then the second proposition may also be treated as a commitment of the same
participant.

Thus our second extension of Hamblin's framework is that
we propose his notion of immediate consequence may be
explicated in the analysis of the circumstantial ad hominem
by relatedness implication. Accordingly, if a participant
is committed to A, even if his commitment is closed under
implication, he need not be committed to A ∨ B if A and B
are not related. If he is committed to ⌐A, he need not be
committed to A → B, and so forth. In general, his commitment-set is determined first of all by what he concedes
according to the rules of (H) plus the optional closure
in some games of this set of propositions under relatedness implication. In addition, the set of propositions
closed under transitive closure (indirect relatedness
implication) will also be considered commitments to particular games (possible variants).

To indicate the pattern of the type of game we have in mind

to model <u>ad</u> <u>hominem</u> argumentation, let us construct one
particular game which we call (H♪). The two participants
are White and Black, each of whom has a commitment-store
containing a finite number of statements. Each must add
or delete commitments according to the rules given below.
White always moves first in beginning a round, then Black
responds, and each continues to make one move at a time.
Capital letters with subscripts, A_1, A_2, . . . A_n, are
variables for statements, always for finite n, in the
meta-language.

In a particular round of (H♪), each participant is
assigned a statement that he must prove by relatedness
logic from the commitments of his opponent, if he is to
win. If neither party succeeds, the game is terminated
after an agreed-upon (finite) number of moves. Axioms
and rules for relatedness logic are contained in the
initial commitment-stores of both participants. In the
game (H♪), commitments of the participants are not closed
under relatedness implication. For simplicity, we
exclude 'Why-questions' in (H♪).

The Game (H♪)

Types of Allowed Locutions

(i)   'Statement A_i' or, in certain cases, 'Statements A_i,
       A_j.'

(ii)   'No commitment A_1, A_2, . . . A_n' for any finite
       number of statements A_1, A_2, . . . A_n.

(iii) 'Question A_1, A_2, . . . A_n?' for any number of
       statements A_1, A_2, . . . A_n.

(iv)   Resolve A_i, for any statement A_i.

Locution Rules

L1. Each speaker contributes one locution at a time.

L2. Question 'A_1, A_2, . . . A_n?' must be followed by

    (a) 'Statement $\lnot(A_1 \lor A_2 \lor . . . \lor A_n)$'

or (b) 'No commitment $A_1 \lor A_2 \lor \ldots \lor A_n$'

or (c) 'Statement A_1' or
'Statement A_2' or
────────── or
'Statement A_n.'

or (d) 'No commitment $A_1, A_2, \ldots A_n$'

L3.   'Resolve A_i' must be followed by

(a) 'No commitment A_i'

or (b) 'No commitment $\lnot A_i$.'

Commitment-store Rules

C1.   'Statement A_i' places A_i in the speaker's commitment-store unless it is already there, and in the hearer's commitment-store unless his next locution states '$\lnot A_i$' or indicates 'No commitment A_i.'

C2.   'Statements A_i, A_j' places both A_i and A_j in the speaker and hearer's commitment-stores under the same conditions as in **C1**.

C3.   'No commitment $A_1, A_2, \ldots A_n$' deletes from the speaker's commitment-store any of $A_1, A_2, \ldots A_n$ that are in it and are not axioms of $\mathcal{S}$.

C4.   'Question $A_1, A_2, \ldots A_n$?' places the statement $A_1 \lor A_2 \lor \ldots \lor A_n$ in the speaker's store unless it is already there, and in the hearer's store unless he replies with 'Statement $\lnot(A_1 \lor A_2 \lor \ldots \lor A_n)$' or 'No commitment $A_1 \lor A_2 \lor \ldots \lor A_n$.'

(H$\mathcal{S}$) is to be regarded as a base system upon which closure requirements of various strengths may be added for the purpose of modelling different contexts of realistic ad hominem argumentation. We emphasize again that commitments are not closed under implication in (H$\mathcal{S}$), but to model the notion of immediate consequence, commitments could be closed in a stronger variant under relatedness implication, or in yet stronger variants under transitive closure of relatedness implication. What follows is a sample round of (H$\mathcal{S}$) that should convey an idea of what dialogues are like.

	White	Black
1.	Question B?	No commitment B.
2.	Question ⅂B?	Statement ⅂B.
3.	Question D?	No commitment D.
4.	Question ⅂D?	Statement ⅂D.
5.	Question R(B,D)?	Statement R(B,D).
6.	Question ⅂(B ∨ D)?	Statement ⅂(B ∨ D).
7.	Question A?	No commitment A.
8.	Question C?	No commitment C.
9.	Question A ∨ C?	Statement A ∨ C.
10.	Question A → B?	Statement A → B.
11.	Question C → D?	Statement C → D.
12.	Question ⅂B?	Statement ⅂B.
13.	Question ⅂A?	Statement ⅂A.
14.	Question ⅂D?	Statement ⅂D.
15.	Question ⅂C?	Statement ⅂C.
16.	Question R(A,C)?	Statement ⅂R(A,C).
17.	Question (A ∨ C) → R(A,C)?	Statement (A ∨ C) → R(A,C).
18.	Question A ∨ C?	Statement A ∨ C.
19.	Question R(A,C)?	Statement R(A,C).
20.	Resolve R(A,C)?	No commitment ⅂R(A,C).
21.	Question ⅂A ∧ ⅂C?	Statement ⅂A ∧ ⅂C.
22.	Question (⅂A ∧ ⅂C) → ⅂(A ∨ C)?	Statement (⅂A ∧ ⅂C) → ⅂(A ∨ C).
23.	Question ⅂(A ∨ C)?	Statement ⅂(A ∨ C).
24.	Resolve A ∨ C.	No commitment (A ∨ C).

By way of commentary, here is what has transpired. Black
commits himself to both ⌐B and ⌐D in separate answers.
He then concedes that B and D are related. At move 6 he
commits himself to ⌐(B ∨ D). He would have been in a
questionable situation to answer any other way at 6, for
(⌐B ∧ ⌐D) → [R(B,D) → ⌐(B ∨ D)] is a tautology in relatedness logic. At move 12, Black reiterates his statement
at move 2. Black is virtually forced to concede ⌐A at
13, because he has already conceded A → B at 10, and ⌐B
at 12. (Remember that modus tollens is a correct inference in ♪). Similar remarks apply to Black's acceptance
of ⌐C at 15. At 17, Black has no good choice but to concede (A ∨ C) → R(A,C) for that is a tautology of relatedness logic. By modus ponens, White thus compels Black at
19 to concede R(A,C), thus contradicting his acceptance
of ⌐R(A,C) at 16. White asks Black to resolve the point,
and Black then withdraws his commitment to ⌐R(A,C). At
21, Black should accept ⌐A ∧ ⌐C in light of his previous
separate acceptance of ⌐A at 13, and ⌐C at 15. At 22,
Black accepts (⌐A ∧ ⌐C) → ⌐(A ∨ C) because it is a tautology. Thus once again at 24 he is forced to make a
choice and he withdraws his commitment to (A ∨ C), by
virtue of modus ponens, move 22, and move 21.

In this round, Black falls into inconsistency of commitments several times, but extricates himself in the face
of White's questioning by retracting commitments.

To fix the analysis of ad hominem, what one wants to do
is to find some particular variant of (H♪) that perfectly
models the argumentation appropriate to the ad hominem
fallacy. However, this is not easy to do because it is
difficult to construct the perfect game to set the criteria
nonarbitrarily by which each participant may win (or lose)
the game. In some traditional games of dialectic, including the obligation game--see Hamblin (1970a, pp. 260-263)--
the objective is to trap one's opponent in a contradiction
by a series of questions. Such a strategy is certainly
the objective of the ad hominem attacker, but in realistic
argumentation, as we have seen, very often the attacked
participant can effectively reply to the allegation of
inconsistency, and carry on the dialogue beyond the point,
even of a successful demonstration that he has contradicted
himself. Thus the strategy of fixing inconsistency upon
an opponent would seem to be one substrategy of a larger
overall strategy in a game of dialectic. How the attacker
uses this proof of inconsistency of his opponent's commitments is what should determine our evaluation of the

fallaciousness or correctness of his argument.

So there is a kind of dilemma for dialectic here. A game
where demonstration of opponent-inconsistency is a win-
strategy nicely models the core objective of ad hominem
argumentation but fails to model the overall strategy or
flow of ad hominem interchanges in argument. A symmetrical
game like (H), where each participant has as a win-strategy
the goal of proving some designated proposition using his
opponent's commitments as premises seems more generally
appropriate. It models the idea that each participant
moves towards a positive, ultimate goal in his construction of arguments. But it is not obvious in this type of
game what the value of proving one's opponent inconsistent
is supposed to be. Does a proof of opponent-inconsistency
count for some points to the attacker, or is it just a way
of forcing your opponent to reorganize or prune his commitments? If the latter, what is the strategic advantage?
These are the interesting questions.

Suppose White shows, by a sequence of questions, that
Black is committed to some set of propositions that he
shows to be inconsistent in $\mathcal{S}$, in the sense of leading
White to 'Statement A' and also 'Statement ¬A.' Such a
sequence of moves may not seem to amount to anything very
much in (H$\mathcal{S}$), because, after all, commitment-stores are
not required to be consistent. But notice that if Black
does not retract commitments in such a way as to remove
the inconsistency, White can always win the game at the
next move. An inconsistent proposition, taken together
with any proposition related to the proposition White
needs to prove, always implies the proposition that White
needs to prove in relatedness logic. For example, suppose
White needs to prove C follows from the commitments of
Black in order to win. Suppose that Black is committed to
A ∧ ¬A, as White has shown. Then all White has to do is
find some proposition related to C that Black accepts.
For example, since all participants are committed to axioms
of $\mathcal{S}$, Black accepts ¬(C ∧ ¬C). But in $\mathcal{S}$ the following is
a tautology: [(A ∧ ¬A) ∧ ¬(C ∧ ¬C)] → C. Thus by closure
of commitments Black is committed to C, and White can
prove it.

Therefore, there is a powerful strategic value in demonstrating opponent-inconsistency in (H$\mathcal{S}$). For if your
opponent does not immediately move in such a way as to
remove the inconsistency, you can always win the game at
the next move. In (H), a similar and even more direct win-
strategy is likewise available, because (S ∧ ¬S) implies T,

for any S and T in classical propositional calculus.

How should Black cope with a demonstrated allegation that he is inconsistent? Clearly he will have to remove the inconsistency on pain of losing the game. But he may not want to retract commitments other than those that will get him in trouble. How is he to organize his commitment-store to react most rationally against the charge of inconsistency? That is another question to be addressed.

RESPONSES TO AD HOMINEM ATTACK

When two disputants are arguing and one accuses the other of the circumstantial ad hominem, let us suppose that the attacker is on good grounds and that in fact the defender is committed through his actions and/or his assertions or recommendations to a set of propositions that is demonstrably inconsistent. Advancing the dialogue can only proceed by the defender's retraction of some of this set of propositions. But how can retraction be rationally organized?

There are two ways to respond to the allegation of pragmatic inconsistency. One is to subtract information by reducing the set of propositions alleged to be inconsistent. For example, if one is accused of bringing about A while at the same time committing oneself to the rejection of A, one seems committed to the set {A, ⌐A}. Thus one response is to drop or withdraw one of A or ⌐A.

Consider a case where one disputant points out that his opponent is committed, by means of actions she has brought about or said should be brought about, to the following set: {p → q, p, ⌐q}. The opponent, convinced by the truth-table below that this set is inconsistent, must contemplate selecting some consistent subset.

	p	q	R(p,q)	p → q	p	⌐q	
(1)	T	T	T	T	T	F	Reject ⌐q.
(2)	T	T	F	F	T	F	
(3)	T	F	T	F	T	T	Reject p → q.
(4)	T	F	F	F	T	T	
(5)	F	T	T	T	F	F	
(6)	F	T	F	F	F	F	
(7)	F	F	T	T	F	T	Reject p.
(8)	F	F	F	F	F	T	

The opponent has a straight three-way choice in this situation. She may accept $\{p \to q, p\}$, $\{p, \neg q\}$, or $\{p \to q, \neg q\}$. How to choose? If avoiding allegations of connectibility is part of one's strategy of defense in an ad hominem allegation, then a reasonable policy would be to give preference to sets where the member propositions are not related to each other. In this case, the policy dictates accepting $\{p, \neg q\}$, since in both other sets the component propositions are related.

The defender is looking at a set of actions or act-outcomes, and he must ask questions concerning the coherence of this set. Rescher (1976) recommends the preference of the most plausible maximal consistent subsets by placing a plausibility filter on the inconsistent set. However, that is not the only possible solution. In the case of ad hominem allegations, one needs to take into account the connectibility by practical reasoning of the different act-outcomes. What we propose is a connectibility filter on the maximal consistent subsets. Given all the maximal consistent subsets, we give preference to those that have propositions with the least number of connections between the member propositions. The motivation for this strategy is to enable the defender to be in the best position to rebut further allegations of connectibility that might lead to subsequent ad hominem attacks. In short, one has to take into account relationships among the propositions defended and attacked over and above their truth-values.

The second way of reorganizing commitments in the face of a successful ad hominem attack is to add information to one or both of the two propositions in order to remove the contradiction. For example, if the act-descriptions are {moving, not moving}, they may be changed to {moving quickly, not moving slowly}. And, of course, it is perfectly consistent to advocate moving quickly while at the same time not moving slowly oneself. Or if the act-descriptions are {lying, not lying}, they may be changed to {lying, not lying except to save somebody from a greater harm} in order to restore consistency.

A variant on the theme of the sportsman's rejoinder will serve as an example of the second method of response.

1. Businessman: I protest the killing of laboratory animals for neurobiological research. These animals often have to suffer in great agony for prolonged periods, and most often the research turns out to be useless anyway.

2. Scientist: I happen to know that you are person-
                   ally in the meat processing business.
                   You are directly engaged in the killing
                   of animals for profit. How can you
                   accuse me of killing animals when you
                   yourself engage in this very same act
                   every day? You are inconsistent!

3. Businessman: The animals in my slaughterhouses are
                   killed painlessly and humanely. In
                   scientific experiments, animals are
                   often killed and maimed in a way that
                   means they are in fear and pain for
                   prolonged periods.

4. Scientist: That is not true, at least not as much
                   now as it used to be. With the advent
                   of anesthetics, animal experimentation
                   can be carried out painlessly.

5. Businessman: I doubt that. If you look at caged,
                   drugged, and maimed laboratory animals,
                   they do not look any too happy.

6. Scientist: I concede that these animals have to
                   suffer to some extent, but the goal of
                   research is scientific knowledge. If
                   it is permissible to kill animals for
                   food, then it is permissible to kill
                   animals for knowledge.

7. Businessman: Well, I disagree. We need food, you
                   know. Without it we would starve, and
                   humans would die.

8. Scientist: Not true. There are perfectly nutri-
                   tious vegetable substitutes for meat
                   protein that are economical to produce
                   and make available without killing
                   animals.

9. Businessman: Well, scientific experiments do not
                   require the killing of animals. Neuro-
                   biological research can be carried out
                   by means of tissue and cell studies, and
                   also by computer simulations of animal
                   functions. And, as I said, most experi-
                   ments are useless anyway. They do not
                   turn out to lead to new knowledge at all.

10. Scientist: It is the nature of scientific method
                   that many experiments turn out to be
                   useless. That is just the way of scien-
                   tific research. Not every experiment
                   can be guaranteed to be a breakthrough.
                   Moreover, it is just not true that neuro-
                   biological research can be carried out

11. <u>Businessman</u>:

exclusively by computer models or chemical or pathological investigations without using tissues from live animals. We have to observe what happens when the function of a living system is modified, and there is no substitute for examination of experimental results on living creatures.

11. <u>Businessman</u>: I still do not think you can argue that knowledge is more important than food. Scientific research has led to nuclear power that is not only polluting the world and killing humans and animals, but may well lead to the destruction of the world. There is nothing wrong with killing animals for food if we need the food and the killing is humane.

This dialogue starts with an allegation of inconsistency. At 2, the scientist alleges that the businessman is pragmatically inconsistent: the latter condemns the killing of animals but is himself in that very business. This is indeed a pragmatic inconsistency. The businessman condemns the killing of animals yet himself engages in that very act.

The interesting question here is, How does the businessman try to get out of it? The answer is that he redescribes the action in question so as to remove the inconsistency. Instead of sticking with the action 'killing animals,' he shifts to the more specific descriptions 'killing animals painfully' and 'killing animals nonhumanely.' While conceding that he kills animals, he counters that neither of the latter more specific actdescriptions are attributable to him, whereas they are attributable to the practice of the scientist. The businessman in effect alleges that the correct actdescriptions for his own practices are 'killing animals painlessly' and 'killing animals humanely.' In other words, the businessman is retracting what seemed to be his original position; it is not the killing of animals per se that he condemns.

The scientist's <u>ad hominem</u> has succeeded quite nicely. On pain of pragmatic inconsistency, which he quite correctly wants to avoid, the businessman reformulates, or at any rate clarifies, his position.

After some further badinage, the scientist at step 6
finds himself in a hard place to argue from, and initiates a shift at 7 to yet another act-description. He
advances from 'killing animals' to the more specific
'killing animals for food' and 'killing animals for
knowledge,' thus differentiating between his practice
and that of his opponent. Here he shifts the burden of
proof back onto the businessman. Since knowledge is
presumably a more lofty goal than food, the businessman
is finding himself in another position of inconsistency.

The scientist alleges that his opponent is committed to
the following propositions.

(1)   If it is permissible to kill animals for food,
      it is permissible to kill animals for knowl-
      edge.
(2)   The businessman kills animals for food.
(3)   It is not permissible to kill animals for
      knowledge.

Here is the inconsistency. From (1) and (3) it follows
by modus tollens that (4) it is not permissible to kill
animals for food. But (4) is pragmatically inconsistent
with (2). The businessman wisely responds by denying
(1), claiming that food is necessary for survival.

Then follows a disagreement over how necessary killing
animals is for human nutrition and scientific research.
What the businessman has done at 7 is to shift once again
the act-description under contention. Here we shift from
'killing animals' to 'killing animals unnecessarily.'
This latter description is a more culpable one, and probably impossible to defend oneself of practicing. Naturally, neither is willing to accept it and in the end the
businessman comes back at 11 to (4), which he then disputes on a different basis.

FINAL COMMENTS ON McAULIFFE'S ARGUMENT

The various specimen arguments we have evaluated have
usually been dialectically two sided, and both sides have
been represented. In the case of McAuliffe's argument
studied in Chapter 5, only the one side is represented.
The press has not really been given the opportunity to
reply to the allegation of pragmatic inconsistency. Moreover, McAuliffe's argument is different from some other

purposely simplistic mock dialectical exchanges we have
devised ourselves. These other exchanges involve real
issues, like McAuliffe's argument, but they are not nearly
as realistic in several ways. McAuliffe's argument is a
deeply real-life specimen of argument on a highly complex
and vexatious issue of public policy. It is one part, a
very interesting one, of a large and complicated real-life
dialectical sequence that could be carried on in many
possible directions. Can we offer anything meaningful in
the way of advice on how "the press" (or other opponents)
should or could reply to McAuliffe?

First, let us note that the issue is a delicate one for
the ethical position of the media. The news media present
themselves as serious purveyors of factual news and information. Reporters, other writers, and media workers quite
correctly feel that in a free society they have a serious
and important role to play as disseminators of information.
If this is so, it would seem to follow that they are in a
position of "public trust" to report the news accurately
and fairly. And if this is so, then according to McAuliffe's
argument it would follow that there should be ethical guidelines on how this position of public trust should be fulfilled. Such guidelines might well hamper a journalist's
"freedom of inquiry," or at least seem to, from the point
of view of a working journalist. So the targets of
McAuliffe's argument are in a delicate position. No doubt
they want to acknowledge their important role as factual
informants on matters of public policy, but on the other
hand they are not likely to want to be too heavily regulated by "ethical guidelines." Their position is that of
being open to criticism and by concentrating on their
actions by ad hominem reasoning, McAuliffe's arguments are
remarkably effective in forcing them to abandon what is
taken to be their present position.

McAuliffe's argument succeeds in showing a circumstantial
inconsistency in the position of the media. This is not
to say that McAuliffe's argument should be taken to imply
that the media's unethical practices wholly invalidate its
criticisms of others in a position of public trust. However, McAuliffe's argument still has a force of powerful
and legitimate criticism by questioning the coherence of
the media position.

The effect of the argument is to "put the ball in the
media's court" by challenging the coherence of their position, given their apparent advocacy of a double standard.

For the effect of practicing a course of actions, while
recommending as a general policy the condemnation of
that type of action as applied to others, opens one's
own stand to legitimate questioning and criticism. This
is so especially if the one who practices such actions
has not justified his own conduct as a legitimate exception to the general policy at issue. Unless the ostensibly inconsistent position can be modified or defended,
it is quite appropriate to think it a vulnerable position,
weak and open to doubt and challenge.

It is a question of commitment in dialogue. If an arguer
sets out to persuade an arguee to adopt the arguer's
position, his stated goal carries with it a burden of
proof to produce arguments for that position. But this
positive thrust carries with it certain negative obligations as well. If the arguee challenges the arguer's
position by raising certain questions that open that
position to the vulnerability of inconsistencies within
itself, the arguer may be obliged to defend his position.
In short, there is a certain burden of proof on the
arguer to defend the consistency of his position.

We can see therefore, that the criticism of a position
can have legitimate validity as an argument even if it
falls short of a knock-down refutation of that position.
It can be a legitimate criticism by shifting the burden
of proof, quite rightly, onto the defender of the position to maintain consistency of his commitments. That a
failure to maintain inconsistency represents a losing of
the argument in a rational game of dialogue designed to
persuade another arguer to accept one's position is
mirrored in our common practice of according loss of
credibility to the arguer who is caught in positional
inconsistency.

Commonly, and with justification, we reason: if this
person can sincerely make policy recommendations evidently
meant to cover the sort of instances where he himself acts
in a manner contrary to the policy, he cannot truly be
committed to this policy. Either his words are hollow,
we infer, or his deeds are wayward. Either way, his commitment is impeachable and open to question. Therefore
his argument to persuade me of the worth of his viewpoint
lacks substance. Commitments that are shown to lack
stability and consistency cannot function as a sound
basis of persuasion to adopt a position.

The suggestion harks back to Hamblin's statement that the

ad hominem often has the function of shifting the burden
of proof "not unjustly" to the adversary in an argument
(Hamblin, 1970, p. 174). McAuliffe's argument fills in
enough evidence to make a good argument that the position of the media, as he fills it in, admits of inconsistencies. This charge suggests that the media is
involved in advocating a "double standard." Hence
McAuliffe's argument places the burden on the media as
a profession to defend their position as an institution
of public trust and confidence. True, the media falls
back on the doctrine of freedom of the press. But why
should the media have any more freedom than any other
profession in a position of public trust? Failure to
answer this question leaves the most plausible interpretation of the media's position open to severe challenge. They must defend that position by further argument at the cost of losing credibility. The onus of
proof is shifted onto the respondent to defend. This is
the negative obligation of proof in any process of dialogue and persuasion.

The precise rules of pragmatic structure underlying this
conception of dialogue as rational persuasion will be
given in Chapter 11. For the moment, let us make the
point in concrete terms by offering a "Socratic" dialogue
analogous to the positional thrust of McAuliffe's argumentation. This dialogue is yet another variant on our
"smoking" theme.

Socrates: Can we accept the proposition that health is
             a good thing? I mean health is worth having,
             both as an excellence of the body and mind,
             and as a means to the good life. Can we
             accept that?
Bob: Of course. That's a motherhood and apple-pie
             question. Although, if you think of it,
             neither motherhood nor apple pie may be as
             sure to be free of unqualifiable acceptance
             today as their use as an example suggests.
             But seriously, I can hardly deny that health
             is a good thing.
Socrates: All right. Now is a good thing worth pursuing?
             I mean if something is good then undertaking to
             bring about that good thing is a course of
             action to be recommended. Is it not so?
Bob: Well, all things being equal, perhaps. But
             pursuing a good thing can be full of pitfalls.
             I may undertake the good thing and cause all
             kinds of bad things to happen along the way.

Socrates: Well, yes, of course. Caution is admirable,
and nature is uncertain in cooperating with
our plans. But surely a good thing is worth
pursuing if there are no bad things known to
be connected with this pursuit, or if the good
thing far outweighs the bad side-effects.

Bob: Well, yes. I'll go along with that. Good
things are worth pursuing. But there are so
many good things to pursue. How can you pursue one when there may be many others to pursue that could be even better?

Socrates: Well yes, there are sometimes these sorts of
selective choices to be made. But suppose
you can bring about something which leads to an
acknowledged good thing without being so difficult or time-consuming to prevent you significantly from pursuing other good things.
Shouldn't you do it?

Bob: Well, yes. I can hardly deny that. If there
is very little cost, and the thing is clearly
and abundantly good, you ought to carry out
something that will accomplish it.

Socrates: Now is good the opposite of bad?

Bob: Well, I suppose so. It depends on what you
mean by 'opposite' and so forth. But generally speaking, 'good' and 'bad' are mutually
exclusive terms if you add 'at the same time,'
'in the same respect,' and so forth (Bob is
inclined to be analytically minded at times).

Socrates: O.K. You agree then, in light of our previous
conversations, that if something bad is about
to occur, and you can prevent it without
significant costs or complications, you ought
to?

Bob: Well, yes. I'll go along with that. It is
consistent with our previous discussions.

Socrates: Now, I want to discuss a recent medical con-
troversy. It seems to be increasingly accepted
by doctors that cigarette smoking is a primary
cause of congestive lung diseases, including
emphysema, that are in turn significant causes
of many medical problems and shortening of
life. Not only that, many of these medical
problems are very expensive to treat, and cause
many economic effects in the workplace.

Socrates and Bob now have a long discussion about these
recent medical findings too complicated to reproduce here.

The upshot is that Bob agrees that smoking causes congestive lung disease and that congestive lung disease is
unhealthy.

Socrates: Well, that was a long discussion and very com-
             plicated. Let's get back to something more
             philosophical. Not that medicine is an unphil-
             osophical subject, but it is not my main inter-
             est of the moment. One more empirical question
             though, if you'll forgive my apparent digres-
             sions. You smoke, don't you, Bob?
Bob: Well, er, yes. I do, and have done so for many
             years.

It does not take too much imagination at this point to see
where the dialogue is going. Socrates is about to "lower
the boom." Bob will have to be ready with some fast foot-
work if he is to extricate himself from Socrates' web.
Bob might admit that even though he agrees that smoking
is unhealthy and therefore a bad practice, he is unable
to give it up in his own particular circumstances. Socrates
will, of course, refuse to accept this way out, and hammer
away at the idea that if you are truly committed to a
policy of doing good, you will carry out acts falling
under this policy in your own personal conduct. Socrates'
position, speaking in historical hindsight, was impeccably
preserved in maintaining such consistencies of personal
conduct to the point of death. So he is a hard person to
argue against ad hominem.

One can see then that personal-positional inconsistency
can be a legitimate basis of argument and criticism in
dialogue even short of conclusive refutation. Socrates is
clearly winning the argument short of pinning Bob in
irrevocable inconsistency even as he mounts up a heavier
burden of proof against Bob's position. Just so, McAuliffe's
arguments shift a heavy burden of proof onto the media's
position even if the position fairly attributed to the media
remains open and malleable to the extent that further dialogue is quite possible. McAuliffe shifts the burden of
proof onto exponents of the media position to defend that
position such as it exists in the context of the current
dialogue.

The key observation here is that since the press collectively has not taken or enunciated some position in the
form of a unanimous declaration, set of ethical principles,
or other form of pronouncements or statements, the usual

methods of propositional analysis cannot be brought to
bear.   However, certain statements have been made by
some members of the press, and McAuliffe's strategy is
to align these propositions with act-descriptions that
may also be attributed to members of this same profession.   Thus ad hominem refutation is not only perfectly
appropriate, it is remarkably effective.   It is not
clear how the press should respond, but it is clear that
they should respond somehow unless they are happy to
concede that their position is pragmatically inconsistent.   Nobody wants to admit to inconsistency, and if
our analysis is correct, they are quite justified in
such a reluctance.   The novelty of ad hominem criticism,
how it differs from more usual refutations by showing
inconsistency, is that "position" takes into account not
only expressed propositions but also actions of a
disputant that indicate commitment to a line of argument.

PRACTICAL REASONING AS SEQUENTIAL SEARCH-
PROCEDURE

The notion of an ad hominem argument appealed to by the
foregoing considerations requires that an argument is
(1) a set of propositions, (2) a set of truth-values
(the true and the false) taken on by these propositions,
(3) a sequence of practical inferences such that each
proposition is connected to a network of related propositions, and (4) in a given sequence we can determine
whether any pair of propositions that lie on it are
directly related or not.   Thus a proposition is more
than a bearer of two truth-values, as in classical logic,
it is also something that can be brought about in an act-
sequence.   This means that 'sufficient condition' is
defined differently from classical logic.   A model is
defined not only as a truth-value valuation, but also by
a relatedness relation (see Epstein [1979]).

By these lights, an argument is a set of premises and a
conclusion, but in evaluating it we must take into
account how the individual propositions in the argument
are related to each other.   Just as in classical logic,
when we evaluate validity we may not know in fact whether
or not these propositions are true or false, so in an ad
hominem disputation we may not know in fact whether these
propositions in act-sequences are directly connectible
or not.   Instead, we take into account all possible

combinations of relatedness and truth-values.

Accordingly, when we interpret implication in this action-theoretic way, it is appropriate to call it pragmatic implication. If we are to adjudicate allegations and refutations of ad hominem of the circumstantial act-theoretic sort, then we must take act-sequences into account as an intrinsic part of the logic of the argument itself. Only so considered is the ad hominem a logical fallacy or argument in any proper sense.

However, there is a sense in which our treatment of the logic of the circumstantial ad hominem has been minimal, even austere, in its assumptions. Although, as indicated in the next chapter, in order to study the fuller structure of act-sequences a modal approach would be useful, we have kept at the level of propositional logic. Moreover, the system $\mathcal{S}$ we have utilized is even weaker than classical propositional calculus. Clearly there is more to be said about the structure of act-sequences than we have ventured to account for. The system $\mathcal{S}$ is as close to propositional calculus as possible except for the deviance required to introduce a pragmatic notion of the connectibility of propositions in a sequence of actions.

No doubt many will find the very idea of pragmatic implication novel. Spatiotemporal actions and implication have rarely been thought to be partners in the same relationship. No doubt in the Tarski-Davidson tradition such a partnership would seem illegitimate or even perverse. However, the notion of the circumstantial ad hominem, as we have construed it, demands such a conjunction of logic and act-sequences. Otherwise ad hominem of the action-theoretic sort here studied would be even at its worst, an ethical breach of conduct rather than a failure of logic. Insofar as one can make a plausible case for a logic of action propositions, there is thereby a case to be made for ad hominem as a logical fallacy, otherwise not.

The system proposed here for the evaluation of ad hominem disputation may find more of a home in the idealist tradition than in the truth-conditions framework of much recent philosophy of logic. When disputants are arguing ad hominem, they need to take into account the coherence of the propositions in a position within the structure of a given network of action-theoretic world lines. In such disputations, it is presumed that the participants have

information concerning the different ways propositions
can be brought about. We assume that determinations can
in principle be made that pairs of propositions are
directly related in an act-sequence, or not. Given the
possibility of such determinations, we can then specify
conditions under which sets of propositions are consistent, related to each other by implication, and so forth.
We are concerned, then, with not only whether each of
these individual propositions obtains (is true) or not,
but how it is related to other propositions in a pragmatic sequence of actions.

We do not mean to maintain that the relation of connectibility is the only suitable relation to study when one
is interested in the coherence of a set of propositions
relative to logical implication. Indeed, we have suggested that informational inclusion is another such
relation. And other possibilities are not to be excluded.
We conclude that when two or more disputants are in ad
hominem argumentation, each of them begins with certain
items of background information against which their allegations may be understood. The first set of items consists of a set of actions attributed to the agent, representing different ways a proposition could come about or
be made true. Then each of these propositions in the
allegation must be fitted into the overall network of
actions or intentions implicit in the agent's position.
This position, or plan of the agent as we know it,
includes the different ways that proposition can be made
true, according to what the disputants know of the likely
and usual order of events in natural sequences. Then,
given any two propositions, the participants can argue
about whether they are directly related as being approximately coincident in an act-sequence. Of course, the
participants may know this or not in a given case, just
as they may know whether or not the propositions in an
argument are true. System $\mathscr{A}$ takes into account all possible combinations of truth-values and relationships on
a given set of propositions.

It is to be expected that participants in ad hominem disputations may have at their disposal considerable background information on how propositions are made true or
could be made true in the context of a specific dispute.
By the conventions of dialogue, the participants can then
begin with the bits of information that each participant
has conceded as part of his commitment-set. Then the

participants can determine whether the information
included in one proposition is also included in another,
as in an internal act-sequence. In this conception of
argument, a proposition is more than a truth-value. It
is also a subset of a collection of bits of information
with which the participants begin. In ad hominem disputation, these bits of information represent ways the
propositions are made true.

Let us consider an example of an act-sequence to see
what is meant by connectibility of propositions in such
a sequence. In describing movement in golf as a source
of aesthetic satisfaction, Arnold Palmer (Radio Times,
September 15, 1973) used these expressive words.

> What other people may find in poetry or art
> museums I find in the flight of a good
> drive--the white ball sailing up into that
> blue sky, growing smaller, then suddenly
> reaching its apex, curving, falling and
> finally dropping to the turf to roll some
> more, just the way I planned it.

In an act-sequence like that described by Mr. Palmer, we
might distinguish a number of propositions that are made
true by what he did.

1. A swinging movement of the arms and upper body
     took place.
2. The club described an arc through the air.
3. The club head contacted the ball.
4. The ball was driven forward.
5. The ball sailed up into the blue sky.
6. The ball curved into a long trajectory of flight.
7. The ball dropped to the turf.
8. The ball rolled toward the green.
9. The ball rolled onto the green.
10. The ball came to rest near the cup.

In this sequence, there are three distinct objects that
each successively takes the part of the subject--Mr.
Palmer's body, the golf club, and the ball. Thus, over
the sequence genidentity is not preserved--the act-sequence
through the various stages does not encompass only one
continuing spatial object through time.

A sequence of practical reasoning runs through all ten of
these propositions. It falls into the given temporal

sequence and extends spatially from Mr. Palmer's body to
an area near a cup on a green. There is room for alternative possible developments running through different
propositions. For example, if 7 were changed to 7*,
'The ball dropped into the river,' and 8, 9, and 10 were
also changed, we would have an alternative world line,
diverging at 6.

By bringing it about that 1, Mr. Palmer brought it about
that each of 2 through 9 was also realized, either
directly or indirectly. By bringing it about that 1,
Mr. Palmer directly brought it about that 2. Reason:
1 is approximately spatiotemporally coincident with 2.
Whatever can make 1 true can directly make 2 true because
Mr. Palmer's hands are grasping the club. Similarly, 2
is directly related to 3, 3 is directly related to 4, and
4 is directly related to 5. However, 1 is not directly
related to 5. But 1 is connectible (indirectly) to 5 via
2, 3, and 4. We can say that 2, 3, and 4 are between 1
and 5 in the act-sequence. There can be action at a dis-
tance only because there is an approximate spatiotemporal
coincidence between intervening stages of what was made
true.

One aspect of practical reasoning in realistic argumentation that makes it complex concerns the fact that inferences may be linked together in a sequential process.
When an agent formulates an intention, he may do so in
quite general terms. He may then cast around for some
way of making this intention come to be realized. But
such a process can often involve many intermediate steps.
One thing may be necessary for another, so the process of
carrying out an intention may involve a lengthy chain of
practical inferences.

The notion that actions are characteristically linked
together in sequences is familiar to us. But it is important to recognize that practical reasoning is also
strongly tied to act-sequences. Single practical inferences are linked together in a series when an intention
to carry out some objective is realized. Aristotle gives
an excellent example in the Metaphysica (Z.7 - 1031b25 -
1032b29) of the reasoning of a physician who goes through
a sequence of steps in order to arrive at some state of
affairs he can produce by an available procedure.

        The healthy subject is produced as the result
        of the following train of thought:--since this
        is health, if the subject is to be healthy

this must first be present, e.g. a uniform
state of body, and if this is to be present,
there must be heat; and the physician goes
on thinking thus until he reduces the matter
to a final something which he himself can
produce. Then the process from this point
onward, i.e. the process towards health, is
called a 'making' (1032b6 - 1032b11).

The physician's job or task is to produce "health."
Aristotle's physician defines health as a "uniform bodily
state." But how to produce it? In this situation, the
doctor sees that the patient needs warmth to produce this
uniform state. But how to produce warmth in this instance?
The physician might see that the best way is to rub the
patient.

The chain of practical inferences can be represented as a
sequence of the following sort.

    1. Objective: to produce a healthy patient.
    2. It is necessary for a patient to be in a uniform
        state in order to be healthy.
    3. Problem: how to produce a uniform state in this
        instance?
    4. To produce a uniform state in this patient, it is
        necessary to produce heat.
    5. Problem: how to produce heat?
    6. If I rub the patient, heat will be produced.
    7. Resolution: I must set myself to rub this patient.

One can well imagine that these sequences of steps in practical reasoning can be lengthy. A simple example will
indicate how commonplace these sequences are.

Suppose I form the intention to wash the car this morning.
In order to begin, I know that I have to park the car on
the driveway within reach of the hose. I have to hook up
the hose to the tap in the backyard. And finally I have to
have a bucket of soapy water and a sponge. In order to
move the car, I have to have the keys. I go to the kitchen
and check. The keys are there. I then go to get out the
hose and find it is split. To repair the split I need tape.
To get tape I must drive to the store, take along some
money, and perhaps do some other things as well.

Returning with the tape, I repair the hose. Then I attach
the hose to the backyard tap. It works satisfactorily. I

go into the garage, get the ladder, climb up and get the
bucket. I go to the kitchen, put soap in it, and fill it
with water from the hose. Then I carry the bucket around
to the driveway and start washing the car. Let us review
the sequence of actions so far mentioned.

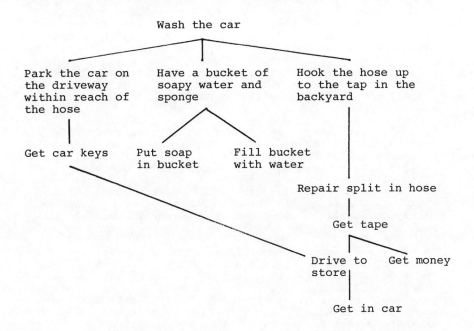

The above review of my act-sequence is of course quite incom-
plete. For example, to get to the store I had to perform a
long sequence of actions.

According to Simon (1977) the method of <u>maximizing</u> is an
appropriate principle of decision-making if every one of a
set of possible outcomes is given and your problem is which
outcome to choose. An alternative method of arriving at a
conclusion when your problem is how to do something is
called <u>satisficing</u> by Simon. It is the process of searching
for "good enough" solutions, where the comparison of all
possible outcomes with each other is not feasible.

An example Simon (1977, p. 173) gives is the problem of

finding the sharpest needle in a haystack where needles are distributed at random through the uniformly dense haystack. The maximizing method is to find all the needles and compare them for sharpness. A less demanding method of producing some chance of finding the sharpest needle is to search some portion of the haystack. But when should we stop searching? An economist would say to stop when the searching starts to cost more than likely improvements in sharpness will be yielded by additional searching. However, Simon notes that this answer is not always helpful if in practice it is easier to define "sharp enough" than to define "marginal value of additional sharpness." He suggests that in a particular situation, a better rule might be to stop when we find a needle sharp enough to sew with.

Hence the characteristic of satisficing as a method of deciding how to proceed is to "compare each possible solution as it is generated, with a standard" (Simon, 1977, p. 173). So you don't need to compare all possible solutions with each other, as in the method of maximizing. A lot depends on what standard you set up to begin with however. The first needle you find may be very sharp but also highly radioactive, and would kill anyone who used it to sew.

In practical reasoning you start out with some objective or goal you have in mind, a state you want to bring about. For example, I intend to drink this glass of water. Sometimes an end can be brought about directly. The normal way to drink this glass of water is to bring it up to my mouth and pour it in. I may conclude that this is what I should do, in order to bring about my objective.

But suppose the usual procedure for drinking water is not available in the circumstances. Suppose my hands are handcuffed to the desk. Then I have to look around for some other way to do it.

So I search around for a way to do it. I look around for some procedure I can do that might lead to a way of making it possible to drink the water. Perhaps there is a straw on the next desk, and by various contortions I can bring it about that the straw is in the glass of water. The actions involved in achieving this could involve quite a complicated sequence to describe.

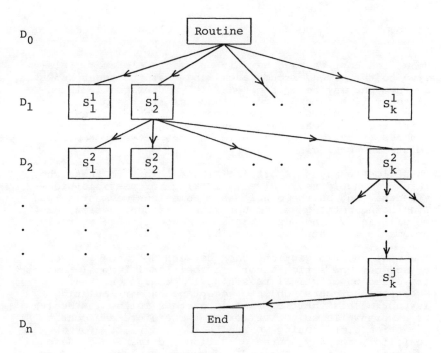

The process takes the form of a search-tree for states S_k^j
where each state is a sufficient condition of some state
at the next depth D_i. k is the <u>width</u> of each level, and j
is the <u>depth</u> of the tree. If we take into account necessary conditions as well as sufficient conditions, the
structure will be more complex. Any state might have certain prior states needed to be brought about in order to
bring that state about. In practical reasoning, we have
restricted the agent's plan to what he knows, never mind
unknown side-effects. Our inference by these models is
satisficing rather than maximizing because we need only
choose among the conditions we already know are sufficient
(necessary). So too the conclusion is limited, requiring
the agent to do A_i in light of his present knowledge.

Our models of practical inference are therefore epistemi-
cally limited to a <u>known</u> plan of action and all the <u>known</u>
conditions that are practically relevant. If new intentions are added to the premises, or if new knowledge about

acceptable consequences is added in, closure may cease
to hold.

Hence the best we have here is pragmatic closure. Relative to the given circumstances and what the agent knows
of them, he may be criticized fairly of pragmatic inconsistency if he accepts an instance of all the premisses
of n.c.s. or s.c.s. but not the conclusion. Yet such a
criticism is defeasible in the sense that new circumstances or fuller consideration of the act-sequence may
refute the criticism.

This closure may seem artificial and unfair to those who
think we should never give up looking for possible side-
effects. But on the other hand, sometimes we must act.
Even doing nothing may amount to significant action, as
we will see in the next chapter. Hence closure is truly
pragmatic in practical reasoning.

The dialogue two sections back between Socrates and Bob
brings out how action-theoretic positional inconsistencies
are based on practical reasoning. The argument that
Socrates engineers Bob into accepting and articulating
as part of his position runs in part as follows. "Health
is a worthwhile objective for me. Therefore any course
of action contributing to health is good policy for me
to follow, and any course of action undermining or defeating health is to be avoided. However, smoking is bad for
health, and runs counter to health. Therefore, if I am
to follow sound policy based on these premisses, I should
not smoke." This much of the sequence of reasoning fixed
upon Bob by Socrates' questioning is an instance of
practical reasoning, clearly. But then the fact is that
Bob admits to the practice of smoking when questioned.
Hence Bob's practice is flatly inconsistent with the
practical syllogism that has premisses Bob has freely
committed himself to. Hence Bob's real conduct makes
clear that he is committed to the negation of that conclusion whose premisses he accepts. Here then it is
clear that Bob's argument is practically inconsistent in
the same sense of 'practical' that the practical syllogism is a valid form of argument. The practical syllogism infers the acceptability of policy that dictates a
certain course of action as acceptable or ration relative
to the carrying out of stated objectives. Having publicly
gone on record by giving commitment to these objectives,
it is practically inconsistent to then retract that commitment in practice by acting in a contrary way.

8

Complex Act-Sequences

Having now made our positive recommendations on the
analysis of the ad hominem, it remains to examine some
partially solved and unsolved problems raised by the
analysis. Many times we have touched on the topic of
omissions and negative actions in ad hominem arguments.
This topic is a difficult and controversial one, but it
is incumbent upon us to attempt to unravel some of the
implications of our analysis for allegations of pragmatic inconsistency where omitting or refraining is at
issue.

ANALYSIS OF THE ARMS EXPORTER ARGUMENT

In the analysis of the arms exporter argument given in
the third section of Chapter 3, we alleged that there is
a practical inconsistency between (e) and (f). The
inconsistency is a direct one, easily perceived: a makes
it that A (weapons are sold), and at the same time a
asserts that A should not be made true. The propositional
form of a's joint recommendation and action is A ∧ 7A.
What other subsets of (a) - (i) could be the basis of an
ad hominem attack?

We noted that (g) and (i) exhibit a practical inconsistency. However, in (i) the linkages between the various
connected stages are in terms of what the various agents
intentionally and knowingly plan to do. Thus we must ask
whether the connections in (i) that produce a conflict
with (g) are logical connections or more in the nature of
ethical connections. Let A = the proposition that some
weapons are manufactured by a first party, B = the proposition that some second party buys these weapons, C = the
proposition that some third party acquires them from the
second party, and D = the proposition that this third
party uses these weapons for unjust wars and the persecution of some innocent fourth parties. Now some connections
between A, B, C, and D are there, but they do not seem to
be logical connections, at least as the argument is
expressed.

Consider the connection between A and B. No doubt the
first party makes it true that A at least partly in order
to make it true that B. There is a teleological connection
between A and B. But can we clearly state that some of the

ways in which A could be brought about are also ways in
which B could be brought about? Are some of the ways in
which these weapons are manufactured also ways in which
it is brought about that somebody buys these weapons?
Well it could be, but then it could also be that how
the weapons are manufactured has no direct connection at
all to how they are sold. If these two propositions are
connectible, it is up to the ad hominem attacker to show
us how they are. However, even if connectibility could
be established, it is by no means clear that A is a
sufficient condition for B. Thus on neither basis are
we warranted in claiming that A → B is a premiss that
the student has to accept. Similar remarks apply to the
connections between B and C and between C and D.

We may conclude that the individual a of whom (g) and (i)
are both true may be morally culpable for planning to set
into operation a sequence of events that he knows may
eventuate in an outcome that is inconsistent with what he
himself advocates as a moral norm. But a cannot be said
to have made true a set of propositions that are demonstrably inconsistent in the action-theoretic interpretation of relatedness logic. Thus a is not pragmatically
inconsistent in precisely that way.

What this shows is that there are teleological connections
among actions that outrun our analysis of action-theoretic
inconsistency given here but that may nonetheless be
thought to be of real importance in evaluating the circumstantial ad hominem.

We could say that the inconsistency between (g) and (i)
has to do with the modality of bringing about. There is
a sense of 'a makes it true that p,' which means that
relative to something a does (or does not do) p is true at
some point in every possible historical development as
planned by a. In this sense, an agent strategically
(deliberately) brings about some outcome by structuring
a situation such that every possible line of development
will eventuate in that outcome at some point. This is a
modal sense of 'p is made true' because its logic is
similar to the necessity operator of alethic modal logic.

We will not attempt to give a full theory of strategic
bringing about here. The theories that best capture this
notion, those of Ingmar Pörn (1977), Stig Kanger (1972),
and Lennart Åqvist (1974), are surveyed and evaluated in
the critical study of Douglas N. Walton (1979). Here it

will be sufficient to make some informal comments on the
modality of bringing about and keep the formal development at the level of propositional logic.

First, it is important to note that 'p is made true by
something done by an agent' and 'p is allowed to be true
by something done by an agent' are interdefinable as
double negations of each other, like necessity and possibility in alethic modal logics. Thus 'p is allowed to
be true' is equivalent to 'it is not the case that not-p
is made to be true.' It is easy to understand this
equivalence if we see that 'a lets it be true that p'
means that relative to something a does (or does not do),
p is true at some point in at least one possible historical development as planned by a.

The upshot of defining bringing about and allowing in
this modal way is that we have to think of a world line
or possible historical development in a different way
than we have so far. Moreover, sequences of negative
actions can be shown to admit various permutations.

An introduction to these new features of act-sequences
is best brought about by looking to some distinctions
originally due to St. Anselm of Canterbury. St. Anselm
distinguished between direct action, 'bringing it about
that p,' and indirect action, 'bringing it about that q
where q is a sufficient condition for p.' As he put it,
an agent can bring about something itself (facere idipsum
esse), or bring it about through some other state of
affairs (facere aliud esse). The Anselmian approach is
now capable of perspicuously distinguishing six varieties
of agency. Using St. Anselm's illustration of the action
of killing, we can set these out as follows.

1.	Killing directly	Facere idipsum esse
2.	Not making not dead, (not raising the dead man to life, should one have the power so to do)	Non facere idipsum non esse
3.	Making the killer have arms (arming the killer)	Facere aliud esse
4.	Not arming the victim	Non facere aliud esse

5. Making the victim not
    armed (disarming the   <u>Facere</u> <u>aliud</u> <u>non</u> <u>esse</u>
    victim)

6. Not making the killer
    not armed (not disarming   <u>Non</u> <u>facere</u> <u>aliud</u> <u>non</u>
    the killer)   <u>esse</u>

The logical forms exemplified by these six varieties of
agency can be brought out by the following awkward para-
phrases.

1. directly bringing it about that the victim is dead

2. not bringing it about that the victim is alive, that
    is, allowing him to remain or become dead

3. bringing about some state of affairs q such that some-
    body else kills the victim (q = the killer has arms)

4. failing to bring about some q such that somebody else
    does not kill the victim (q = the victim has arms)

5. bringing it about that some q fails to obtain where
    the q is such that somebody else does not kill the
    victim (q = the victim has arms)

6. not bringing it about that some q fails to obtain
    where q is such that somebody else kills the victim
    (q = the killer has arms)

These action-theoretic distinctions show that while we
are sometimes held responsible for omissions, allowings,
or other inactions, one has to be extremely careful in
drawing the distinction between act and omission.

The arms exporter alleged that the student was practically
inconsistent in acting as stated by (b) and also by (j).
The act-description (b) was that $\underline{a}$ attends a university
that has invested funds in corporations that manufacture
arms, and the act-description (j) was that $\underline{a}$ condemns the
selling of weapons to nations that use them for unjust
wars and the persecution of innocent persons.

Of course, the claim here of pragmatic inconsistency is a
questionable one, for manufacturing arms is by no means
directly connectible to selling them to persons who use
them for unjust purposes. So the burden of proof is

definitely on the arms exporter to fill in the links of
connectibility, if he can, between these act-descriptions.
However the interesting thing about this allegation is
that the student is presumably being accused of a negative
act: by attending a certain university and failing to
investigate the investments and holdings of that university,
and also failing thereby to withdraw from connection with
that university, the student has allegedly allowed arms
manufacturing to take place. By something he has not done,
he has allowed a certain practice to take place. Further,
the allegation is that this latter practice is connected
to some outcome the student has morally condemned.

The argument is that the student has committed a circumstantial ad hominem by not doing something. It is not
that his action and pronouncement are inconsistent.
Rather, the allegation is that what he omitted to do is
pragmatically inconsistent with what he has advocated.
Here we have a negative circumstantial ad hominem. Such
an argument is curious enough to bear some investigation
of negative act-sequences.

COMPLEX NEGATIVE ACT-SEQUENCES

Given the building blocks from St. Anselm's remarks, we
can now go ahead to see how negative and nonnegative
actions can be combined into certain characteristic patterns of sequences. Some instances that will turn out to
be of special interest can illustrate how the basic grammar
of actions can be studied.

1. S brings it about that q.
2. S does not bring it about that q.
3. S brings it about that not-q.
4. S does not bring it about that not-q.
5. By bringing it about that p, S brings it about
   that q.
6. By bringing it about that not-p, S brings it
   about that q.
7. By bringing it about that p, S brings it about
   that not-q.
8. By bringing it about that not-p, S brings it
   about that not-q.
9. It is not the case that S brings it about that q
   by bringing it about that p.
10. By not bringing it about that p, S brings it about
    that q.

11. By bringing it about that p, S does not bring it about that q.

12. By not bringing it about that p, S does not bring it about that q.

13. By not bringing it about that not-p, S brings it about that q.

14. It is not the case that S does not bring it about that not-q by bringing it about that p.

The key thing to notice about these grammatical permutations is that negation can function in various different ways in an act-sequence. Initially one might tend to think that a negative action is a simple not-doing after the pattern of 2. But that is only so because we often tend to think of actions as more or less discrete spatio-temporally localized events, such as my moving a finger. But actions are not always as simple; often they can be spread out over a complex and far-reaching act-sequence.

To get an initial idea of what is involved in the different varieties of negation, consider the example of an intern who is considering giving a certain medication to a patient. By a positive act of administering the medication herself, she can bring it about that the patient has the medication, as in 1. Or, as in 2, she can elect to not bring it about that the patient is medicated. Suppose the nurse is about to administer that medication. Then, as in 3, the intern by intervening could see to it that the patient does not receive that medication--here we have a positive act with a negative result.

Suppose again that the nurse is about to administer the medication, as usual. Then another possibility is for the intern not to bring it about that the patient does not have the medication. That is, she can let the patient be medicated as usual. Thus we see that a letting happen (4) is a double negative of 1, in effect a positive but passive mode of action. So far we have looked at action (inaction) as a simple one-step procedure, but it is also possible to view it as a binary sequence.

Consider 5: by bringing it about that a statement is written on the patient's chart, the intern could bring it about that the patient is medicated. In other circumstances, the intern could bring it about that the patient is medicated by not writing something on the chart, that is, by not countermanding the usual procedure. The reader can easily see how the remaining sequences could be illustrated, but one or two remarks may be helpful. First, note that in 7 a negative action is brought about by means of a positive one. So it would be easy to become confused here about whether the action is positive or negative. For example, is driving without a licence a positive or negative act? Similarly in 10, we have to be careful to note that a positive act is brought about by means of a negative one. The lesson is that we should never ask simply whether an act-sequence is positive or negative, but always look carefully to see the possible different ways negations function in the sequence. This lesson is one we can apply repeatedly as we proceed.

We also have to be very careful because negative action descriptions can often be handled as if they were positive, for example, "They also serve who only stand and wait." St. Anselm clearly pointed out that 'to do' can also have 'not to do' as an instance (see Desmond Henry [1967, p. 123]). Thus great care is needed in firmly labelling an action as intrinsically positive or negative--a lot may depend on how you choose to describe the action (inaction) sequence.

Let us now turn to distinguishing between refraining and omitting by giving an analysis of each of these negative concepts in turn.

CRITIQUE OF BRAND

The most clearly worked out, systematic, analytical attempt to confront the natural language of not-doing is that of Myles Brand (1971). A major weakness is that causality is used as a basic concept, but as is well known, this problematic concept is too unclear to function as a primitive basis. Nonetheless we will begin by looking at Brand's analysis, and then try to improve on it by using relatedness instead of causation as a primitive. The key definition is that of an agent refraining from performing an action. Like us, Brand begins by taking a notion of positive action as primitive--he takes as a given undefined 'Agent S performs action $\underline{a}$.' And he takes a binary relation (three-place if you consider the agent) also as primitive: '(a person) performs (an action) in order that (an event) occur.' This relation corresponds to our binary by-relation at the beginning of this chapter.

In order to work up to the definition of refraining, Brand then defines his preliminary notions of the causal sort.

1. One event is said to be causally relevant to another when the former is either causally necessary or sufficient for the latter or the former is causally necessary or sufficient for what happens when the latter does not occur (p. 48).

Then causal prevention is defined as follows.

2. e_1 causally prevents e_2 from occurring if, and only if, (i) e_1 occurs, (ii) the date of e_1 is not later than the date of e_2, (iii) it is causally impossible that e_1 occur and e_2 occur, and (iv) e_1 is causally relevant to e_2.

Given these definitions, we move on to define "a person causally prevents something from happening" as follows. S causally prevents e from occurring if, and only if, there is some action a that S performs such that S's performing a causally prevents e from occurring. Finally, we reach the third of these definitions.

3. S refrains from performing a if, and only if, (i) it is not the case that S performs a, and (ii) there is some action b that S performs in order to prevent himself from performing a (p. 49).

This is a very systematic and careful even if problematic program for giving an account of refraining. It is one, in general outline, that we will endorse and accept, but it requires major revisions on at least two counts: first, there are problems with the preliminary causal vocabulary; and second, we find particular problems with the way refrain is defined, apart from the unclear causal modal expressions used as a basis. Let us therefore turn to some criticisms of Brand's approach.

It can be shown that clause (iv) is redundant in Brand's definition of causal prevention. To see why, first note that Brand postulates that the modal prefixes 'it is causally necessary that' and 'it is causally impossible that' be thought of as parallel to logical necessity and impossibility in modal logic (p. 48). It would follow that 'it is causally impossible that e_i occurs' is equivalent to 'it is causally necessary that e_i does not occur.'

Given the truth-functional equivalence of 'p ∧ q' and
'⅂(p ⊃ ⅂q),' it follows that 'it is causally impossible
that e_1 occurs and that e_2 occurs' is equivalent to 'it
is causally necessary that if e_1 occurs then e_2 does
not occur.' But it follows from this definition of
causally relevant that if it is causally necessary that
if e_1 occurs then e_2 does not occur, then we have it
that e_1 is causally relevant to e_2. In short, clause
(iv) of Brand's definition of causal prevention follows
logically from clause (iii). Thus clause (iv) is
redundant.

Clearly Brand would deny that (iv) follows from (iii),
for he gives an illustration to show that causal impossibility does not have "built in" relevancy conditions
(p. 49). The reasoning is that for any q you like, even
one unrelated in any way to p, if it is not possible
that p then it is not possible that both p and q. The
example is that if it is not possible for a certain bird
to land on a certain tree in Argentina, it is not possible for the rains to fall in Boston and this bird to
land on that tree. Brand proposes that without the
requirement of causal relevance, we would have to say
that the falling of the rains in Boston prevents the
bird in Argentina from landing in the tree there.

However, the problem is that, despite Brand's highly
reasonable avowal that causal impossibility does not
have "built in" relevancy conditions, (iv) does indeed
follow from (iii) on the three assumptions that (a) 'it
is causally impossible that e_i occurs' entails 'it is
causally necessary that e_i does not occur,' (b) 'p ∧ q'
implies '⅂(p → ⅂q),' and (c) causal relevance is defined
the way Brand defines it.

The problems here stem from the general assumption that
implication, negation, and conjunction of the classical
truth-functional sort must be presupposed as a base
logic in causal language. One way of obviating the
problems that flow from this assumption is the following.
In a relatedness logic, 'p ∧ q' is not equivalent to
'⅂(p → ⅂q)' provided we are thinking, as seems reasonable
here, of conjunction as classical, that is, not requiring
relatedness of p and q, but thinking of implication as
requiring relatedness of p and q. We require only that
p and q be related in the sense of being approximately
spatiotemporally adjacent. This does not require that
we use causation as a primitive at all. But we can think

of 'p is related to q' as meaning that p can cause q in
the sense that p and q are adjacent points in the same
act-sequence.

Thus a way to solve Brand's problems is to rewrite causal
relevance as a relatedness relation 'e_1 is adjacent to e_2
in the sense that e_1 and e_2 are related' as described in
the first section of this chapter. We are thereby spared
the necessity of requiring that it is necessary that if
e_1 occurs then e_2 does not occur, if e_1 and e_2 are incompatible. After all, e_1 and e_2 may be incompatible simply
because one by itself is impossible. It need not therefore follow that if one occurs, the other by necessity
does not occur, for they may be unrelated as actions in
the same sequence of events.

REFRAINING

The upshot is that clause (iii) should be rewritten to
read: it is necessary that if e_1 occurs then e_2 does not
occur. Here the 'not' is classical negation, but the
'if-then' is relatedness implication. Furthermore,
clause (iv) should be rewritten to read: e_1 is related
to e_2. So construed, clause (iii) is independent of
clauses (i) and (ii). However, since relatedness implication requires that e_1 and e_2 be related where e_1 implies
the negation of e_2, it turns out that the new version of
(iv) follows from the new version of (iii). Consequently,
clause (iv) may be dropped in the revised definition of
causal prevention.

With the above modifications, we can accept some of the
basic outline of Brand's framework of definitions. Now
let us proceed to our own definition of refraining.

There is another problem, however, with the Brand definition of 'a person refrains from performing an action,'
definition 3 above. Take the example of the patrolman
who shouts "Stop or I'll fire" to a fleeing youth, then
fires and misses. He did not shoot the youth, and he did
perform some action in order to prevent himself from
shooting the fleeing youth. It follows that by Brand's
definition, the patrolman refrained from shooting the
fleeing youth. Most of us would presumably feel that it
is incorrect, however, to say in this case that the
patrolman refrained from shooting the fleeing youth.

One way out is to say that the policeman did refrain,
but then when he fired he ceased refraining. If we
break the act-sequence into subactions, we can say that
the first act was a refraining, but it was followed by
another action, firing the gun, which signalled that
the refraining was over. Removing the temporal gap
makes this strategy of dividing the actions less plausible, however. What are we to say of the policeman who
fires even while shouting "stop!"? Does he refrain from
shooting even while shooting?

Another way to deal with the problem is to add a clause
(iii) to the definition: S's performing b does causally
prevent S from performing a. But even this addition
does not cope with the sad case of Cass.

Suppose that Cass, in order to prevent herself from eating and thereby worsening her growing problem of the
weight-watcher's sort, sees to it that she has an operation to wire her jaws shut. But two weeks later, overcome by the sight of a chocolate cake, she pitifully
attempts to gorge herself despite the wired jaws. It is
hardly correct to say that she refrained from eating the
cake, despite the fact that she did not succeed.

One way out would be to require more than Brand that the
events in question be in the same causal sequence.
Accordingly, to refrain from bringing about q by bringing
about p, not only must it be true that S brings it about
that not-q by bringing it about that p, but p and q must
be directly related in the sense of being directly
related in the act-sequence. It is not enough merely
that they both be somewhere in the same act-sequence. By
these lights, a fourth clause must be added to the definitions of refraining: (iv) what S brings about in performing a is directly related to what S brings about in performing b.

This requirement might appear to be too strong, however,
in ruling out instances of refraining by means of an
indirect act-sequence. Let us take the case of a person
who begins to recognize he is an alcoholic. He usually
begins to drink in the afternoon as a matter of habit,
but decides to stop drinking on one particular afternoon.
He knows that he gets a strong desire to take a drink in
the afternoon. Hence, this morning he prevents himself
from drinking on this particular afternoon only by locking
it in the closet and arranging with his wife to hold the

key and not give it up. Suppose also that he is successful and does not drink that afternoon. Here he refrained
from drinking--by locking the alcohol in the closet and
giving his wife the key. But his locking the alcohol in
the closet is not directly related to his not drinking
the alcohol because the act-sequence may be described as
follows. Let p = the closet is locked and his wife has
the key, q = the closet door is not opened, r = the alcohol
is not taken out, and s = the alcohol is not consumed.
Then we may say that by bringing it about that p, he
brought it about that q. By bringing it about that q, he
brought it about that r. Hence, by bringing it about that
p, he indirectly brought it about that r. But by bringing
it about that r, he brought it about that s. Hence by
bringing it about that p, he indirectly brought it about
that s. The upshot is that if it is right to say he
refrained from drinking the alcohol then (iv) is too
strong.

Looked at more carefully with a view to specifying the
time of the alleged refraining, however, the case of the
alcoholic may not be so different from that of Cass. The
following refutation can be mounted. In the morning, he
did not refrain from drinking the alcohol in the afternoon because it was not afternoon yet, so he did not yet
have the opportunity to drink it in the afternoon. But
in the afternoon he did not refrain from drinking the
alcohol either insofar as we are presuming that he had no
choice in the matter then, the closet being locked and
his wife having the key. The strategy is to split the
act-sequence into subactions by specifying the time of
the alleged refraining precisely. According to the refutation, it is not true to say that he refrained from
drinking the alcohol at any time. Rather, he put himself
in a position where there was no need to refrain. If,
like Cass, he had tried to smash open the closet, surely
he would have not refrained, despite his earlier actions
to prevent drinking. The earlier actions, according to
this view of the matter, should be treated as independent
of his refraining or not at the later time.

Here we are at something of an impasse. Some observers
might not think of Cass or the incipient alcoholic as
truly refraining because they lacked the opportunity, at
the time, to indulge themselves, even if they tried. Yet
possibly there is a sense in which it is correct to say
that they indirectly refrained, in virtue of something
they freely set into motion earlier. Whatever the final

word on indirect refraining is, the lesson is to distinguish direct and indirect refraining in the act-sequence.

A second problem, perhaps not quite as serious if equally
perplexing, is that the Brand definition always requires
that if I refrain from doing something, there is something that I do in order to prevent myself from performing it. But if I refrain from eating a pastry, it is not
clear that I need have done anything in particular in
order to prevent myself from eating it. Of course, a
defender of this sort of definition could always retort
that I did not eat the pastry in order to prevent myself
from eating it. But this strikes me as being somehow
question begging or vacuous much like a reply attributed
to Richard Daley when asked why somebody was not elected--
"He didn't get enough votes."

The best solution to this problem is to concede that I
could prevent myself from eating the pastry by not doing
something, such as not move my hand in the direction of
the pastry. Once again, the lesson is to see that negation can enter into an act-sequence at more than one
point.

We have described refraining as an essentially binary
sequence like (7) or (8). We now turn to an analysis of
omitting, which we see as basically a negative action of
form (2).

OMITTING

By contrast with refraining, the analysis of omitting is
very simple: omitting is simply not-doing, as in the
paradigm form (2). Even this simple analysis is not
unproblematic, however. What does it mean, for example,
to say 'Jones does not take his medication'? Taking our
cue from Davidson (1966), we should point out that 'Jones
brings it about that his medication is not taken' will
not do as an analysis because it is not equivalent to
'Jones does not take his medication.' The first statement could be true by virtue of Jones's seeing to it that
Smith does not take Jones's medication, unlike the latter.
Nor does 'It is not the case that Jones brings it about
that his medication is taken by Jones' seem to be exactly
equivalent. If he took it unwillingly, the latter might
be true, yet it would hardly be correct to say he did not
take his medication. Are we stymied by negation?

The best way out of this impasse is by way of the concept
of a pure action proposition defined in the beginning of
the chapter. We say that 'Jones takes his medication' is
a pure action proposition just in case the following is
true: Jones takes his medication if, and only if, Jones
brings it about that Jones takes his medication. If
'Jones takes his medication' is indeed a pure action
proposition, then its negation is simply this: it is not
the case that Jones brings it about that Jones takes his
medication. We see incidentally that pure action propositions contain an element of deliberate agency--that is
what characterizes them. However, if the original negative proposition is not the negation of a pure action
proposition then two possibilities remain: (i) we have
to pursue the analysis of the structure of the act-
sequence to see if the proposition in question is related
by an act-sequence to a pure action proposition, or (ii)
we may not be able to analyze it as an omission within
the present theory.

The lesson here is that the present approach enables us
to deal with omissions and actions more adequately as
the element of rational deliberation in bringing about
an outcome is emphasized. Any action proposition we can
negate is a pure action proposition, and therefore contains an implication of deliberate action or inaction.
However, this limitation is one we might expect studying
the logic of actions. In short, the problem of assigning
an analysis to 'Jones does not take his medication' is
not insurmountable, given the requisite limiting assumptions about the analysis of nonnegative action statements.
'Not' is just classical negation, something we all know
and love. We now turn to formulating our proposal for
the analysis of the concept of an omission.

The underlying syntax of omitting, as proposed in the
second section of this chapter, can be given by the
appropriate permutations on 'bringing about' (both unary
and binary) and classical negation. Thus paradigmatically,
to say that S omits $\underline{a}$ is to say that S does not bring it
about that p, where $\bar{p}$ is what is brought about by S's
doing $\underline{a}$.

But then as G. H. von Wright (1968) has pointed out, the
use of the expression 'S omits $\underline{a}$' in ethical contexts
suggests that omission is not purely action-theoretic,
but contains an implicature of 'being able to do $\underline{a}$' and
perhaps also 'being expected to do $\underline{a}$.' And it is indeed

these usual implicatures that lead to Brand's criticism
below that the von Wright approach begs the Free Will
question. It seems to me that the only favorable solution to this apparent impasse is to postulate that 'omits'
has an underlying action-theoretic structure of bringing
about and negation, but also has normative overtones of
opportunity and expectation. Thus a fully adequate normative analysis of "omit" will incorporate normative
notions, and thereby appear to beg some normative questions.

It has often been noted that "omitted" commonly contains
an element of expectation. Thus even if (2) obtains and
S is able to bring about p, as von Wright would require,
we are still not fully satisfied to say that S omits to
bring about p. We do not say of the surgeon that he
omits to save his patient dying of renal failure even if
it is possible to save him by extracting a kidney from
an unwary passer-by in the hospital corridor. Brand
(1971, p. 52) deals with this normative element by
defining omission as a purely legal concept. However,
are there not omissions where legality is not at issue?

But Brand also criticizes G. H. von Wright and Arthur
Danto's proposal that 'S refrains from doing a' means
'S does not do a but is able to' on the ground that it
begs the Free Will question. The proposal implies,
apparently oddly, that if I refrain from doing a, I can
do a. For von Wright (1963) and Danto (1966), 'S
refrains from a' entails 'S can perform a and S can
refrain from performing a,' which in turn entails 'S is
free to do a.' But Brand suggests that refrainings can
be the result of coercion or compulsion, the same as
other kinds of action. Note that, on their views, 'S
performs a' does not have the same entailments. There
is a reputed nonparallelism between performing an action
and refraining from performing it, and that seems odd.

So we seem to be stuck in a dilemma. If we bring in
elements of opportunity or expectation, we beg some normative questions. But if we do not, we can scarcely seem
to have a realistic and adequate analysis of omissions.

A theory of Åqvist (1974) shows how the structure of the
act-sequence can clarify the problem. Åqvist thinks of
an action h as an ordered pair $\langle q, q' \rangle$ of decision
points in a game-tree where q' occurs at time $t(q)+1$.
Each decision point in a tree (excluding end points) is

assigned to exactly one agent as his 'move.' An agent x
is said to omit to perform h in a world w at time t if,
and only if, q is a decision point for x but ⟨q, q'⟩ ≠ h
(p. 78). Thus an Åqvist game-tree can be thought of as
an act-sequence graph of the second section of this
chapter. An act-sequence is again a sequence of binary
action relations. So Åqvist's account of omissions is
quite comparable to our own.

What about cases where an agent decides to do something
and even tries to do it, but does not do it? Are we
required to rule that she omitted to do it? It would
seem so, and this would seem to be a problem. If a
physician decides to implant a kidney in a particular
patient, but transplantation is not successful, surely
it is false to say that she omitted to do the transplant.
Yet, according to Åqvist's condition, she decided to do
it, but did not do it. And therefore it follows that by
the above condition, she omitted to do it.

How could the logic of the act-sequence cope with this
problem? I believe that it can be dealt with by bringing
out the binary nature of (5) in the second section of
the chapter as extended and enriched by Åqvist. According to his full account (p. 81), it is ruled that "by
having just performed h in w at t, x caused (brought it
about, saw to it) that q was realized in w at t'" is
true if, and only if, (i) x has performed h in w at t,
(ii) q is realized at t', (iii) x could reasonably have
omitted h in w at t, (iv) by having omitted h in w at t,
x could reasonably have avoided that q was realized in w
at t', and (v) the performance of h by x in w at t is
historically sufficient for the occurrence of q in w at t'.
This analysis can be nicely illustrated by an example in
the form of a directed graph, as in Figure 1 below.

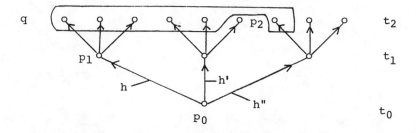

Figure 1

We can say that an agent x, by having just performed h at
t_0, brought it about that q was realized at t_2, provided
all five required conditions are fulfilled: (i) x has
performed h at t_0, that is, $\langle p_0, p_1 \rangle$ is an action for x;
(ii) q is realized at t_2; (iii) x could have omitted h at
t_0, for example, x could have performed h' or h"; (iv) by
having omitted h, x could have avoided that q was realized
at t_2, for example, if x had performed h', then p_2 might
have been realized at t_2 instead of q; (v) once x had performed h, then this was sufficient for the occurrence of q
at t_2.

Now we understand this analysis, we can see how it can be
applied to analyze the following expression: by having
just omitted h in w at t, x brought it about that q was
realized in w at t'.   The basic structure of this expression corresponds to (10) above in this chapter's second
section.   The expression is analyzed as a conjunction of
the five clauses above except that clause (i) is altered
to read 'x has omitted h in w at t.'   Interestingly,
clause (iii) now reads 'x could reasonably have omitted
to omit h in w at t.'   This may seem subtle, but is easily
understood in an Åqvist game-tree.   An omission for x is
simply a pair of points $\langle q, q' \rangle$ that is not a performance
for x, that is, q is a decision point for x, but $\langle q, q' \rangle$
$\neq$ h for x.   But to say that x could reasonably have omitted
this omission is simply to say that there is some point
$q" \neq q'$ accessible from q.   This situation can be illustrated by Figure 2 below.

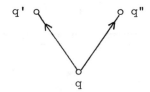

Figure 2

A potentially obscure notion is given a precise explica-
tion by seeing how it can be expressed as an act-sequence
structure.

The significance of what has transpired here bears general
comment.   It has been shown how the notion of an omission

can be ambiguous, even treacherously so. We can think of
an omission in a simpler, minimal way as a negative action,
something we did not do, but by a decision not to do it.
But, second, we can have an enriched notion of what an
omission is that can explain its wider role as a species
of inaction that in turn can explicate its causal role in
an act-sequence. In this richer framework, we can see
and understand a notion that at first seems highly paradoxical, namely that of an omission (a negative action)
bringing about (positively) some outcome. It almost seems
that an omission, so described, is a nonnegative action,
and in a way it is. Accordingly, we might say that someone's failure to treat a patient brought about the death of
that patient.

The implications of this framework are highly relevant to
ad hominem reasoning where it may be assumed that omissions
can always be equated with the notion of a person allowing
some outcome to occur. On the contrary, the binary structure of the act-sequence shows how we can clearly understand the notion of an omission positively bringing about
some outcome. The language of inactions is more subtle
than it is commonly thought to be.

Now back to our original problem, which is solved as follows.
In an artificial and narrower sense of 'omit,' it is correct
to say that the physician omitted to transplant the kidney.
However, all this means is that she did not transplant it,
despite her decision to try. Hence this conclusion is only
warranted insofar as we are thinking of its role as an
action in the wider causal nexus. Taking a more extended
and more accurate view of the act-sequence, what she failed
to do is not correctly describable as an omission. Reason:
although she omitted to do it, it is not true that she
could reasonably have omitted to omit to do it. In other
words, her conduct cannot be described as an omission in
the fuller sense insofar as we presume that she could not
have avoided the negative outcome of transplantation failure.

Some might say that this view compels us to equivocate by
giving us two meanings of "omit," at least one of which is
not by itself completely adequate. I would counter that
this is no equivocation, but rather the discovery of a
deeply important ambiguity that genuinely pervades the
subtle language of inactions and not-doings. Here the
by-relation shows by its binary aspect that negations play
a complex role in causal chains of actions. I can bring
about q' by not bringing about q, but I can also bring about

not-q' by bringing about q, and so forth. The binary
aspect of the act-sequence gives us a clear basic structure for dealing with these complexities of negations.

Does not the richer definition of omission still seem to
beg Free Will questions? The nice feature of adopting
the definition is that it provides an edifying answer to
this puzzle by its stance that omission can be ambiguous.
If we are thinking of omission in a narrower, purely
action-theoretic sense that abstracts from the indirect
relatedness of the act-sequence, then there may be no
need to bring in questions of whether the agent could
reasonably have done otherwise and other accoutrements
of Free Will. Yet if we do wish to consider a richer
notion of omission, more adequate to the wider act-
sequence framework, then assumptions about historically
possible alternatives need to be brought in.

The question of Free Will is not begged because the theory
indicates precisely where and how the parameter of historical alternativeness can be introduced. The question is
not begged because we do not always have to introduce
Free Will. But we can introduce it if we wish to adopt
a richer and more complex definition of 'omission' that
is in turn more adequate to the language of actions,
possible alternatives, and responsibility. The question
is not begged, but divided.

To sum up, the relationship between omitting and refraining, as we have analyzed these notions, can be generally
put as follows. If I omit to do a, this means that I do
not bring it about that p, where p̄ describes what is
brought about in a. Thus an omission is a not-doing. But
if I speak normatively, then I omit a only if, additionally, I can do a and I am expected to do a. However, we
have seen that the syntax of omitting can be complex, once
we bring in the binary notion of bringing about. In this
sense, I may omit to do something by doing, or not doing,
something else. A refraining is a kind of omission where
the by-relation incorporates not-doing by self-prevention.
I refrain from doing a where something else I do, b, makes
it happen that I do not do a, and b is related directly
to a. Finally, a letting happen is a variety of refraining whereby S refrains from preventing something from
happening. Letting an outcome happen may be compatible
with that outcome not happening. And a letting happen
need not always be simply described as an omission.

It is clear enough that an ad hominem criticism alleges
a positional inconsistency. But how do we fairly judge
what an arguer's position commits him to? In real arguments, we do so by judging his actions. However, as
this chapter has shown, there are many subtleties in the
judgment of actions. Sometimes actions express commitments of the agent, sometimes not. Moreover, the
strength of an arguer's commitment to propositions he
has brought about or allowed to obtain may vary with
many factors.

To determine an arguer's position, we need to look at
the whole network of his practical reasoning with regard
to the actions alleged to define that position. We need
to examine the agent's plan of action, including his
intentions, his actions, his omissions, or any steps he
may have taken to realize some outcome. Building up a
network of practical reasoning to understand an agent's
plan involves an understanding of the language of actions,
omissions and refraining. In practical terms, it is by
means of the deployment of this language in argument that
an agent's position is defined, defended, or refuted in
the context of ad hominem disputations.

9

Nailing Down the Fallacy

In concentrating on actual specimens of argumentation in our previous case studies, one problem we have occasionally confronted is that of "nailing down" the fallacy (this phrase is coined by Hamblin). It is all very well to warn against the existence of a possible occurrence of ad hominem, but proving that a determined opponent has definitely committed the fallacy is quite another thing.

However, we have shown how to prosecute such a charge in several types of ad hominem disputation. By process of dialectic, a pragmatic inconsistency can be reduced, or shown not to be reducible, to logical inconsistency. By the use of formal models of relatedness logic and plausible inference, other species of ad hominem can be resolved. But there are certain cases where nailing down an ad hominem fallacy is problematic. And it would be unfair not to examine some cases of this sort. We select two representative problem cases for this chapter. They represent open problems for future research.

ETHICAL REASONING

Johnson and Blair (1977) offer an example that they think illustrates the fuzzy boundary between the red herring fallacy (failure of relevance) and the ad hominem fallacy. However, since it is my thesis here that failure of relevance is one aspect of the ad hominem fallacy, it is not too surprising that the two failures are connected in the practice of argumentation. At any rate, the example they give is an interesting one. In an article in the Globe and Mail (September 1975), an opposition party member charged that the Canadian government was "too slow to act on mercury poisoning in the Kenora area and lung cancer dangers facing uranium miners in Elliott Lake until the [opposition party] screamed for action." The government health minister at the time responded as follows, according to Johnson and Blair (p. 57).

> [I am] tired of people complaining about health
> hazards facing Indians in Northwestern Ontario
> while the complainers go on killing themselves
> with what [are] called diseases of choice by
> exercising too little and smoking too much. I
> get a bit cynical about reactions of [a] society

that totally ignores my warnings about smoking
and wearing seat belts, killing more people
every day than mercury ever will.

According to Johnson and Blair, the reply given above was
irrelevant to the accusation and invited a digression onto
the topic of the government's critics and their heeding
of warnings about seat belts and smoking. Is the reply
really irrelevant? Well, interestingly, it does indeed
seem that here a good case could be made for arguing that
there is no subject matter overlap of common topics
between Canadians who smoke too much and fail to exercise
and wear seat belts, on the one hand, and those who are
susceptible to mercury poisoning in Kenora or lung cancer
from radiation in uranium mines in Elliott Lake. Switching from the one set of problems to the other does indeed
radically change the topic to something quite different
in many ways, yet that is also vexatious and problematic.
It could indeed serve nicely as a distraction. However,
we must be careful about potential ambiguities in the
concept of relevance. Perhaps there is a sense in which
the reply is not altogether irrelevant.

In both instances, we have people engaging in activities
that are hazardous for their health. Is that not relevance of a sort? Or is it? When you look at it carefully,
this reply cites an alleged inconsistency between two
propositions: (1) people are complaining about health
hazards facing Indians in northwestern Ontario, and (2) a
society is ignoring warnings about seat belts, smoking,
and exercising. Now, of course, there is no logical inconsistency in recklessly driving around, smoking, with no
seat belt instead of exercising, while at the same time
decrying mercury poisoning in Ontario. So we have to look
carefully to see whether there is some sort of pragmatic
inconsistency between (1) and (2). The two cases do seem
somehow parallel, but how?

As the actions are described in (1) and (2), there is no
pragmatic inconsistency either. There is no inconsistency
in recommending that mercury poisoning and lung cancer
from radiation should not be brought about while at the
same time bringing it about that one smokes or failing to
see to it that one wears a seat belt.

Perhaps, though, it is possible to extract a pragmatic
inconsistency out of (1) and (2) by redescribing the
actions expressed in them. What (1) may be presumed to

condemn is the needless risk of deadly health hazards--
hazards that could be corrected by appropriate cautionary
measures. But that very type of state of affairs condemned
in (1) is the action taken in (2). By smoking, not wearing seat belts, and failing to exercise, the very persons
who condemned correctible allowance of health hazards in
(2) are themselves bringing such hazards about. Surely
that is the pragmatic inconsistency that is really being
alleged by the government health minister.

Note, however, that (1) and (2), as stated, are not pragmatically inconsistent. The actions they describe must
be appropriately redescribed for the inconsistency to
emerge. One has to take great care in indicating what
are the precise pair of propositions alleged to be inconsistent. There are some similarities between the activities expressed in (1) and (2)--both are remediable health
hazards. But it might be alleged by the opposition sup-
porter to whom the government minister's ad hominem is
addressed that there are differences as well. He might
point out that many of the Indians have to fish out of
their lakes in order to provide food for themselves, but
there is no like pressure of necessity requiring people
to smoke cigarettes or forgo doing up their seat belts.
Many miners have to work in the mines in order to support
their families, even if they know it is dangerous. Again,
the same economic pressures do not apply to the actions
of smoking or exercising. So the opponent of this argument would surely cite these differences as counting
against the claim of circumstantial inconsistency. Who
is right?

The best way to proceed here is to rule that the argument
as expressed does not constitute a pragmatic inconsistency.
Therefore, the ad hominem, as stated, has not been justified or successfully pinned onto the persons to whom it
is directed. The fallacy has not yet been nailed down.
In order to establish that an ad hominem has been committed,
the actions of (1) and (2) must be redescribed. This means
that different premises need to be justified as applicable
to those against whom the allegation is being mounted.
The government minister's argument operates on the basis
of certain presumptions that the indicated redescriptions
may reasonably be made. These likely presumptions are not
hard to root out, on analysis, but the point is that they
are not proven--in the argument, strictly as stated--and
the participant in the argument accused of fallacy should

have an opportunity to argue against them if he wishes.
In short, the argument needed to substantiate a successful prosecution of the ad hominem, as it stands, is not
complete; it requires the addition of further premises
which should be precisely stated and conceded.

This case thus turns out to represent the classical
problem of nailing down a circumstantial ad hominem by
filling in gaps between act-descriptions in order to
try to close up the pragmatic inconsistency. It comes
largely down to questions of how to describe certain
alleged actions and link these descriptions together
into causal sequences. Often, then, the problem is one
of interpreting what the arguer has really said. What,
in other words, is the participant committed to by virtue of the written or spoken transcript of the given
data?

Thus, as we emphasized in chapter 1, a large part of the
analysis of ad hominem disputations concerns the pin-
pointing of the actual propositions, as stated, that are
alleged to be inconsistent. Any redescription of these
propositions must not be treated as a concession of the
arguer unless he clearly and specifically concedes it.

In this case, however, the gap between the cited act-
descriptions is even wider than in previous cases in one
regard. The actions of smoking and harvesting mercury-
infected fish are altogether distinct actions, and are
not just different act-descriptions of what might be
called the same action. Nor are they presumably alleged
to be causally connected to each other, as in the arms
exporter case study. Instead, the claim here would seem
to be that they are parallel because they both lead to
the same type of effect and because they are both presumed to be needless health hazards for the persons
involved.

Note also that rebutting the attack, as suggested above,
likely involves not denying that this pair of actions
has the same type of effect, but denying that the one act
is as much of a purely voluntary act as the other.
Clearly, therefore, the pattern of dialectic needed to
resolve this disputation is one we have not met up with
yet. In basic outline, this case is similar to the other
cases of pragmatic inconsistency. But it raises some
ethical factors that seem to outrun our previous analyses.

The rebuttal of the parallel raises the question of whether there could be an excusing factor present in the one act but not in the other, even granting that both actions are deliberate. This move seems to bring in ethical considerations beyond the scope of our analysis.

The reason why it is problematic in a case like the one above, to try to specify in advance the precise dialectical moves needed to reduce the pair of alleged propositions to a logical inconsistency, has to do with the fact that there are many more excuses that allow one to escape the charge. A useful example of the open texturedness of this type of moral defeasibility is given by G. E. Hughes (1958). Suppose Jones says in the course of a conversation, "It's wrong to join the army." But then the next day, while passing the recruiting office, we see Jones at the point of enlisting. This is what Professor Hughes calls a "logical eyebrow-raiser." Did Jones really understand what he was saying? We can be reassured that he did, if he makes any one of the following sorts of replies given in Hughes to our further query: (1) "Yes, but my case is a special one. I meant last night that in general it is wrong to join the army; of course there are exceptions, and my case is one. I could have gone into this last night, but someone changed the subject"; (2) "Yes, but I've been doing some hard thinking overnight, and I have come to the conclusion that I was mistaken"; (3) "I'm afraid I haven't got much moral fiber; I can't bring myself to do unpopular things" (p. 112f.).

In any of the cases, we will conclude that Jones really did understand what he had said the night before. His utterance is therefore not pragmatically inconsistent with his action the next day in the sense that it is dialectically reducible to a logical inconsistency. True, in the case of the third response, Jones may be guilty of a moral fault. But that, of course, does not mean that he has committed a logical fallacy.

What these cases illustrate, then, is that sometimes where we suspect a pragmatic inconsistency, we may find that further dialogue carries us into an ethical dispute concerning the excusability from full responsibility for the action at issue. Sometimes pragmatic inconsistency, or even logical inconsistency, is excusable. Sometimes people change their minds and retract their commitments.

That does not mean, however, that pointing out the original inconsistency is not worthwhile or valuable. It
does remind us, though, that there are some ethical
escape routes from the charge of circumstantial ad
hominem.

THE BORDERLINE BETWEEN ABUSIVE AND
CIRCUMSTANTIAL

Previously we have accepted the traditional distinction
between the abusive and circumstantial categories of ad
hominem fallacy. We have analyzed the circumstantial
ad hominem in terms of pragmatic inconsistency. The
circumstances said to be inconsistent are concessions
of the arguer, or act-descriptions that can dialectically be shown to be equivalent to concessions of the
arguer. These act-descriptions represent actions of
the arguer, and acts that represent states of affairs
he deliberately brought about and does not now disavow
or reject.

The abusive ad hominem has been analyzed as a fallacy
of relevance in some cases, in others as a species of
plausible reasoning. True, several cases, like the one
in the previous section, have indicated that in actual
argumentation there seems to be some overlap between
these categories. Sometimes a circumstantial ad hominem,
for example, may exhibit a failure of relatedness of
subject matters, and also may qualify as an abusive
personal attack.

An illustrative case of a borderline abusive circumstantial ad hominem attack can be found in Hansard (Canada:
House of Commons Debates, volume 3, second session, 1970,
p. 2298). The topic of this debate was the situation
in Biafra at the time. A Canadian observer team was
being sent to Biafra, to obtain information. However,
the question arose of whether commercial aircraft were
presently available for flights to Biafra.

At this point in the debate, Mr. MacEachen asked the
Prime Minister, Mr. Trudeau, whether he would consider
sending the Jet-star aircraft, if it is available. The
dialogue then proceeded as follows.[1]

Mr. MacEachen: Would he consider sending the Jet-star
                if it is available?

Mr. Trudeau:	It would have to refuel in the middle of the Atlantic Ocean.
Some hon. Members:	Hear, hear!
Some hon. Members:	Oh, oh!
Mr. Hees:	Mr. Speaker -
Mr. Speaker:	I suggest to the hon. member -
Mr. Hees:	On a point of order, Mr. Speaker, I bought the plane for the government and I know it can make the flight with the proper stops on the way.
Mr. Speaker:	The hon. member for Nanaimo-Cowichan-The Islands.
Mr. Trudeau:	I do not think it would have to stop if the hon. member went along and breathed into the tank.

Mr. Trudeau has committed an abusive ad hominem attack here by implying that Mr. Hees is an alcoholic. The suggestion may even be that Mr. Hees was drunk at the moment of the debate, and therefore that his argument should not be taken seriously. Here is a use of the ad hominem that is the flip side of the ad verecundiam. Mr. Hees's authority as a credible expert on the Jet-star aircraft is attacked by Mr. Trudeau's remark.

Perhaps, however, Mr. Hees had been a knowledgeable source of information on the capabilities of this aircraft. For all we know, the Jet-star may have been capable of the flight, as Mr. Hees proposed. Mr. Trudeau's personal attack simply dismisses that possibility by rejecting Mr. Hees as a credible spokesman.

The use of sarcasm or other forms of humor can demolish an argument by making one's opponent appear foolish or incompetent. In the adversarial context of parliamentary debate, this strategy can be all too effective. The suggestion that a man is so intoxicated that his breath could fuel a jet aircraft was no doubt found to be quite diverting by many of the audience of this debate. The humor disguises the severity of the personal attack. Drunken conduct is a form of personal circumstance incompatible with the conscientious performance of duty by a member of parliament in session. Mr. Trudeau offers no proof of such dereliction of duty. But his sarcastic remark is sufficient to achieve its effect of alleging a circumstantial inconsistency. At the same time, his remark constitutes a direct personal attack.

The next case will also sharply challenge the mutual

exclusiveness of the circumstantial and abusive categories. It will suggest that sometimes personal circumstances are used to function as part of what would
undoubtedly be described as a traditional ad hominem
refutation. But these circumstances are not purely
abusive, nor are they concessions or actions of the
arguer who is attacked.

It is all very well to describe the ad hominem as an
argument that unfairly brings in the personal circumstances of one's opponent in a disputation. However,
a case study approach of looking at an actual argument
of this general sort quickly makes it clear that this
description is far too imprecise to function as a helpful analysis of the ad hominem fallacy. What counts as
"personal circumstances"? Does this phrase refer to
the arguer's personality, her previous avowals or statements, her profession, her motives, her deeper psychiatric urgings, or perhaps her moral persuasions or practices? The problem is that it could be legitimate to
refer to some of these circumstances in some arguments,
whereas in other arguments such references could commit
all sorts of lapses of correct argument. The following
case study will help to indicate these problems inherent
in trying to sort out whether the allegation bringing
in personal circumstances is fair or not.

THE POWERLESS THEORETICIAN

This particular argument was put forward in the context
of a discussion of paternalism in a recent issue of the
journal, Man and Medicine (5, no. 3 [1980]). Recently,
physicians have been criticized for being paternalistic,
that is, for presuming the moral right to make decisions
on behalf of their patients. Allen Buchanan is a philosophy professor who has made particularly strong
attacks on physicians' rights to make such decisions.
Dr. Nicholas P. Christy, a medical practitioner and
professor of medicine, criticized Buchanan's arguments
in a commentary entitled "Who's in Charge Here?" (Man
and Medicine, pp. 203-206). Dr. Christy's arguments are
very carefully reasoned, with admirable scholarly precision. However, towards the end of his article, he takes
a different, more personal approach and ventures to
speculate on what he calls the "roots" of Buchanan's
reasoning. In this section, Dr. Christy poses a number
of questions and suggests that Professor Buchanan may be

arguing from a position of powerlessness as a university
professor of philosophy. We are asked to consider,
therefore, whether Professor Buchanan's argument might
stem from an unconscious wish to strip physicians--a very
powerful class of professionals--of their paternalistic
authority. Dr. Christy suggests, again very cautiously,
if it could be possible that these "thwarted theoreti-
cians" are really harboring a fantasy of taking over this
power of decision making themselves. The suggestion of
a kind of philosophical Dr. Strangelove, obsessed by a
fantasy of usurping the heady power of clinical decision
making--the thwarted theoretician disassociating the
doctor from his white lab coat, donning it, and then
marching boldly into the medical wards to make decisions
--is perfectly absurd. It is funny enough, yet contains
enough of a kernel of cunning appeal to make it a devastating ad hominem. Professor Buchanan's motives are so
subtly and thoroughly undermined that his credibility,
in the minds of most readers, is likely to be utterly
destroyed.

Quoted below is the kernel of the passage in question
(p. 206).

> I assume that Professor Buchanan is a philos-
> opher. Philosophers are, by the nature of
> their field, theoreticians. It is entirely
> natural for a theoretician to feel some
> frustration when he sees lofty matters--
> individual freedoms, for instance--tampered
> with. I suggest it is conceivable that a
> well motivated theoretician might be moved
> to a degree of resentment when he sees, from
> the relatively powerless position of, say, a
> university department of philosophy, an
> unqualified and incompetent but powerful
> group (doctors) paternalistically making a
> mockery of the freedoms of helpless patients.
> Might there not be an unconscious wish to
> strip that powerful class of its authority?
> And if physicians are incompetent to do the
> decision making, would it not be prudent to
> substitute for them those who are qualified:
> professional moralists, ethicians? It is
> possible that the thwarted theoretician har-
> bors a fantasy of this sort: "Let us deprive
> the doctors of their decision making power
> and supplant them by us ethicists. Then our

decisions, my decisions, will control clinical practice. I will be in charge."

Dr. Christy goes on to add that this fantasy reminds him
of the astronomer in Samuel Johnson's _Rasselas_ who, after
years of observing the planets, eventually came to believe
that he controlled their movements. He then adds that
any resemblance between these fantasies and the ones he
attributes to Professor Buchanan, are "purely coincidental."

ANALYSIS OF THE CASE

What precisely are the personal circumstances brought into
play by the argument above? First, Professor Buchanan is
categorized as a philosopher, a theoretician. Immediately
the suggestion is introduced--one that will no doubt have
its not so subtle effect on many readers--that he is
thereby completely disqualified as an authority worthy of
serious consideration. But is it fair to accuse Dr. Christy
of propounding this suggestion? It is hard to rule one way
or the other.

Dr. Christy is not--at least overtly--arguing as follows:
Buchanan is a theoretician, therefore what he says is
incorrect. His argument never positively affirms that step
to the conclusion that what Buchanan says is false. Dr.
Christy is merely "speculating" on the "roots" of Buchanan's
reasoning. However, such speculations are far from harmless, are not likely to be taken by many readers as mere
harmless speculation at all, and are therefore not as
innocent as claimed. The problem is that the harm done is
more by way of innuendo than by articulated propositions.
An innuendo is not necessarily an argument--minimally a set
of propositions--and can hardly therefore be pinned down
as a definite fallacy. We are at the edges of the ad
hominem fallacy, but we cannot nail it down. True, the
fact that Professor Buchanan belongs to a particular profession does not mean that his arguments are wrong, but Dr.
Christy has not affirmed, as far as I see, that they are
wrong for that reason.

However, the argument goes on to propose that a theoretician, because he is powerless, is resentful of those who
have the power that he lacks. Here Dr. Christy's argument
is at the edge of a damaging accusation. He is suggesting
very strongly that his opponents' arguments could be
prompted by the resentment of the powerless theoretician.

In effect, his opponents are characterized as unqualified and frustrated meddlers, interfering with doctors because they are resentful of the doctor's powers.

The picture conveyed here is a rhetorically powerful one. Many readers no doubt would be strongly inclined to accept the proposition that arguments on public interest decision making are likely to be prompted by the arguer's own professional interests and affiliations. Indeed, it is a sad fact that professional groups do tend to lobby for their own special interests on topics like medical policy decision making. Lawyers will tend to argue that such issues should be decided in the courts. Doctors tend to feel comfortable with the idea that the doctor should make the decision. And philosophers like the idea that ethical committees (no doubt composed of philosophers) should have input. There are many exceptions, but the point is that an audience is likely to believe, with some justification, that professional interest groups are likely to favor their own special interests.

While Dr. Christy does not explicitly argue that Buchanan's view is wrong because it is based on self-interest or even baser motives like professional resentment, nevertheless, because of the antecedent beliefs of many readers of his article, it is quite likely that many readers will interpret it that way and accept that argument.

Of course, Dr. Christy is merely suggesting that it is possible that the thwarted theoretician may harbor a fantasy of powerful role-usurpation. But is he really being coy here? The answer is almost certainly yes. Of course it is perfectly legitimate to speculate about the psychiatric roots of an adversary's reasoning. But if this speculation is likely to be a powerful rhetorical force in influencing a particular tribunal--in this case the readers of the journal--it is really far more than a harmless diversion.

The problem is that the ad hominem fallacy in Dr. Christy's argument is not located in the propositions, the premisses, and conclusions he specifically advances. Rather, it is located in the propositions that many members of his audience are likely to take as the argument from what he writes. Many readers will get the message that Buchanan is a thwarted theoretician acting from resentment, therefore what he says is wrong, and they may be fully ready to accept this argument.

Yet the rejoinder is always open to Dr. Christy: "That
was not my argument. In fact I was not even propounding
an argument at all. I was merely constructing a fantasy
concerning certain possibilities." The defense is this:
if there is no argument, there can be fallacy. To quote
Hamblin (1970a), "A fallacy is a fallacious argument.
Someone who merely makes false statements, however absurd,
is innocent of fallacy unless the statements constitute
or express an argument" (p. 224). In fact, Hamblin
squarely states the very problem we are concerned with,
calling it the problem of "nailing" a fallacy. He asks
us to consider a case where person A makes statement S
and then person B replies with the ad hominem, "It was C
who told you that, and I happen to know that his mother-
in-law is living in sin with a Russian." A, in turn,
objects: "The falsity of S does not follow from any facts
about the morals of C's mother-in-law: that is an argumentum ad hominem." But then suppose B replies as follows:
"I did not claim that it followed. I simply made a remark
about the incidentals of the statement's history. Draw
what conclusion you like. If the cap fits . . ." As
Hamblin notes, this reply may be disingenuous, but even so,
B cannot be convicted of having committed a fallacy unless
it can be proven that he has advanced an argument (p. 224).
That argument must be precisely located and identified
before it can be shown that it is incorrect or fallacious.

In the present case, Dr. Christy quite disingenuously puts
forward his damaging remarks in the guise of a fantasy
about the roots of his opponent's reasoning. He states
only that it is possible that the thwarted theoretician
harbors a fantasy of power and decision making role-usurpation, through his own resentment at his powerlessness.
Rather than making statements, he asks questions: "Might
there not be an unconscious wish to strip that powerful
class [of physicians] of its authority?" Can we affirm
positively that there is an argument here, one that commits
the ad hominem fallacy? Our suspicion is that Dr. Christy's
question is really a rhetorical question, so-called, that
it really makes the statement that there is an unconscious
wish to strip authority from those with power on the part
of those he criticizes.

THE RHETORICAL DEBATE

The point to be made here is that whether the information
conveyed is in the form of a statement or question, whether

it is bold assertion or merely, as in this case, the suggestion of a possibility, still the damage to one's opponents is done. The reason lies not so much in the modality
of the assertions, questions, or whatever, but in the
impact that will be conveyed to the readership's beliefs.
It is a matter of rhetoric, a question of the way the signal will be received by the particular audience towards
which it is directed. However, as Hamblin's remarks indicate, we have to be very careful here. We cannot convict
someone of having committed a logical fallacy on the basis
that his remarks might have such-and-such an effect on
this or that audience. We have to go by what he says, by
what he asserts, by what propositions he actually puts
forward, not by what effects his remarks might have in
some group of receivers.

Part of the problem here is that in a written commentary
like Dr. Christy's, the opponent does not have a chance
to reply, at least right away, to the questions or other
remarks made in print. In a dialectical game, questions
are directly put to one's opponent, who may then reply to
them. Suppose Dr. Christy's opponent, Professor Buchanan,
was able to reply directly to Dr. Christy's question,
"Might there not be an unconscious wish to strip that
powerful class [of physicians] of its authority?" Presumably he would be very upset indeed by such a slanderous
question and could reply, for example, by posing an
equally damaging question about Dr. Christy's motives in
asking such a nasty question. However, as it happened,
Dr. Christy's commentary in this issue followed another
article that was also a criticism of Buchanan's arguments.
No doubt Professor Buchanan or his supporters may still
have the opportunity to reply in subsequent issues of
the journal but, in the meantime, Dr. Christy's questions,
unanswered, will have their intended effect in the minds
of many readers. Here we are at the border between logic
and rhetoric.

The point is that in a formal game of dialectic, both
parties are allowed to respond not only to the arguments
of the other, but also to questions, and even to presuppositions, suggestions, or even querying of possibilities
in the form of fantasies. Moreover, in some of these
games, like the obligation game, the respondent is con-
fined to answering questions and is not allowed to pro-
pound fantasies or otherwise deviate from offering propositions. Finally, the game's win-strategy is defined by
how well the participants perform according to the stated

rules, not by the possibly quite emotional reactions of some target audiences or referees.

In the rhetorical debate, or in an ordinary quarrel, the outcome is decided not by the conformity of the partici- pants' arguments to some precisely formulated set of rules, but by the vote of some target audience. In some debates, a vote is taken among the audience, in others a panel of judges is asked to rule. However, the decision is dependent to a goodly extent upon rhetorical factors, that is, upon the effect or impact of the participants' arguments or moves upon that target audience. In this setting, if Professor Buchanan was not ready or able to respond to Dr. Christy's rhetorically powerful insinu- ations with equally devastating replies, he would be likely to lose the debate. In the actual case studied here, therefore, in effect Professor Buchanan's side loses by default, if we look at the interchange as a debate or quarrel.

That is the problem with trying to study or analyze the ad hominem fallacy at the level of the debate or ordinary quarrel. The question of fallaciousness, or at least the question of how effective this type of argument is as a win-strategy, is determined by the rhetoric of the situ- ation, by the reactions of the audience or referees. These reactions, however, may be irrational or dominated by elusive emotions. What is or is not fallacious is not objectively analyzable. It may not even be clear or determinable whether a participant has offered an argu- ment, let alone a fallacious one.

The lesson would appear to be that the analysis of what is fallacious (incorrect) about the ad hominem can only take place at the dialectical level, where moves and out- comes are more fully determined by objective rules rather than by the psychologically varying reactions of some particular audience. Only then can we use the model of dialectical argument as a tool of analysis to approach the debate or quarrel to ask questions like the following. Is it an argument, or a question? Does the opponent have a chance to reply? Does the sequence of interchange between the participants qualify by the rules as a win- strategy for the opponent or the respondent? In this setting, clearly much that is both objectionable and elusive from a point of view of rational criticism of Dr. Christy's argument would be forced out into the open where it could be confronted more fairly.

This case stretches to the limit how we define the concept
of argument in studying the <u>ad hominem</u> fallacy. We started
by thinking of an argument as a set of propositions. We
then introduced participants in a game making sequential
moves in putting forward these propositions. We utilized
classical deductive logic, then added relatedness logic
and plausibility theory. Can this already rich and diver-
sified conception of what constitutes an argument bear the
strain of including the likely rhetorical effects of the
propositions on a target audience? It seems we should be
very careful in extending our model of argument this far.
But if we do not, I think we cannot handle the argument of
this case study as an <u>ad hominem</u>. However, by the traditional conceptions of <u>this fallacy</u>, most of us would
probably want to include it in that category. We leave
this problem for the reader to think about.

NOTES

    1. I would like to thank John Dorward for drawing
this debate to my attention.

10

Positional Defensibility

IS POSITIONAL INCONSISTENCY FALLACIOUS?

Our analysis postulates that any ad hominem refutation
rests on an allegation of positional inconsistency. The
inconsistency may be logical inconsistency, as in classical logic, or it may be another kind, such as pragmatic
or action-theoretic inconsistency, as modelled in a
relatedness logic. These, at any rate, are the two basic
types of inconsistency we have stressed.

Of course, in many an ad hominem allegation, the inconsistency is derived from a practical sequence of steps.
The accusation is essentially: "You yourself act in such
a manner as to bring about p, but I claim that ⅂p is
practically related to something you brought about."
Venturing into the field of practical reasoning, we have
provided an analysis of the kinds of moves that the participants in logical dialogue need to make to resolve the
issue. We feel it is best for the arguers to proceed by
logical steps and first clarify the action-theoretic core
structure implicit in their allegations of positional
inconsistency before settling their dispute on whether an
ad hominem criticism is justified. We have argued that
any applicable framework of practical reasoning should be
based on a core basis of relatedness propositional calculus
action propositions.

Now according to our analysis, the precise degree of a
well-founded allegation of positional inconsistency is
dependent on the nature of the dialectical game one is
engaged in. In practical terms, however, positional
inconsistency is an extremely devastating and serious allegation. Perhaps it behooves us to try to see just why, to
the extent that we can.

First of all, as pointed out by Trudy Govier (1981), a
position that is pragmatically inconsistent is extremely
vexing to persons who are themselves forced to act in a
manner consistent with the pronouncements of one who fails
himself to act in that manner. One is outraged, for
example, when politicians act in this inconsistent manner,
yet exhort or even force others to comply with the direc-
tives they themselves fail to act on. Certainly, as we
have noted several times, persistence in such inconsistency
can be highly immoral and in fact can appear to violate

fundamental ethical principles of fairness and democratic
government. Moreover, positional inconsistency may be
the best kind of evidence of callousness, moral indifference, or stupidity. Inconsistency can be strong evidence
of the existence of some logical error, because an inconsistent set contains at least one false member.

Positional inconsistencies due to conflicts between propositions professed and propositions deliberately brought
about by an arguer, of course, are preserved in some
cases as provable logical inconsistencies in relatedness
logic by our analysis. Does not this analysis thereby
suggest the fallaciousness of an action-theoretic positional inconsistency?

Of course, we have seen that not all valid classical
inferences are also valid for action propositions. An
inference that is valid under the classical construal of
the conditional, but fails in the logic of action propositions, is the following one.

$$A \rightarrow (B \rightarrow C)$$
$$\overline{B \rightarrow (A \rightarrow C)}$$

Assume that by making it true that the switch is flipped,
an agent makes it true that by his making the light go on
a prowler is warned. Does this conclusion have to follow:
by making it true that the light goes on, the agent makes
it true that a prowler is warned by making it true that
the switch is flipped? We think not.

The reason this inference fails is that, in the particular
instance under consideration, it is false that what the
agent does when he flips the switch is directly related to
his warning the prowler. Even supposing he does turn the
light on, it need not follow that it is his flipping the
switch that warns the prowler. Rather, it is the illumina-
tion of the light that directly warns the prowler.

If we look at the form of inference above, we can see that
the premiss is true if A, B, and C are all made true. A
is related to B and B is related to C. However, even with
these values, the conclusion must be false if A is not
(directly) related to C. Interchange of the directly
related propositions in an act-sequence is not always
permissible.

Nonetheless, enough classically valid inferences are

retained in relatedness logic to give our analysis bite
in cases where a disputant advances the premisses but
rejects the conclusion of some inferences. We saw in
chapter 6 that certain tautologies of classical logic
hold while others fail to obtain in the logic of action
propositions we adopted there. Let us look at a valid
inference form for action propositions.

$$A \rightarrow B$$

$$A \rightarrow \exists B$$

$$\overline{\qquad\qquad}$$

$$\exists A$$

Suppose an agent's making it true that A is sufficient to
assure that he has made it true that B, and moreover that
his making it true that A is also sufficient to assure
he has made it true that 7B. In such a case, we have to
conclude that the agent has not made it true that A. So
this inference must be generally valid.

We can see why it is valid in relatedness logic. For the
conclusion to be false, A must be true. But if A is true
in both premisses, then at least one premiss must be
false, for B must be either true or false. Hence no case
is possible wherein the premisses are true and the conclusion is false.

Suppose I have made A true and by making A true I have
directly made it true that B. But suppose you, my opponent in disputation, can show that my position commits me
to A → 7B. Then I am pragmatically inconsistent and you
are in a position to refute my argument by means of an
ad hominem refutation.

If an arguer professes the premisses of an inference
through deed or word, and likewise professes the negation
of its conclusion, and the inference is valid in $\mathcal{S}$, then
the position of this arguer is demonstrably logically
inconsistent in $\mathcal{S}$. Should not such a positional inconsistency be judged fallacious?

Moreover, an allegation of positional inconsistency is an
extremely effective refutation, psychologically or rhetorically speaking. It is a deadly retort that often has the
effect of undoing one's opponent altogether in debate. The
best reply may still leave one's credibility badly damaged.

For all these reasons, one may be strongly tempted to think

that positional inconsistency is itself a fallacy, or
should be, regardless of what inference may be drawn from
that inconsistent position in subsequent dialogue. A case
study and some remarks of one commentator in particular
seem to support the suggestion that positional inconsistency is fallacious.

Govier (1981) proposes the following schema which she
claims would constitute a blatant fallacy of relevance.

(*) 1. A advocates that p should be followed.
    2. Ā does not himself follow p.
    3. Therefore, p is false.

However, Govier then suggests that real-life examples of
the tu quoque argument are rarely if ever this simple.
As an illustration, she cites a case where some outdoor
workers went on a bitter strike and eventually settled
for an 8 per cent pay increase, even though some politicians told them that wages had to be kept down to control
inflation (p. 3). A year later, however, these very same
politicians voted themselves a 48 per cent wage increase.
The outdoor workers were so enraged that they tried to
bring the matter to a public referendum, saying, "Council
should remember when they drove us out for 55 days on the
line." The point Govier makes is that (*) does not appear
to constitute an adequate analysis of what has gone wrong
in this case. She writes (p. 3):

> The point here would seem to be not that coun-
> cil members are shown by their actions to have
> said something false when they said it was
> important to keep down inflation, but rather
> that the inconsistency between their advocacy
> of that principle and their quest for a fat
> raise for themselves makes it hard to accept
> from them either the initial principle or the
> subsequent demand for their own higher wages.

This observation is quite accurate. The point is not that
the council's proposition that inflation should be kept
down is false. Indeed, nobody is even alleging that.
Certainly the outdoor workers are not, as the case is presented by Govier's account of it. So where is the fallacy
as analyzed by (*)?

This remark appears to constitute a serious criticism of
our analysis of ad hominem refutation. For have we not

claimed that (*) represents an important yet incorrect form of argument that constitutes the ad hominem fallacy? Yet according to Govier, what is deeply disturbing and characteristic of the wrongness in the case cited is not modelled adequately by (*).

To resolve this problem, we must go back to our own analysis of ad hominem. According to our analysis, an allegation of circumstantial ad hominem may be quite accurate and justified if the argument attacked exhibits a direct circumstantial inconsistency. In such a case, the attacker commits no fallacy. His argument is a successful and correct ad hominem refutation--provided, as we required, that he does not commit additional indiscretions, for example, (*). In this case, it seems fair to judge, on the given information in Govier (p. 3) that the outdoor workers' allegation of action-theoretic inconsistency is quite justified and is therefore a reasonable refutation, as far as it appears to have been carried by its exponents. Thus, by our analysis, no fallacy has been committed.

One exception must be made to this assessment, however. If the workers are justified in their argument, as we concur, then the council has indeed committed a circumstantial inconsistency. Insofar as such inconsistency is "fallacious," therefore, these individuals may be said to have committed an error or fallacy. Thus the question is raised: Is the commission of a circumstantial inconsistency in itself a fallacy?

To respond to this query, we have to go back to chapter 2 and recall our requirement that a fallacy is a fallacious argument. But is an inconsistent position an argument? We saw in chapters 7 and 8 that the outcomes of an arguer's actions can be represented as propositions that he brings about. These propositions can in turn be brought into certain logical relationships with propositions he advances or has committed himself to. Such propositions collectively make up a set of commitments in a dialectical interchange that could represent the position of this particular disputant. To repeat, then, is an inconsistent position an argument?

It seems that the best answer is that such a position is not itself an argument, although it may certainly be part of an argument. However, such a position may be refuted, questioned, or shown to be inconsistent by a participant

in the argument. If the one refuted is thereby shown to
be inconsistent in his position, that need not mean he
has committed a fallacy. Perhaps further dialogue may
explain or remove the inconsistency. Whether or not a
fallacy is committed by the inconsistent position arguer
thus depends on what he does with that inconsistency,
how he proceeds to argue from that point.

But such subtle considerations as these raise a fundamental question about what we mean by "fallacy" in the
common term ad hominem fallacy. As we have seen, this
very term itself prejudicially (fallaciously?) suggests
that all ad hominem refutations and arguments are fallacious (incorrect arguments), and that is a suggestion our
analysis strongly refutes.

THE CONCEPT OF POSITION IN ARGUMENTATION

The existence of the so-called straw man fallacy suggests
that there can be significant mischief in misrepresenting
one's opponent's position in disputation. Moreover, in
the practical analysis of arguments, there are pragmatic
questions about what should count as an arguer's position,
as we saw in the practical problems encountered in chapter 9.
There we tried to adjudicate on an ad hominem allegation
and found difficulties in nailing down the fallacy. In the
case of Dr. Christy's argument, we found we could not con-
firm the commission of a fallacy on his part because we
have to go strictly by the propositions he actually put forward in his allegations. We had to contend with a borderline area where his propositions were not clearly and
definitely advanced, but rather coyly suggested by innuendo
towards a target audience. Here we found ourselves at the
border between logic and rhetoric.

Pragmatic problems are encountered in attempting to determine fairly whether the propositions alleged are truly
concessions or commitments of the one against whom the ad
hominem refutation is directed. Arguments commonly cited
as ad hominem often seem to derive what plausibility they
have from an unjustified, overly inclusive interpretation
of what constitutes an opponent's position. Because one
is female, it hardly follows that one adopts a feminist
position. Or what counts as the Marxist position is likely
to be quite open to disputation. Gratuitous conferring of
such positions on one's opponents is the stuff and substance
of many an ad hominem.

Let us therefore work towards defining "position" more
clearly. A position, P, may be defined as a set of propositions that are commitments of a participant in a
dialectical game. What constitutes a commitment (precisely)
varies with the commitment-rules of the game one has in
mind, or that the players have agreed upon. Thus, in order
to define precisely "position" one needs to specify a game,
or a class of games. What class of games is appropriate
for the ad hominem has been a main concern of this book,
and we now turn to narrowing this class even further.

Given the notion of a position, the ad hominem argument
amounts to just this: if one participant argues that the
set of propositions that make up his opponent's position
is inconsistent, then that participant mounts an ad hominem
attack (allegation, trial refutation). If inconsistency is
demonstrated, according to the rules of the game, then a
successful ad hominem attack has been carried out. (That
it is successful does not mean that it cannot be rebutted
by further dialogue--"successful" may be defined relative
to a point in the dialogue, although for some games, as we
will see, a successful refutation signals the winning [end]
of the game.) In some instances moreover, a successful ad
hominem criticism may be advanced, even though the position
criticized is not thereby refuted. An ad hominem fallacy
occurs where the advancer of the attack argues from the
inconsistency of P to the falsehood of some (consistent)
subset of P.

The above two paragraphs give, in general, our analysis of
the ad hominem (attack, criticism, refutation, fallacy).
What needs to give the analysis depth is an account of what
constitutes a position. Notice already one fact, however.
By this form of analysis, the ad hominem argument is not
always fallacious.

One's position may also be defined as a set of propositions
that form a basis for acting when one is formulating a plan
of action. A position, then, is a sort of code, a body of
propositions that represent outcomes one plans to bring
about and deliberates to achieve as outcomes of one's
actions. A position may be the code of a group of agents.
For example, it may be a statement by a group of individuals who want to express their resolve to support nuclear
disarmament. Or it may be a statement of commitment to a
professional or group ethic like the Hippocratic oath. On
the other hand, a position may be an individual's statement
of his own goals, an expression of where he or she stands

on an issue. A position may even be a single statement
attributable to an individual, that expresses a stated
goal of that individual. In general, an arguer's position
relative to a specific set of real circumstances is
defined by an account of that arguer's practical reasoning
relative to his stated goals and the actions that may be
fairly attributed to him.

Given the concept of a position, we are now in a position
to elucidate what can be logically aberrant about a circumstantial ad hominem inconsistency of the action-theoretic
sort. If we assume (a) that proposition p is part of the
position of some agent a, we may infer that p forms a basis
for an action plan that a has formulated. In other words,
a has said, as it were that he is committed to bringing it
about that p, as part of his plan of action. But if we
also assume (b) that a brings it about that not-p, we may
infer, by the analysis of chapter 6, that not-p is brought
about by something a did. This leads us to presume that
not-p is related to some proposition that was a deliberate
outcome of the plan of action of a. We need to ask, then,
did a deliberately see to it that not-p? If so, and we can
be assured of it, then we can see that a's plan of action
is incoherent in precisely this sense: his goal of deliberation is to bring about p, but he deliberately acts so as
to bring about ⅂p. Therefore, his plan or practical deliberations, his collective position, is inconsistent.

What is wrong with an inconsistent plan of action? Simply
put, an inconsistent plan can never be carried out. In
relatedness logic, inconsistency is not globally destructive
as in classical logic, where any proposition you like is a
consequence of an inconsistency. But inconsistency is
locally destructive in the sense that any proposition
related to any proposition in the inconsistent set follows
from an inconsistency. Hence a positional inconsistency
results in a nondirective plan. It allows you to follow
any course of action related to your position. For example,
if p is related to q, then you have $(p \wedge ⅂p) \rightarrow q$ and $(p \wedge ⅂p)$
$\rightarrow ⅂q$, so your plan cannot tell you whether to bring about q
or ⅂q. It becomes nondirective in informing you how to make
a rational choice between q and ⅂q. In short, a positional
inconsistency makes one's position useless as a rational
plan for deliberate action.

Now we know what is wrong with an inconsistent position in
disputation, we still need to answer the vexing question of
whether such inconsistency is fallacious in itself. To do

this, we investigate a certain type of dialectical game
where the object is to force one's opponent into an
inconsistent position.

THE OBLIGATION GAME

In the twelfth century, the medieval disputatio evolved
into a level of abstraction where the questions debated
no longer represented substantive (material) problems,
but even false or bizarre propositions were entertained
as suppositions, and evidently true propositions were
questioned. This level of abstraction signalled that the
moves in a disputation came to be regulated by systems of
rules that were essentially formal as a structure. The
special art called dialectic by Aristotle in the Topics
and De Sophisticis Elenchis became a part of the curricu-
lum at Paris, Oxford, and other universities. This was
the art of confounding an opponent in argument by finding
errors (sophisms) and rebuttals to serve as refutations
of his arguments. The great logicians William of Sherwood,
Lambert of Auxerre, and Peter of Spain were all exponents
of this dialectical art.

One major pedagogical vehicle of this art was the obligation game, a dialogue usually between master and student
designed to give the student practice in the use of logical
rules of inference. According to Romuald Green (1963),
the structure of an exercise de obligationibus may be
described as follows. It is a disputation between two
parties, the opponent (opponens) and respondent (respond-
ens). The opponent begins by requiring the respondent to
take on the obligation of upholding a particular proposition. This done, the opponent then poses a series of
questions that the respondent must reply to by either
conceding or denying. The aim of the opponent is to
involve the respondent in inconsistency, and the respondent
loses the game as soon as he concedes a set of propositions
that the opponent can show to be inconsistent. Otherwise,
the respondent wins the game after an agreed-upon finite
number of questions have been answered. Usually the
initial proposition set down by the opponent is false, or
else is one that, with enough concessions, is going to
lead to difficulties.

The statements conceded by the respondent do not have to
be true. Indeed, in order to win, he must concede a false
proposition where its negation would be inconsistent with

the _positum_ (the initial proposition he conceded). At
all costs, he must maintain consistency. However, if a
proposition put to him is such that neither it nor its
negation is inconsistent to any of his previous concessions, he must concede only propositions he thinks to be
true. The respondent's essential difficulty is that he
is sometimes forced to choose carefully to fulfill both
these objectives in the assigned priority. An example
will illustrate this problem.

Suppose the _positum_ accepted by the respondent is (1)
Socrates is black. Next he is queried on (2), Socrates
and Plato are the same color. Since (2), in actual fact,
is true, and consistent with (1), the respondent should
concede it. But next he is queried on (3), Plato is
white. Clearly, in order to retain consistency, he must
deny (3). However, had (3) been queried before (2), he
would have had to concede (3) because it is in fact true,
and then deny (2).

So one can see how the game works. The opponent tries
to entrap the respondent by getting him to concede some
proposition that seems factually true but where the
negation of that proposition, unbeknownst to the respondent, follows from his own earlier concessions.

Another example, this based on one given by Green (1963,
p. 69f.) illustrates how the opponent was supposed to
achieve his strategy. In this example, as was commonly
done, the opponent and respondent together may agree on
certain propositions as true by "actual fact" (_rei_ _veritas_),
to make the game even more complex. This makes for further
complications because the agreed-upon "fact" may not be
true, any more than the _positum_ is.

The following dialogue takes place between two disputants
who agree at the outset on the validity of _modus_ _ponens_
and the disjunctive syllogism. The structure of the
dialogue is essentially similar to an exercise in the
treatise _De Obligationibus_, thought to be authored by
William of Sherwood. I did not find the treatise's
example very convincing, at least as I understood it--see
Green (p. 69f.)--so I have somewhat changed the order and
presentation of my version of the dialogue.

Opponent: Will you agree to concede the following two
            propositions as _positum_? First, the disjunction
            'Socrates runs or you are standing,' and second

the disjunction 'Socrates moves or you are
not standing.' Moreover, let us agree as
an actual fact that Socrates does not exist.

Respondent: Yes, I'll concede all those propositions.
Opponent: What do you say about the proposition
'Socrates moves'?

Respondent: Well, I'll have to deny that. For I have
already conceded that Socrates does not
exist. Therefore 'Socrates moves' has to
be false [The respondent is something of a
Russellian].

Opponent: What about the conditional 'If Socrates runs,
he moves'?

Respondent: Well, that seems to be necessarily true. Yes,
I'll accept it.

Opponent: What about 'Socrates runs'?

Respondent: I have accepted the conditional 'If Socrates
runs then Socrates moves.' If I concede
'Socrates runs' I'll have to concede 'Socrates
moves,' because that follows by modus ponens.
But I previously denied that very statement.
Thus to be consistent, I must deny 'Socrates
runs.'

Opponent: All right. By the positum, you conceded
'Socrates moves or you are not standing.'
Right?

Respondent: Yes.

Opponent: But above, you denied 'Socrates moves' is
true. It follows by disjunctive syllogism
that you must concede 'You are not standing.'

Respondent: All right.

Opponent: Now you also conceded, as part of the positum,
'Socrates runs or you are standing.' But
since you now concede the truth of 'You are
not standing,' you must concede that 'Socrates
runs' is true. But that is precisely the
propositions you had to deny, above.

Respondent: So it is. Egad!

The structure of the dialogue can be given in classical
truth-functional logic. Let p = Socrates runs, q = Socrates
moves, and r = You are standing. The respondent does himself in once he agrees to p ⊃ q. For this concession,
taken together with the positum, deductively yields q.

$$
\left. \begin{array}{l}
p \supset q \\
p \vee r \\
q \vee \daleth r
\end{array} \right\} \quad \underline{positum}
$$

$$ \overline{} $$

$$ q $$

The respondent does not realize that however. Right at
the outset he denies q, because the falsehood of q seems
to him to follow from the actual fact. Thus once he has
done that and then conceded p ⊃ q along with the positum,
he has left a win-strategy open to the opponent. At that
point, all the opponent has to do is fill in the missing
steps.

This sophisma is an interesting one, particularly because
the bait is a necessary proposition, 'If Socrates runs,
Socrates moves.' The respondent may therefore be more
inclined to accept it rather than backtrack and calculate,
figuring out that if he accepts it he loses.

We see thus that in the obligation game an inconsistent
set of concessions can be enough to make a participant
lose the game. Does the obligation game therefore support
the thesis that, at least in some dialectical structures,
inconsistency of position is fallacious for the one who
maintains that position? On the presumption, here adhered
to, that a fallacy is a fallacious (incorrect) argument,
a good case can be made for the negative answer. A position, although it is a set of propositions, is not an
argument, and need not constitute an argument. Hence by
itself it cannot be a fallacious argument. It is how one
argues on the basis of that position that determines
whether the ad hominem fallacy is committed.

In an obligation game, if the respondent's position contains an inconsistency it does not follow that the respondent must lose the game. What does follow is that the
opponent has a sure win-strategy at his disposal. That
is, if the opponent, by means of the rules of the game,
can force the respondent to concede an outright inconsistency on the basis of his implicitly inconsistent concessions, the opponent wins the game. Direct, demonstrable
inconsistency from the respondent's position is sufficient
for his loss of the game. Inconsistency of the respondent's
commitments--if implicit as opposed to directly available
in the form A ∧ 7A--means that the respondent can lose at
that point provided the opponent is sufficiently clever and
has enough remaining moves to carry out his win-strategy
attack.

We conclude that for the obligation game, and hypothesize
that for dialectical games in general, inconsistency of
position on the part of a participant is not in itself
fallacious, or specifically itself constitutes the commission

of an ad hominem fallacy. However, it certainly is bad
strategy, and leaves one open to refutations by an opponent. While not fallacious in itself, it nevertheless
makes one's arguments extremely vulnerable. Indeed, so
much so that in obligation, a directly inconsistent position signals a loss of the game, and an inconsistent
position generally offers one's opponent a clear win-
strategy that may be sufficient for one's loss of the
game.

These features of the obligation game reflect the fact
that inconsistency, while not fallacious, is something
to be avoided in formulating or consolidating one's position on an issue. Inconsistency is a sure indicator of
falsehood somewhere in that position (again, on classical
and classically based logical rules). One's position, if
inconsistent, is certainly inadequate as a good position,
as it stands. Thus a well-founded allegation of positional inconsistency is a serious criticism, and that
truth is reflected in the connection between the rules
of strategy and positional inconsistencies in all the
games of dialectic we have surveyed. Accordingly, a
successful ad hominem allegation is a positive move in
argument that thrusts the burden of proof onto the participant, whose position is thus made vulnerable, to
extricate himself if he can. That a successful allegation has been advanced does not mean that either participant has committed an ad hominem fallacy, by our analysis.

ATTACKS, REFUTATIONS, AND FALLACIES

It is important to note that we are dividing what we call
a refutation into two parts. First, there is the allegation, made by the attacker. Then there is the response
of the other disputant to the attack along with subsequent
moves and countermoves by both parties. This following
segment of dialogue, the second part of the refutation,
may then result in the refutation being successful or not.
In this secondary sequence, either party may commit an ad
hominem fallacy. But it is not the initial attack that,
in itself, is fallacious or not fallacious.

As was well brought out by our analysis of the sportsman's
rejoinder, such an attack may be incorrectly formulated.
But it is still not in and by itself fallacious. Rather
the participant attacked must show by his response that
the attack has failed to establish the direct inconsistency

(presumably required by the rules of the game) and that
therefore the initial attacker's argument is open to
rejoinder as a species of ad hominem fallacy (attacker's
ad hominem). Perhaps this is the particular species of
ad hominem fallacy where we come closest to the mark of
claiming that the allegation itself constitutes a form of
the fallacy. Yet, even here, it is more the ensuing
response that determines in fact whether a fallacy has
been committed and by whom.

In general, therefore, we adopt the thesis that it is not
the initial attack that is or is not per se fallacious.
Inconsistency of position, in itself, is fallacious
neither for the defender nor attacker of that position.
However, it is the basis of a serious criticism that may,
or likely will in some cases, lead to refutation.

What sort of criticism is it to show that someone's position is inconsistent? In assessing the seriousness of
such a criticism, we must first of all be reminded that
in an inconsistent set at least one member must be false.
Moreover, if we have in mind an action-theoretic inconsistency, a jointly inconsistent set of act-outcomes cannot
all be carried out. Thus if one's plan of action involves
act-inconsistencies, it will be impossible to carry out
that plan as a totality. A plan of action that includes
pragmatically inconsistent acts is incoherent in the
sense that it can never be realized in practice.

Of course, as our analysis of ad hominem reasoning makes
clear, there need be nothing wrong with an arguer's argument for some particular conclusion, even if the set of
propositions making up that argument is a subset of a
position that is inconsistent.

We must also remember that, in dialogue, inconsistency
can be corrected or resolved by further dialogue. Hamblin,
as we noted, makes a point of not requiring, in general,
that commitment-stores must always be consistent. Thus
there are two sides to this issue, and it is not a trivial
problem to resolve in general.

The first fact that needs to be emphasized in working
towards a resolution of the problem is this: a refutation
of White's position is not necessarily a refutation of
White's argument. Whether the two refutations are connected depends upon the precise connection between White's
position and White's argument. The two need not stand or

fall together (in many games of dialectic). This fact
is the fundamental one in any analysis of the ad hominem
fallacy. In the Hamblin game (H), for example, if Black
shows White's position to be inconsistent, White is not
refuted in the sense that he thereby loses the game. But
White does have to resolve the inconsistency if he wants
to be able to continue the game. Hence in (H) a demonstration of an inconsistent position by one's opponent is
a serious criticism--it is not without force--but it is
not a conclusive refutation in the sense that the perpe-
trator of inconsistency must lose the game forthwith.

By contrast, in the obligation game, the objective of the
opponent is to trap the respondent into inconsistency.
Thus it is a rule of the game that the opponent wins as
soon as he succeeds in demonstrating an inconsistency in
the respondent's position. In this game, a well-founded
ad hominem allegation constitutes a win, a conclusive
refutation of the respondent. The respondent's objective
is to avoid inconsistency until the opponent runs out of
moves.

Thus the second fundamental fact is this: how serious
or conclusive a well-founded ad hominem argument amounts
to as a criticism of one's argument depends on the rules
(in particular, the win-strategy) of the dialectical game
one is engaged in. In particular, note that the obligation game is cumulative in the sense defined by Woods and
Walton (1978a); it allows for no retractions of commitments. In this class of games, inconsistency of position
is much more serious for if the rules are based in classical logic, anything follows from an inconsistency. We
brought out this feature particularly in chapter 8.
Indeed, even in the relatedness game, demonstration of
inconsistency quickly allowed the finder of it to win.

In short, there are plenty of grounds for caution against
acquiescing too quickly in the doctrine that a well-
founded allegation of inconsistent position on the part
of one's opponent constitutes either a conclusive refutation or does not. This exclusive disjunction is a sophistical one and its exclusivity has to be handled carefully.
Rather, ad hominem is a more or less serious criticism or
conclusive refutation depending on the precise nature of
the rules of the particular dialectical framework one has
in mind.

If we remember our main case study of Appendix 1, McAuliffe's

arguments for pragmatic inconsistency were very well justified and supported by plausible arguments. However, we
must always remember that a criticism of this sort is a
unilateral dialectic. Although the position of the press
was represented, the individuals criticized were not
allowed "equal time" in McAuliffe's article for rebuttal.
An elementary condition of dialectic was not (at least
adequately or fully) met. However, let us look at another
case of ad hominem argumentation that is especially interesting as a case study in this connection, because the
attack is unusually effective.

Gordon R. Lowe's review of four works of Thomas Szasz,
reprinted here in Appendix 2, provides an interesting
example of ad hominem refutation at work. As Lowe puts
it, Szasz's books go straight for the jugular--they
severely and remorselessly criticize the fundamental practices and principles of psychiatry. Szasz describes the
typical psychiatric hospital as a "prison," and the science
of psychiatry as "incoherent rhetoric." However Lowe himself goes straight for the jugular, pointing out that Szasz
is himself a practicing psychiatrist and even a professor
of psychiatry. Lowe argues that if Szasz is right that
psychiatry is unscientific nonsense, then Szasz must be in
a position of professing unscientific nonsense to his
students, and practicing it on his patients.

In the last nine paragraphs, Lowe hammers home his ad
hominem attack on Szasz's position with a relentless array
of direct pragmatic inconsistencies. Szasz criticizes the
psychiatric establishment but himself belongs to it. What
Szasz teaches in his classes could scarcely be consistent
with what he writes in his books. Szasz criticizes his
colleagues, but does not apply these criticisms to himself.
Szasz nowhere tries to justify this position--a peculiarly
vulnerable one, it begins to seem.

The interesting aspect of Lowe's argument in particular is
that he shows no sign of yielding to the ad hominem fallacy
of arguing that because of these pragmatic inconsistencies
in Szasz's position, his argument against psychiatry is
wrong. Indeed in the fourth paragraph of the review he
concedes that Szasz's onslaught is "perfectly justified."
Given this careful reluctance to acquiesce in the fallacious ad hominem move of rejecting Szasz's argument per se,
is it conceivable that Lowe's argument is about as good an
example of a correct or successful ad hominem refutation as
you could want. If so, the pointed question is raised of

what precisely we mean by refutation in this context.

The fact that Szasz is a professor and practitioner of
psychiatry implies that he is committed to certain codes
of conduct. True, these codes are not formulated in
specific statements that Lowe has identified. But it is
part of the code of a professor to profess some coherent
knowledge or discipline. And it is a part of the code
of a physician not to harm his patients, say by using
medications or treatments that he knows to be ineffective
or possibly harmful. If Szasz argues in his books that
psychiatry is an incoherent discipline and an ineffective
or harmful mode of therapy, how can his means of earning
his living be consistent with his pronouncements in his
books? A good question, one that Szasz might be hard
pressed to respond to adequately.

The most effective and damaging allegations of inconsistency made in Dr. Lowe's arguments occur on the last two
pages. There are earlier claims that could be taken as
allegations of inconsistency, but instead of being act-
theoretic inconsistencies characteristic of the ad hominem
argument, like those in the last two pages, these three
earlier cited inconsistencies postulate inconsistent pairs
of propositions within Szasz's stated arguments. The
first pair is cited in the allegation, "He decries mental
illness as mythical, but accepts the reality of physical
illness and the medical model." Note that in this allegation and the subsequent two in the same passage, Dr. Lowe
does not explicitly claim that there is a contradiction.
Hence when we say there is an allegation we mean rather
that we propose to interpret the passage in question in
such a way that we postulate a suggestion or implicature
present to the effect that Szasz's argument is inconsistent. In fact, however, there is no inconsistency between
decrying mental illness as mythical (unreal) and accepting
physical illness as real. So we must be careful. Any
claim of erroneous or unsupported allegation on the part
of Dr. Lowe rests on a possibly tenuous claim of implicature.

The second allegation is found where Dr. Lowe writes,
"He [Szasz] castigates involuntary psychiatry as criminal
coercion, but accepts voluntary psychiatry as a game
played by consenting adults." Again there could be an
appearance of inconsistency here, but in fact there is
none, as the statement stands; the difference between
voluntary and involuntary treatment is, at least arguably,

a real one. The third case occurs where Dr. Lowe writes
that Szasz "ridicules the idea that the doctor is the
patient's agent, but accepts the doctor as altruistic
healer." Whether there is inconsistency here perhaps
depends on what is meant by "agent," but certainly if
there is inconsistency, it is far from obvious how it is
to be demonstrated.

Hence we suggest that these three allegations above, if
taken as accusations of inconsistency, are weak at best.
They are perhaps more charitably taken as hints of some
tensions--perhaps short of inconsistency--that Lowe
thinks represent questionable aspects of Szasz's position.
Clearly, however, they are not ad hominem allegations, at
least serious and well-founded ones like those in the
last two pages of Lowe's review.

In another place Lowe makes an allegation that, if taken
as an allegation of inconsistency, would seem to be
inadequately supported: "[Szasz] noisily abuses the
therapist who uses physical treatment to intervene because
suicide is not an illness, yet he regards psychotherapy
as unobjectionable, and indeed generally desirable."
There is certainly no inconsistency in rejecting physical
treatment while advocating nonphysical treatment, viz.,
psychotherapy. However, perhaps Lowe's point here is that
treatment of any sort for a nonillness is illogical or
inconsistent. But is it? Lowe offers no further argument
to show precisely which propositions are supposed to be
inconsistent.

Perhaps the inconsistency is to be established as follows.
Dr. Szasz's arguments take as a focal presumption the
proposition that psychiatry cannot be correctly described
as medical treatment because "mental illness is mythical."
However, he also asserts that voluntary psychiatric help
should be available to anyone who wants it, and that
psychotherapy is "unobjectionable and indeed generally
desirable" (p. 488). It seems, then, to be ostensibly
inconsistent both to denounce psychiatry as an incoherent
discipline and to support it as a discipline that should,
at least in some cases, be practiced. Perhaps Dr. Szasz
could justify exceptions, but surely Lowe is on warranted
grounds here to bring forward what at least appears to be
a prima facie inconsistency. Of course, as Lowe reports,
Szasz only supports voluntary psychiatry insofar as it is
a "harmless game," which seems to suggest only a weak and
qualified form of support.

As a corrective to the one-sidedness of many an ad hominem labelled as a fallacy by textbooks and other critics of arguments, it is well to be reminded that any ad hominem argument should be treated as an essentially two-way inter-action between participants in a game of dialogue. This reminder applies to Lowe's ad hominem criticisms of Szasz's position.

Because Szasz is a practicing psychiatrist who criticizes certain practices in his profession, Lowe asks how Szasz in good conscience can earn a living from the very profes-sion he deplores: "What excuse is there for a psychiatrist who exposes the delusion, sneers at it for twenty years, but keeps practicing it with his tongue in cheek?" Lowe, in effect, is arguing that Szasz, to be morally consistent, should either leave the profession or cease his attacks on its practices.

While I hope to show that Lowe has mounted a well-argued case for circumstantial inconsistency in Szasz's position, nevertheless I will try to show that the refutation is not conclusive, where conclusiveness would imply that Szasz is left no room for rebuttal. Of course, the conclusiveness of any purported refutation must depend on the rules of a particular game of disputation. In an obligation game of refutation by action-theoretic inconsistency, Szasz's posi-tion would quite possibly be refuted by Lowe's attack. But in a more symmetrical game of dialogue that allows for resolution of inconsistency, could Szasz have a way out?

Could Szasz not reply as follows, were he allowed to attempt to justify his position? "By staying in the profession, and continuing to write about the activities therein, I can do more good by bringing these questionable practices to light than by quitting my position. If I leave, people would be less likely to pay attention to my criticisms than they would to a psychiatrist who is not currently in the profession. I can do more for my cause by staying in the profession, thereby maintaining my sources, my information, my credentials, my position, and my credibility. Moreover, although I disagree with many practices of my profession, I feel that I am entitled to my opinions, and that giving up would only weaken my position for advocating reforms and improvements in the profession." We need not go fur-ther to indicate how Szasz could justify his position and perhaps contend with or defuse Lowe's charge of hypocrisy.

Perhaps Szasz, by judicious explanations, could convey to

his students his beliefs in the shortcomings of psychiatry as a discipline and practice, while still at the same time taking a constructive approach to dealing with these problems. Would we want to rule out the possibility that Szasz might be able to defend his position along these lines? I think not. Dialectic requires that he have a chance to reply, at least to try to justify his position. Thus Lowe's argument, while it is a strong one, should not be regarded as a conclusive refutation. In short, even the strongest and best-mounted ad hominem attack should not be treated as a conclusive ad hominem refutation if only one side of the dialectic is given.

In conversational disputations or written criticisms like book reviews, however, the problem with a fair adjudication of an argument is that the rules are not clearly stated or enforced, as they are in formal games of dialogue. In a book review, the author criticized rarely has an opportunity given to reply to his critic, and in fact from a point of view of dialectic such practices may be rightly regarded as, if not unfair, at least misleading by way of incompleteness of the argument. Although the criticism is made, and it may be a good one, the disputation is not complete until the defending party has a chance to reply. As we have seen, many a contradiction in an arguer's position can be resolved by further argument. A game of dialogue is only complete when both parties have been allowed, by mutual agreement, an adequate number of moves to make their cases.

We conclude, then, that Lowe's attack on Szasz's position is a good argument (as a well-argued attack), but that it should not be treated as a "good argument" in the dialectical sense of conclusive refutation of the opponent's position.

Another disputable aspect of Lowe's criticism is the extent to which it goes beyond the circumstantial ad hominem attack and into the area of the abusive ad hominem. Lowe freely makes use of a flamboyant and sarcastic language, for example, "The derisive titles of Szasz's books proclaim that he enters the psychiatric cathedral not to pray but to jeer . . . his chapter headings prick the skin and draw blood." Lowe's major objective, successfully executed, is to criticize Szasz's position, his conduct and pronouncements, but it may appear at times that he is attacking Szasz personally. However, while Lowe's comments are at times colorful and emotional, and do have a moral charge of

hypocrisy contained in them, they can be construed as
essentially criticisms of Szasz's reasoning. At least
this interpretation is legitimate consequent on the argument of this book that the charge of act-theoretic inconsistency can be a criticism of the argument and not merely
the arguer as an individual.

Our point is that an argument should not be treated merely
as a set of propositions so that the arguer himself is
entirely external to the argument. Rather, in dialectic,
the argument is defined as a pair of sets of propositions,
each indexed to a participant in the game of dialogue.
Thus each participant has a set of propositions identified
as his thesis and commitment-store (collectively, his
position). Thus a legitimate goal of criticism is the
establishment of an inconsistency--in some games an action-
theoretic sort of inconsistency--among the opponent's position propositions.

Despite these acknowledgments, however, an attack may
become sufficiently abusive and personal that its contribution to a legitimate circumstantial refutation becomes
questionable. For example, within his legitimate criticism
of what he takes to be Szasz's position, Lowe uses the
phrase, ". . . with a cynicsm that can only be described
as disgusting. . . ." Although emotionally titillating to
potential readers, this language verges on the questionable
abusive form of ad hominem.

Describing the evident inconsistency in teaching psychiatry
while severely criticizing its credentials as a discipline,
Dr. Lowe again resorts to some questionable metaphors: "To
remain in psychiatry while snarling at its evils is about
as graceful as a dog biting the hand that feeds it." The
basic criticism here is a good one, so we concede at least,
but one may well question whether this picturesque metaphor
is a fair way of making Lowe's point. Surely the unnecessary (but possibly very effective, rhetorically) abuse in
these passages is tending to the direction of the abusive
personal ad hominem attack.

Here then is a subtlety of note. The well-founded and
correct circumstantial ad hominem attack is blended in at
some junctures with the highly questionable abusive ad
hominem personal attack. A blanket condemnation or approval
of the argument as a whole would be premature and equivocal.
Analysis calls for a finer sorting of these elements.

It will throw considerable light on what is meant by a

refutation in a game of dialogue if we introduce some
basic structure adopted from Hintikka (1979). Let us say
that a basic game of dialogue has in the simplest case
two participants α and β, and each has his respective
thesis A_O and B_O. As the game proceeds, by a sequence of
question-and-answer moves, each party must try to prove
his thesis. The first one to prove his thesis, that is,
in the least number of moves, wins the game. This basic
game is symmetrical in the sense that the moves and the
objectives of both opponents are similar. In an asymmetrical game, such as the obligation game, one party may be
a defender of his position, the other an attacker of that
position. Here, the attacker wins if he refutes the opponent's position in a finite number of moves, the defender
wins if he defends against a successful refutation by
demonstration of inconsistency.

According to Hintikka, the basic core propositional structure of a game of dialogue is provided by classical logic.
We would of course insist, in the context of ad hominem
argumentation, on a nonclassical propositional structure
of proof, namely relatedness logic.

In a special sort of game of dialogue called a dispute,
the thesis A_O is the negation of the thesis B_O. That is,
the objectives of α and β in a dispute are strongly opposed
in just this sense. α proves his thesis A_O if and only if he
refutes (disproves) β's thesis B_O. And β proves his thesis
B_O if and only if he refutes (disproves) α's thesis A_O.

However, in games of dialogue there may be different types
of refutation. α may prove A_O by deducing it from his own
commitments A_O, A_1, . . . A_i, or he may disprove B_O by
deducing $\neg B_O (=A_O$ in a dispute) from B_O, B_1, . . . B_i, the
commitments of β. Both of these types of proof may be
called strong refutation in the sense that they count as
proofs that A_O is true or that B_O is false. However, in
weak refutation, α may show that β's thesis is not yet
proven by β's arguments, even if α has not shown by deduc-
tion that B_O is false.

Strong refutation, in some games of dialogue, counts as a
win for one person and as a loss for the other (in a zero-
sum game of dialogue). However, weak refutation may not
count as an outright win if the other party still has moves
remaining. Rather, weak refutation shifts the burden of
proof onto the other participant, meaning that this party
will lose if he fails to counter by resolving the criticism.

We can see, then, how in some games of dialogue a criticism can have a certain force in contributing to the
outcome of the game without, by itself as a single move,
constituting a conclusive refutation of the opponent's
position. Here, then, is the theoretical structure that
allows a proper evaluation of Lowe's argument. Although
we can evaluate it positively as a well-mounted ad hominem
criticism of Szasz's position, there is still room to
argue that it should not be evaluated as a conclusive and
strong refutation of the argument criticized.

CONCLUDING REMARKS ON AD HOMINEM ARGUMENTS

We saw in the preface that the Gricean implicature strategy of conversational analysis of cooperative contexts of
discourse that factors of relevance and causal connectedness are informal, background matters, external to struc-
turally well-defined (formal) truth-conditions. However,
by introducing a relatedness relation on sets of action
propositions and embedding the structure of these relations in a complete, sound, and applicable formal system
of logic, we have given a formal core structure to ad
hominem circumstantial reasoning. Is there a conflict
here?

It seems not, because more is involved in an ad hominem
refutation than the core allegation of circumstantial
inconsistency, even if it is justified as a certifiable
logical inconsistency in $\mathcal{S}$. For we saw in chapter 7 that
the dialogical context of the allegation is also part of
the refutation. Thus a successful refutation, even if
it is a demonstration of action-theoretic inconsistency
in the opponent's position, is still not the last word
in the argument. Rather, a successful refutation is
defined in relation to its objective of shifting the
burden of proof onto the attacked participant to remove
the inconsistency. Moreover, our case studies have shown
that in many cases the attack is only partially successful as a refutation, or even may be unsuccessful to the
point of being fallacious, so that much ad hominem reasoning is in the adjudication of such partial refutations.
As we saw, further dialectic is the method to fill in the
missing steps. Thus perhaps the Gricean approach is justified in presuming that much of the essential machinery of
even disputative conversation theory will have a degree
of informality. In practice, our case studies have shown
that ad hominem allegation needs a lot of tightening up

before the resources of our formal system can be fairly
and charitably brought to bear on a given argument in
order to determine whether the ad hominem attack is a
successful ad hominem refutation.

It is good now to amplify our thesis that much of the
prevailing standard treatment of ad hominem rests on the
superficial assumption that ad hominem allegations are
always, in some sense, fallacious. By now it is clear
that we cannot accept such an approach. Instead, we
have distinguished the following:

(1)   Ad hominem attack (allegation)--a disputant
       brings forward a set of propositions alleged
       to belong to the position of his opponent.
       Propositions belonging to the position of the
       opponent are very often propositions made true
       by something the opponent deliberately did, in
       the sense of belonging to his/her plan of
       action.

(2)   Ad hominem refutation--an attack becomes a
       successful refutation if the set of proposi-
       tions in (1) can be shown by the attacker to
       be inconsistent in the applicable system of
       logic. In the case of circumstantial action-
       theoretic arguments, a relatedness logic is
       the appropriate vehicle.

(3)   Ad hominem fallacy--a refutation can go badly
       wrong in a number of characteristic ways we
       have catalogued. A number of steps may need
       to be filled in. For example, the attacker
       may determine that A and ꟽB are part of his
       opponent's position, but instead of determin-
       ing A → B in that position to clinch the refu-
       tation, he may only find some indirect link-
       ages between A and B that need to be filled in
       by further steps. Or in another way of commit-
       ting an ad hominem fallacy, he may misdescribe
       A or B by an alternative act-description that
       is nonequivalent in such a fashion as to fail
       to yield an inconsistent set. In yet a third
       form of ad hominem fallacy, the attacker may
       secure a contradiction in the position of his
       opponent but then, in a non sequitur move,
       declare one member of the inconsistent set to
       be false or unjustified per se.

Our thesis, then, is that ad hominem is not always a

fallacy. Indeed, under the right conditions, we rule
that an ad hominem refutation can be successful. Hence
in our view, the ad hominem can be a correct form of
argument. Yet, if certain conditions fail to be met,
the refutation can fail to be correct, and hence be a
fallacious form of argument.

Does this mean that the ad hominem, when it is fallacious,
is formally invalid? Our dialogical approach suggests
that invalidity in 𝒥 is neither necessary nor sufficient
by itself for the fallaciousness of an ad hominem refutation. However, room for dispute on this question
remains open to the extent that choice of a formal dialectical system and the extent of the formality of that
system still remain open to us. Some further comments
on the range of systems open to us in the study of ad
hominem are therefore in order.

Our treatment of the ad hominem and related fallacies has
shown that the theory of the fallacies will be to a certain important but limited extent a formal theory. The
formal part, at least in its primary applications, will
not be classical logic. The informal part is modelled
in dialectical games of disputation. These games, however, also have a formal character, and to the extent
that ad hominem moves in dialectical disputation are
adequately modelled by formal dialectical games, ad
hominem refutations--the part of them over and above
their core propositional structure--can be studied formally as well. However, as Hamblin points out, dialectical games can be studied both as purely formal structures and as practical cases of actual argumentative
interchange. Therefore, in adjudicating on case studies
of actual argumentation, a degree of informality is
appropriate.

In evaluating actual disputations, therefore, it is often
best to ask not whether the argument is simply valid or
invalid as it stands, but rather whether it is vulnerable
(to ad hominem attack). Or in the case of an attack, one
should sometimes ask not whether or not it is a fallacious
or correct argument, as it stands, but whether it is
tenable as an allegation (attack), perhaps with some further filling in. It may be defined as tenable if it is
not demonstrably fallacious by its opponent as it stands,
and if by further dialogue it can be made into a successful ad hominem refutation of the opponent's position.
Such judgments are therefore sometimes most charitably

made as being relative to further continuation of a dialectical sequence.

Thus Massey's prognostication that the standard treatment
of the fallacies fails by way of being (a) too vague and
(b) putting on undue emphasis on the negative aspect
(invalidity) is borne out by our findings. Understanding
the negative element of ad hominem fallacies, we saw,
involved mapping the dialectical geography of attacks,
defenses, refutations, and justifications of positions.
There is both a positive and a negative element. In
studying allegations of positional inconsistency, the
positive aspect of validity of action-theoretic inferences
is of key importance in providing well-written propositional guidelines for propositional validity. Massey is
therefore certainly right that the present state of development of fallacy theory is in its tottering infancy.
However, we believe we have shown how his gloomy suggestions that no systematic and coherent theory of the fallacies is possible may be offset by our positive analysis
in the case of the ad hominem.

Further work in this area should utilize the formal
methods of dialectical games of the types developed by
Lorenzen, Hamblin, Rescher, and Mackenzie. But the study
of ad hominem refutations also calls for the pragmatic
step of applying theories of the structure of action
propositions developed by Pörn and Davidson, and applying
nonclassical systems like those of Epstein. Additionally,
the union of logic and actions is nicely modelled by some
recent work of Krister Segerberg (1982). At least in the
case of ad hominem, we hope to have shown that the study
of the fallacies is not lacking in applicable theoretical
resources. Finally, we should mention deontic logics as
a resource for further study.

Certainly we have brought out many subtleties of the moves
made in realistic bits of argumentation in order to attack
or defend a position in the ad hominem manner. A pragmatic structure adequate to model or regulate these moves
of argumentation is clearly going to need several components of increasing richness. Yet we have seen that the
basic framework we need to support these various components
is that of the logical dialogue-game. Does our study of
ad hominem argumentation indicate that one particular
class or type of dialogue-game is best suited as a basic
framework? This is the question of the next chapter.

11

Structures of Logical Dialogue-Games

Out of our pragmatic studies of ad hominem realistic
specimens of disputes has arisen a need to understand
the move and countermove of argument as a dialectical
interchange. We have found that in order to study ad
hominem reasoning perspicuously, we need to distinguish
attack from criticism and refutation, and work from
there to studying why, how, or whether ad hominem is a
fallacy in different dialectical contexts.

The games of dialogue we used for these purposes were
certainly revealing, far more helpful than any other way
of approaching ad hominem as a fallacy of argument has
been, or perhaps could be. But these formal games admit
of certain limitations of design, and it is time to discuss some of these limitations.

HAMBLIN AND HINTIKKA GAMES REVIEWED

The Hamblin-Mackenzie games were the most valuable tools
in setting out the basic categories of ad hominem moves
in argumentation. However, a basic limitation of these
games is that they do not have clearly or decisively
formulated win-loss rules as part of the game itself.
Consequently, in such a game it is often not clear what
the respective objectives of the players are supposed
to be in making their moves. It seems to follow that
utilizing such a game to define precisely yet fairly the
point at which an ad hominem attack should be ruled
either a failure (fallacy) or a successful refutation of
an opponent's argument is not a hopeful project.

The problem is that the Hamblin games lack a well-defined
win-loss rule to determine the strategy of a player in
making the sequence of moves he makes. It is not made
clear by any rules of the game (H) what each player's
objective of play should be in order to win an instance
of the game. Perhaps in the end it should not be too
important who wins or loses the game. But for purposes
of ruling on ad hominem disputes of the sort we have considered, win-loss criteria would seem to be required in
order to enable us to know when an ad hominem refutation
should be thought successful.

Of course, not all the games that Hamblin considers lack
win-loss rules. In the Obligation Game, the one who

commits an inconsistency in his replies immediately loses
the game. But, as we saw in our case studies, this rule
may not always be appropriate or most helpful in sorting
out ad hominem allegations and disputes.

Hamblin (1977) writes "that the purpose of the dialogue
is the exchange of information among participants"
(p. 137). What precisely counts as "exchange of information" is not defined, but Hamblin's general presumption
that games of dialogue should be "information-oriented"
(his term, p. 137), does affect how he designs (H), and
that affects how fallacies are analyzed in (H). For
example, Hamblin suggests that there is no point in asking
a question if one is already committed to one of the
answers (p. 137), and the rules of Hamblin games tend to
reflect this information-oriented design of rules for
questioning.

But the problem is that these linkages are too loose, and
one needs to know how the purpose of a game, its informa-
tion-orientation, specifically affects the strategy of
the players.

The Hintikka games of dialogue do not share this open-
ended quality in win-loss determination. Quite to the
contrary, the win-loss rule for a Hintikka game of logical
dialogue is precisely defined. A player wins if, and only
if, he deduces his own thesis from his opponent's commitments. In this regard, a Hintikka game is precisely
regulated. It is quite clear how the objective of each
player is set. And therefore, in general outline, it is
possible for each player to plan a strategy to achieve
that outcome within the rules of the game. Consequently,
the overall direction and nature of play in a Hintikka
game can be clearly understood.

In a Hintikka game, trapping one's opponent in a positional inconsistency is a preferred strategic move. If
the logic element of such a game is classical logic, the
next step for the winning player is to prove his thesis
from the inconsistency. If the logic is a nonclassical
logic, like relatedness logic, such a strategy is not
directly available. Yet if some relation between the
thesis to be proved and the set of propositions that make
up the inconsistency can be introduced into the opponent's
position by further dialogue, a win is similarly assured.

In modelling fallacies like the ad hominem fallacy, the

Hintikka structure for dialogues therefore is a theoretical advance over the Hamblin systems, in one decisive way
at any rate. In Hamblin's game (H), if the questioner
poses a yes-no question of the form 'S?' the answerer has
three options. He can answer 'S' (yes), '⌐S' (no), or
'No commitment S.' The third option has the worrisome
consequence that a skeptical player can always prevent
the other player from winning or exchanging information
by the strategy of always replying "No commitment" to
every question; hence the problem posed for (H) by the
lack of win-loss rules. What happens if a sophistical
player always answers "No commitment"? There appears to
be no effective way of excluding or otherwise managing
this sort of strategy in (H). But this problem is a
reflection of the failure in (H) to define "information
orientation" in win-loss rules formulated as part of (H)
that must be followed by the players.

This problem is resolved in the Hintikka (1979, p. 237)
structure for games of dialogue by the following rules
of questioning. A "tableau" is partly like a score sheet
that we may think of as similar to a commitment-slate in
(H).[1]

> Interrogative moves can be of either of two
> different kinds.
> (i) A move may consist in a question addressed
> by the player who is making the move to his
> opponent. The opponent provides a direct full
> answer to the question. The answer is added
> to the list of theses which the addressee of
> the question is defending. It is entered into
> the left column of the tableau of the player
> making the move and into the right column of
> the other player. The presupposition of the
> question is added to the theses of the player
> who is making the move. . . .
> (ii) In an interrogative move, the opponent
> may refuse to answer. Then the negation of
> the presupposition of the question is added to
> one's opponent's theses.

In effect, what this set of rules means is that the 'No
commitment' option is not open to an answerer. He may
answer yes or no, but if he refuses to answer by a yes or
no, the negation of the presupposition of the question is
added to his commitment-set. Thus Hintikka dialogues are
less open than Hamblin or Mackenzie dialogues. The Hamblin

'No commitment' response is not as fully available in the
Hintikka dialogues. In effect, the answerer may be forced
to commit himself either to the presupposition of a question or its negation.

That the questioner should have the power to pose questions
with this much bite is an advantageous feature in modelling
certain kinds of dialogue-interchanges. The questioner
can press forward with revealing questions and thus the
game must move along rapidly if the questioner is skillful.
On the other hand, we have seen that the management of
question-asking fallacies and ad hominem criticisms suggests some kinds of dialogue-interchanges where the questioner should not always be allowed to press so hard without allowing the answerer defenses or escape routes if they
can be justified. In erotetic logic, one defines the presupposition of a yes-no question 'p?' as the disjunction
'p ∨ ⌐p'. But the negation of this disjunction is '⌐(p ∨ ⌐p)'
which is equivalent (in classical logic, but not relatedness
logic) to 'p ∧ ⌐p.' Hence in a Hintikka game with rules
strong enough to yield classical logic, an answerer who
refuses to answer any yes-no question could be shown by his
opponent to have become committed to an inconsistency.

Our previous case studies of the fallacies might lead us to
question the universal applicability of this way of managing
questions in regard to some of the fallacies. We might not
always want to leave this opening to a criticism of inconsistency of position as a burden on an answerer who fails
to respond "yes" or "no." Perhaps some milder alternatives
should be explored as well. If the answerer in a game of
dialogue is not allowed the 'No commitment' option freely
enough, in effect he may be forced by the questioner who
asks him a yes-no question to reason as follows: "I have
to answer yes or no, but I do not have any proof which
answer is correct if one is. Either way I answer, I commit
the ad ignorantiam of arguing from my lack of knowledge to
a definite yes or no" (see Woods and Walton [1978b]).

Clearly a lot turns here on how we define presupposition of
a question. In the usual approach to erotetic logic, presupposition is defined in relation to so-called propositional questions, where the relevant alternatives are propositions. Hintikka (1976) is, however, primarily concerned
with wh-questions, where the relevant alternatives are
values of a bound variable. That is, a question like 'Who
lives here?' poses a set of alternative instantiations of
the open sentence, 'x lives here.' According to Hintikka

(p. 27), the presupposition of this question should be
given as '($\exists$x)(x lives here).'   Thus the presupposition
of the spouse-beating question 'Have you stopped beating
your spouse?' is ($\exists$x)(you stopped beating your spouse at
x), where values of x are moments of time.   This approach
to managing the spouse-beating question in dialogue means
that the participant who refuses to answer claims, in
effect, that there is no such time.

I am not sure yet how this approach can be extended
towards a solution to the pragmatics of the spouse-beating
fallacy or to ad hominem dialogues, but my own limited
concerns in the previous chapters have been with propositional logic and propositional questions and dialogue-
games.   Moreover, our case studies suggest the interest of
a weaker variant of Hintikka's dialogue-structure where
refusal to answer need not always commit one to a denial
of the presupposition of the question asked.

What we shall want to move towards, then, is a Hintikka
dialogue-structure in basic outline with a somewhat different type of question-rule as an option for some contexts
of dialogue.   Hintikka's own proposal of extending games
of dialogue to take into account the tacit knowledge of a
participant provides a clue.

Let us review the game (Hδ) utilized in chapter 7 as a
basic structural model of dialogical argument.   In (Hδ),
'No commitment' was freely allowed as a response to any
question, in the Hamblin style.   Now ad hominem arguments
stand or fall in the consistency of a player's position at
a stage of the game.   There were two kinds of positional
consistency recognized.   One, inconsistency of commitments,
where a player is committed to A and also 7A is included
in his set of commitment-statements.   The other, ambivalence,
occurs where a player replies 'No commitment A' when in
fact he has A as one of his public commitments.

The problem is how to curb the 'No commitment' response in
a nonarbitrary way or at least a way that does not cause
question-asking problems or otherwise lead to difficulties
in the management of ad hominem replies, criticisms and
dialogues.

In the Obligation Game, this problem is resolved by ruling
that any player who commits an inconsistency immediately
loses the game.   But as we saw, that solution is rather
drastic to be as generally useful as we would like.   Could

the players be regulated to manage their inconsistencies
of position in a gentler way?

Now in the Hintikka framework, we have a notion of strategy. A player might hope to trap his opponent into a
subtle inconsistency in $\mathcal{S}$ so that he can have suitable
premisses for proving his own thesis by the rules of $\mathcal{S}$
from his opponent's commitments. But obvious inconsistencies are not useful if the opponent is moderately careful
in his strategy as well. Could we then structure the
rules so that one player, a questioner, has to point out
to the answerer any obvious inconsistencies of position
brought in by the answerer's reply, and ask the answerer
to resolve the inconsistency? Moreover, it might be part
of the game that the answerer has to resolve such an inconsistency one way or another.

This approach would mean that the 'No commitment' response
to a question would be regulated to a certain extent by
the rules of questioning and answering. A certain "surface
rationality" is thereby built into the play of the participants in this new type of game. A player's position does
not have to be consistent. For example, it could contain
A → B, A, and ⅂B without either player noticing or having
to take this inconsistency of position into account in a
compulsory next move. But if a player replies 'No commitment A' when in fact he is committed to A, the other player
must ask him to resolve the inconsistency. And then the
first player must make a choice. He must reject either A
or ⅂A or lose the game immediately.

This approach would tighten up (H$\mathcal{S}$). It would be stricter
than Hamblin's structure but looser than Hintikka's in its
regulation of 'No commitment' moves in question answering.
It seems a suitable way to handle contradictions in dialogues as far as <u>ad</u> <u>hominem</u> dialogues are concerned. But
of course it is not the only way.

In this new sort of game then, direct ambivalences or
inconsistencies in a player's position must be challenged
by the other player and resolved by the first player.[2]
Thus, some but not all inconsistencies or ambivalences are
allowed in play. There is also another way <u>ad</u> <u>hominem</u>
argumentation suggests an enrichment of (H$\mathcal{S}$) to which we
now turn.

DARK-SIDE COMMITMENT STORES

In managing ad hominem allegations and disputes, we saw
that the main problem is in determining whether or not a
statement at issue really does belong to the position of
a disputant. In practice, many arguments take place in
realistic circumstances where one player does not know
the commitments of the other, or perhaps does not even
fully know his own position in the argument. Yet most
often in arguments we do have some plausible even if
perhaps dim idea of where we or our opponents stand in
an argument on a topic. Usually, none of us comes to an
argument with a blank commitment-slate. But at least at
the beginning of the argument, it is not entirely clear
where we stand, or where our commitment precisely comes
down as a public set of statements or theses.

To take yet another quite ordinary example of ad hominem
argument, consider the following objection: "You, a
Catholic, of all people, think that you can have an abortion because your fetus has a birth defect. Abortion is
contrary to the Catholic position, and you're being inconsistent if you think you can make an exception in your own
case!" This criticism can be nicely analyzed by the
methods now familiar by their use on many similar examples
in preceding chapters. But this example raises a difficulty in the application of those methods common to the
other case studies as well. How do we in fact determine
what is the position of the Catholic church on this issue?

In fact, the problem is that, realistically speaking, we
cannot really claim to know what the position of the
Catholic church on abortion is, from our point of view as
evaluators of this ad hominem criticism. We cannot realistically presume that we are all equipped to give defini-
tive answers on Catholic casuistic queries in moral
theology. It would seem that in some, perhaps very
restricted circumstances, abortions could be ruled permissible by Catholic moral teachings. But exposing the fuller
structure of the official Catholic position on this issue
would be a further undertaking.

Thus the position of the arguers is really that both have
some idea of what the Catholic position is. Both know and
agree that the Catholic position is a stand against abortion. But what that stand comes down to, in specific
instances where exceptions may or may not be permissible,
is not known. Specific commitments of the position are at

best a matter of plausibility or conjecture, perhaps best
resolved or clarified by further argument and dialectic.

Whether the criticism of inconsistency is fairly justifiable depends, moreover, on what the position is of the
person allegedly considering abortion. This defender of
a position, let us call her Smith, must try to defend her
position as a Catholic, depending on how she interprets
the Catholic teachings on this matter as it affects her
case. It could even be, for example, that the Catholic
position is currently being discussed and modified by the
church, that it is currently open to dispute in respect
to certain types of cases. What matters, then, is Smith's
position as she takes herself to be a practicing Catholic.
Can she defend her position against this criticism or not?

Realistically speaking, Smith may not know very clearly
what her own position is. Perhaps she had not really
thought very deeply about her commitments as a Catholic
on this issue and what these implied, given the shock of
her recent discovery about the birth defect. True, there
is a definite set of statements in official church pronouncements that help to define the Catholic position,
but she only has a general idea of what these are. She
knows that Catholic theology is against killing and for
the flourishing of life. She knows that there may be no
obligation to insist on the preservation of life in certain circumstances, however, if such an insistence may
constitute a grave burden of suffering in hopeless circumstances. But in relation to her own specific circumstances and that of her baby, Smith is not able to spell
out more fully the Catholic position, or how it should
best be interpreted.

And if you think of it, that is most often the situation
in all the ad hominem criticisms we have studied. The
arguer knows some of his opponent's commitments quite
definitely, but the opponent's fuller position on the
issue may not be known, and may only begin to emerge as
the argument unfolds. Moreover, one's own position may
be clear in some respects, but extremely murky on others.
One finds oneself hotly defending commitments that, before
the argument, one did not think important or even realized
one had. In fact most arguments are curiously revealing
and informative precisely by virtue of more sharply articulating one's dimly held commitments.[3]

In the present case, it may be that Smith has many commitments as a practicing Catholic and as a thoughtful and

concerned person on the subject of abortion and the preservation of life. No doubt, her critic also has many
deeply held commitments relevant to this issue as well.
But neither may know precisely what these commitments are
until their tenability is tested in the heat of argument.

In a discussion in the Logic Seminar of Victoria University of Wellington on this topic, Max Cresswell proposed
that we might think of the commitment-set of a player as
having a "dark side" as well as a "light side." Some
examples of games of dialogue incorporating this idea
have been studied in Walton (1984). We remember that in
the game (H𝛿) in chapter 7, all commitments were thought
to be on a public slate, after the fashion of Hamblin
games. By this conception, the light side contains the
initial commitments of the player, plus all the commitments he has incurred by the commitment-rules during the
course of the game. The dark side contains commitments
not known to the player or his opponents in disputation.
But the commitments on the dark side are a definite set
of statements. Moreover, they play a role in the game
because certain commitment-rules dictate that, under
certain circumstances of play, a statement is transferred
from the dark side to the light side.

The motivation of bringing in dark-side commitment-sets
is that in many familiar arguments we begin and end with
the same set of statements, perhaps feeling that the argument really has not gone anywhere. Yet if we think of it,
such arguments are often curiously revealing in that they
more clearly articulate or make us aware of commitments
we or our dialogue partners hold deeply, but have not
been brought out until the argument took place.

Hintikka's approach sharpened the Hamblin notion of a
game of dialogue by bringing in strategic rules to define
what counts as a win and loss. But perhaps Hamblin is
right in the end that if such games are to model realistic dialogues or manage the fallacies in a constructive
way, the game should be information oriented. Perhaps
the important thing should not be who wins or loses, at
least entirely, but what the players learn from the game.
In practice, it is often much easier for an arguer to
defend his position if he has fewer commitments, a simpler
position to defend against criticisms. This ease or
difficulty of winning the argument varying with the richness of one's commitments could or perhaps should be
reflected in the nature of the game itself. At any rate,

this new way of structuring commitment management in games of dialogue seems much more favorable if our aim is to model realistically ad hominem positional criticisms and fallacies.

When we say that this dark slate is not known to the players, we do not intend some psychological interpretation of it as lurking in the recesses of the player's mind or some such thing. We agree fully with Hamblin that there is no place for this sort of psychologism in logical games of dialectic. The dark-side commitment-set is simply a set of statements; no more, no less. The only difference between our approach and Hamblin's in this regard is that the dark-side set is not on public view to the players. Members of it only become known to the players during play of the game, according to commitment-rules regulating the transfer of statements from the dark side to the light side of a player's commitment-set.

THE DIALOGUE-GAME 𝒮BZ

The proposed new way of structuring dialogue ties together all the elements we have now found useful. In this new style of logical game, we will have (1) relatedness propositional calculus as a logic element, (2) dark-side commitment-stores for the players, and (3) regulation of insertion and erasure of a player's commitments governed by challenge to resolve surface inconsistency or ambivalence. The way in which the last two elements are combined is through the adoption of a new type of rule, below.

> (RDS)   If a player states 'No commitment S' and S is in the dark side of his commitment-store, then S is immediately transferred into the light side of his commitment-store.

Adoption of an (RDS)-type rule means that regulation of 'No commitment' answers relates to the dark side of a player's position. Below is given a logical game of dialogue including (1), (2), (3), and (RDS).

The Game 𝒮BZ

Locution Rules

1. Statements: Statement-letters, S, T, U, . . . are permissible locutions and truth-functional compounds of statement-letters.

2. <u>Withdrawals</u>: 'No commitment S' is the locution
   for withdrawal (retraction) of a statement.
3. <u>Questions</u>: The question 'S?' asks the hearer
   whether or not he wants to reply that S is true.
4. <u>Challenges</u>: The challenge 'Why S?' requests some
   statement that can serve as a basis of proof for S.
5. <u>Resolutions</u>: The resolution 'S, ⅂S?' requests the
   hearer to select exactly one of the pair {S, ⅂S}.

<u>Dialogue Rules</u>

1. Each speaker takes his turn to move by advancing
   exactly one locution at each move.
2. A question 'S?' must be followed by (a) a statement 'S,' (b) a statement '⅂S,' or (c) 'No commitment S.'
3. 'Why S?' must be followed by (a) 'No commitment S'
   or (b) some statement 'T.'
4. For a speaker legally to pose a resolution request
   'S, ⅂S?' the hearer must be committed to at least
   one of the pair {S, ⅂S}.
5. A (legal) resolution request must be followed by
   a statement 'S' or a statement '⅂S.'
6. If a statement S and also its negation ⅂S become
   included in the light side of a player's commitment-
   store, the opposing player must pose a resolution
   request 'S, ⅂S?' at his next free move.
7. If a speaker states 'No commitment S' but S is in
   his light-side commitment-store, the hearer must
   pose a resolution request 'S, ⅂S?' at his next move.

<u>Commitment Rules</u>

1. After a player makes a statement, S, it is included
   in his commitment-store.
2. After the withdrawal of S, the statement S is
   deleted from the speaker's commitment-store.
3. 'Why S?' places S in the hearer's commitment-store
   unless it is already there or unless the hearer
   immediately retracts his commitment to S.
4. Every statement as shown by the speaker to be an
   immediate consequence of statements that are commitments of the hearer then becomes a commitment
   of the hearer's and is included in his commitment-
   store.
5. No commitment that is an immediate consequence of
   statements that are previous commitments of the
   hearer may be withdrawn by the hearer, unless the
   speaker agrees.

6. If a player states 'No commitment S' and S is
    included in the dark side of his commitment-store,
    then S is immediately transferred into the light
    side of that player's commitment-store.
7. Whenever a statement S goes into the light side
    of a player's commitment-store, if its negation
    ⅂S is on the dark side of that player's store, it
    must immediately be transferred to the light side.
    Similarly, S must go from the dark (if it is there)
    to the light side as soon as ⅂S appears on the
    light side.
8. No commitment may be added to or deleted from a
    player's store except by one of the above seven
    commitment rules.

Strategic Rules

1. Any player who makes a move other than those per-
    mitted by the seven dialogue rules immediately
    loses the game.
2. The first player to show that his own thesis is an
    immediate consequence of a set of light-side com-
    mitments of the other player wins the game.
3. Both players agree in advance that the game will
    terminate after a finite number of moves.
4. If nobody wins as in (2) by the point agreed on
    in (3), the game is a draw. Or if it becomes
    evident to all the players that the dark sides of
    their commitment-stores are empty, the game may be
    ended by universal consent. In the latter case,
    the players may agree to maintain their light-side
    commitment-stores and begin with a new set of dark-
    side commitment-stores.

Clearly, there are games that have (RDS) or an equivalent
rule and yet are weaker than 𝒥BZ. We might have a game
otherwise like 𝒥BZ except that it lacks commitment rule
C(7) so that a player's total commitment can contain
direct inconsistencies of the form 'S, ⅂S,' provided one
of the pair is on the dark side and the other on the light
side. Or we might have games with or without C(7) but
lacking one or both dialogue rules D(6) and D(7). In these
games, an answerer is not forced by the rules to resolve
his opponent's immediate inconsistencies or ambivalences.
In these latter games, the onus is on the one whose position is directly inconsistent to sort out and reject these
surface inconsistencies at the peril of remaining in a
weak strategic position. Indeed if S is related to the

opponent's conclusion, such a directly, positionally
inconsistent player will lose the game at his opponent's
next move, if the opponent uses his best strategy. However, in the other sort of games, those having D(6) and
D(7), the onus is on the questioner to challenge immediately and resolve any surface inconsistency in an
answerer's position. If he fails to so challenge when
the rules D(6) and D(7) dictate, he immediately loses
the game.

These families of games represent different ways of handling positional inconsistencies. Some make play easier
for the answerer, some make it easier for the questioner.
Which games are the most natural or best to model and
manage ad hominem argumentation? Our case studies have
suggested that the onus of defense against positional
inconsistency lies on the one whose position is inconsistent. This approach would suggest that the most usual
framework of argument for many ad hominem disputes would
be the weakest in the family of games considered above.
This is the game ↯BV, the game that has all the rules of
↯BZ except L(5), D(4), D(5), D(6), D(7), and C(8). In
↯BV, there is no onus on the questioner to resolve or
point out direct inconsistencies in the answerer's position. An answerer incurs any such inconsistencies or
ambivalences at his peril.

↯BV is perhaps less friendly or less rational than ↯BZ,
depending on how you look at it. It represents more of
a disputational than a cooperative type of play and
strategy than the stronger games ascending up to ↯BZ.
Yet any of these ways of handling surface inconsistencies
and ambivalences is quite legitimate, depending on the
context of argument.

If the participants in argument are careful and correct,
they will make clear at the outset of the argument which
game they are playing, that is, which of the above sets
of rules apply. However, as we have abundantly seen, in
the ordinary marketplace of argumentation, the rules may
not be at all clear to the participants. Small wonder
that ad hominem allegations too often degenerate into
unresolvable incoherence or vicious illogicality and are
never adequately resolved by arguers.

These games provide a structure that gives us the answer
to the question, What is wrong with positional inconsistency or ambivalence? What is wrong from a point of view

of a participant in a logical game of dialogue is that
any inconsistent position he adopts can be effectively
used in his opponent's strategy to defeat him by the
rules of the game. For example, if Black is committed
to A, A → B, and ᒣB as part of his position, White can
win the game, assuming that modus ponens is a rule of
inference of the game. In the axiomatization for ᔔ given
by Epstein (1979), the rule of modus ponens is an inference rule. At his next free move, White can show, by
applying the rule 'A, A → B, therefore B,' that B is a
commitment of Black. Now let us say that T is White's
thesis that he is set to prove. White can ask Black:
"Do you accept B v T?" Presumably, Black must answer
yes because he has already conceded B, presuming that B
is related to T. If Black does not answer yes, White
can ask him "Are B and T related?" Here Black should
answer no if he uses prudent strategy, but suppose that
B is related to T and White concedes it. Since disjunctive syllogism is also a theorem of ᔔ and a rule of ᔔBV,
White should argue: "You accept B v T, and you accept
ᒣB, ergo you must accept T, my thesis." Here, White
wins the game.

What is wrong with positional inconsistency, therefore,
especially in a set of commitments that are related to
each other, is that they leave one in a weak strategic
position in a game of ᔔBV. So why is ad hominem a fallacy? It is a fallacy essentially because ᔔBV and its
extensions represent a certain standard of rational argument, a dynamic sense of argument having to do with the
proprieties and strategies of allegations of positional
inconsistency, replies to these allegations, and criticisms and refutations within the rules of questioning
and answers that are consequent upon such allegations.
In short, we now have a general framework for managing
positional inconsistency.

POLITICAL DEBATE AND THE TWO WRONGS FALLACY

A kind of argument often described as a fallacy by current informal logic texts is called "two wrongs make a
right." According to Kahane for example, this fallacy
involves the inference from one's opponent doing some
evil to the conclusion that, therefore, it is all right
for me to do it as well. It is not clear on the surface
precisely what the fallacy is alleged to be in this sort
of reasoning, if there is one. And some sort of moral

point would seem to be involved as well, which makes one
wonder whether the error, if there is one involved, could
be more of a moral shortcoming than any specifically logical fallacy.

Leo Groarke (1982, p. 10) cites two interesting cases for
discussion that, he thinks, exemplify fallacious instances
of two wrongs reasoning.

> Suppose, for example, that some government
> accuses another of subjecting dissenters to
> torture and other abuses that contravene the
> United Nations charter on human rights. In
> response to such charges, one can imagine
> the government in question replying that the
> nation which has leveled the charges employs
> similar--or worse--practices in its treatment
> of dissent. Here we have a clear case of
> two wrongs reasoning which illustrates why
> such reasoning is sometimes illegitimate, for
> the government in question does not deny such
> practices, but simply directs attention to
> other cases. In reply, it may be said that
> even if its charges could be substantiated,
> this doesn't make abusive practices acceptable,
> and does not excuse the acts in question. At
> most, it shows that both governments are
> guilty of the wrongs such acts entail.

Quite clearly this example is nothing other than a classical case of circumstantial ad hominem refutation. The
replying government spokesman alleges that his critic is
circumstantially inconsistent: "You accuse my country of
torture, but your government is itself involved in torture
of dissidents. Your criticisms indict us for carrying out
the very same practices you yourselves engage. Ergo,
your position is inconsistent." It seems then that the
so-called two wrongs fallacy is nothing other than the
classical circumstantial ad hominem.

Given our previous analysis of the ad hominem, we are now
in a position to see precisely what is or is not fallacious
in the inferences supposedly drawn in this particular
example. First, it should be remarked that it may be quite
legitimate for the respondent to mount a criticism of circumstantial inconsistency if in fact the government in
question has committed the alleged acts of torture. As
we have argued throughout, there need be no fallacy per se

in such an attack or refutation.

However, the inherent possibilities of fallacious inference present in ad hominem refutations are certainly worth
remarking on in this instance as well. It does not follow,
for example, as Groarke rightly points out, that the
abusive practices in question have been shown in themselves
to be acceptable or justified. From the refutation of the
opponent's position, the falsehood of his conclusion by
itself is not thereby demonstrated, as the analysis of the
classical ad hominem refutation clearly shows us. In
short, then, the first example cited by Groarke is precisely the now-familiar ad hominem refutation.

Where Groarke goes astray in his analysis is that he overlooks that the refutation by circumstantial inconsistency
could itself be a correct or at least not fallacious move
in argument. What is good in his analysis is the percep-
tion that it is incorrect to conclude directly from this
circumstantial inconsistency to the proposition that torture by the one party is in itself an acceptable or justifiable action. For although both governments may be
guilty of the wrong of torture, the one may also be in the
absurd position of committing acts of torture while at the
same time condemning all acts of torture as wrong and
indefensible. That inconsistency of position is in itself
worth criticizing, or so it has been contended by this
analysis of ad hominem disputation. What needs to be added
to Groarke's analysis, then, are the various possibilities
of inference involved in this ad hominem disputation, some
fallacious and others not.

Much the same type of analysis is applicable to the second
example given by Groarke, quoted directly from Kahane
(1976, p. 29).

> Senator Robert Dole, then Republican National
> Committee Chairman, was guilty of two wrongs
> make a right when he defended President Nixon
> against charges of impropriety in the ITT
> case. (The charge was that ITT had received
> favors in an important antitrust suit in
> return for its huge donation to Nixon's 1972
> reelection campaign.) Dole's counter-attack
> was to schedule a news conference to disclose
> "improper activities involving the Democratic
> National Convention involving vast sums of
> money improperly received from big business."

> Dole hoped his attack would take some heat
> off Nixon, and it did until the Watergate
> scandal brought ITT back into the public
> eye.

Groarke is justified in his allegation that Dole's attempt
to excuse Nixon is fallacious. But only on the assumption
that Dole's sole conclusion is that Nixon was guilty of no
impropriety. What is overlooked is that Dole may be
making a legitimate dialectical move if he is justified
in his claim that the Democrats are themselves engaging
in the same actions that they condemn. Such a counterattack may be justifiable as a move in a logical game of
dialogue, and of course need not be fallacious in itself.

In short, then, it seems that the so-called two wrongs
fallacy is nothing else but the very paradigm of the
circumstantial ad hominem refutation, containing the
classical possibilities of ad hominem fallacies. Any
further concern with two wrongs as a separate fallacy
would therefore seem to be redundant. We can now see
that it is simply a special case of the classical ad
hominem pattern of criticism.

Political debate in parliaments, congresses, and legislatures tends to be heavily positional in its argumentation. It is virtually always constrained and regulated
by the position of the speaker's party and the position
of the adversary parties. In democratic assemblies, all
argumentation is set against a triangle of objectives and
constraints.

perceived position
or opinion of voters

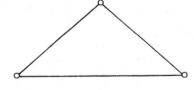

position of   position of
speaker's   opponent party
party   (or parties)

This triangular analysis is often a simplification, since
there may be a multiplicity of other positions necessary
to take into account. Various lobbies and pressure groups

outside one's party may have visible positions that need
to be taken into account. Sometimes a morally courageous
congressman or member of parliament may argue contrary to
his party's position and follow the lonely path of his
conscience or his own argument, most often thereby drawing fire from both sides. Nevertheless, a good deal of
political argumentation can only be understood and fairly
evaluated by studying its positional relationships on the
model of the triangle above.

Usually ad hominem criticism of an opponent's position
amounts to an allegation that some action or commitment of
the opponent is inconsistent with that position. However,
criticism based on an adversary's position can take
various forms. In one case of political argumentation, a
member of the Canadian House of Commons criticized an
opposing parliamentarian's recommendation on the basis
that it was implied by that opposing parliamentarian's
position. In Hansard (Canada: House of Commons Debates)
one member criticized the argument of another on the topic
of juvenile offenders (May 17, 1982, p. 17494).

> I suspect that the secret of the hon. member
> for Burnaby, certainly, is that he enjoys
> having that kind of a state role in juvenile
> affairs, that he wants to have a state enter-
> prise in the juvenile system and to move into
> those areas which are properly the family
> areas. I suspect that that has more to do
> with ideology than it has to do with the wel-
> fare or prescient understanding of where the
> children or the young people are at.

This argument appears to be of the ad hominem sort, but
the critic is saying, I think, that the member for Burnaby's
advice is suspect precisely because it does follow logically
from his ideological position. This criticism could be in
effect saying "If you don't accept his position, don't
accept his advice in this instance either." Or it could
amount to the allegation "His conclusion is merely reflexive
party line advocacy, and no result of dealing with the
real problem." In either case, the criticism is an ad
hominem attack.

Political argumentation very often is less concerned with
the internal consistency of an opponent's argument or its
validity than with the consistency, coherence, and justi-
fiability of the opponent's position as a whole in relation

to the issue of the particular discussion. Therefore,
as one might expect, circumstantial ad hominem attack is
a characteristic and powerful form of criticism in parliamentary debate.

One index of the power of ad hominem refutation in political argumentation is its well-established effectiveness
in influencing voter behavior. Recently a Democratic
gubernatorial candidate attacked the Republican party for
"seeking to monopolize the American dream by such elitist
devices as tax shelters." A favorite over her Republican
opponent, she then released a financial statement admitting that she and her millionaire husband had paid no
state income taxes and only a small amount of federal tax
due to their paper losses on real estate investments. The
Republicans, of course, accused her of hypocrisy in attacking tax shelters while at the same time profiting from
them. This ad hominem refutation evidently succeeded with
the voters, according to newspaper reports, and posed such
an issue that it "stopped her campaign dead in the water."4

The effectiveness of ad hominem criticism is of course only
too well known to those in the political arena. In the
above instance, the inconsistency cited was between the
candidate's recommendations or exhortations and her own
personal actions. However, the position of her party was
obliquely involved, since the Democratic party has an
ideology that tends to be supportive of criticism of
elitism, tax shelters, or other matters likely to be perceived as privileges of affluent corporations.

In many other cases it is not the actions of the speaker
that provide a basis for attributing a position to him,
but rather it is the party position that is utilized.
Thus if a speaker's proposal can be shown by the opposition to be inconsistent with the position of the speaker's
own party, that is regarded as quite a serious criticism.
It reflects not only on the tenability of the speaker's
particular argument, but may also impugn the coherence of
the party's position as a whole.

In political argumentation, the position of a party may be
defined quite generally as its ideology, or more specifically as a certain set of statements the party has gone on
record as committing itself to. In the clearest cases,
position is defined relative to a specific set of statements acknowledged as commitments. However, in many ad
hominem disputations, the position at issue may be a set

of general statements. In such a case, the defending
party or arguer may be striving to bring these general
commitments into relationship with a particular topical
issue in order to formulate a specific position on that
issue. Thus, there may be room for argument concerning
what one's position is or should be on a particular
question.

Naturally, too, a political party will adjust its position on a specific issue if it perceives a shift in
public opinion. Hence, in the triangle of political
debate, there is always a connective link between ad
hominem refutation and ad populum argumentation. Sometimes, in fact, these two types of argumentation almost
seem to merge into a single thread of attempted refutation.

We are now in the fortunate position of seeing how a
number of the traditional informal fallacies we have
studied are all closely connected within the basic structure of logical dialogue-games. The ad hominem has to
do with criticisms concerning an arguer's position, or
set of commitments in dialogue. According to the structure of dialogue here adopted as the theoretical framework for reasonable argumentation, the objective of an
arguer should be to argue for his own conclusion using
his opponent's premises or commitments. The goal is to
argue from your opponent's position in dialectic. Certain ways of doing this badly or incorrectly may be
judged as instances of the ad hominem fallacy. Other
ways of doing it may constitute reasonable ad hominem
criticisms of an opponent's position. But the ad populum
fallacy also has to do with positional argumentation. If
your adversary in argument, your target audience, is a
broad constituency, then it may be perfectly reasonable
to argue from premises likely to have broad popular
appeal. Such a strategy is in fact dictated by the
objective of reasonable dialectic, namely to argue from
your opponent's premises. You are supposed to argue from
your opponent's commitments in order to play the game well
and fairly. Hence what might be called ad populum argumentation need not be fallacious in every instance. It
is only the specific violations of this form of argument
previously remarked upon that lead to the charge of
"fallacy" where this position-based form of strategy is
used badly.

Similarly, problems due to the unfair asking of loaded

questions have to do with misconstruals of an answerer's
position. A question is said to be loaded with respect
to an answerer if the question contains presuppositions
that are not reasonably and fairly deemed to be part of
that answerer's position. It is the misuse of loaded
questions in certain contexts that can lead to cases of
the fallacy of many questions. And similarly again, the
straw man fallacy arises from the unfair attribution of
certain propositions to an arguer in dialogue, where it
can be shown that those propositions are not truly part
of his position.

The essential point to be noted in the analysis of all
these kindred informal fallacies, and the dialogue mechanisms of criticism and defense that are part of them,
is that for an arguer to use the commitments of his
adversary in dialogue as premisses, to argue towards a
certain conclusion, need not be fallacious in every
instance.

Admittedly, such arguments are "subjective" in a sense.
But this sense of "subjective" only need mean that they
are dialectical arguments. And logical games of dialectic can be reasonable if they have fair and clearly
agreed upon rules of dialogue, win-loss rules, commitment rules, and clear canons of valid argument. These
types of arguments therefore, need not always be intrinsically subjective in the sense of being emotional,
irrational, or psychological in nature. For an arguer's
commitments are not necessarily his beliefs, feelings,
or other psychological states.

In the case of all of these traditional informal fallacies then, the solution to the analytical problem posed
proceeds from the first step of recognizing that each of
them can be basically a reasonable form of argument in
the context of logical games of dialogue. The second
step is to sort out the incorrect uses of such moves in
games of dialogue where clear and appropriate procedural
rules are formulated. The "fallacy" can then be located
as the violation or misuse of some procedural rule of
dialogue as an identifiable type of move. In the cases
of the fallacies presently at issue, the abuse is the
unfair attribution of a position.

The realities of party politics in political debates and
arguments mean that any political position is not likely
to be adequately represented as a fixed public set of

statements in an arguer's commitment-store. In fact we
often do not know, but can guess, whether a particular
statement is included in the position of some participant
in the arena of political disputation. Political positions are forged and strengthened in caucus and debate,
and thereby become better known, both to their advocates
and the less committed.

It follows that one benefit of adversary political debate
can be the evolution of a more sophisticated and balanced
political program brought into the light side of an arguer's
position. So despite all the pitfalls of ad hominem argumentation we have uncovered, it seems that sometimes there
can be an underlying positive value in such criticisms if
they are managed well and carefully. Hence dialectic,
despite all its negative implications as a theory of fallacies and errors,[5] can indirectly lead us towards the truth.

The fact about the practice of argumentation in the marketplace of disputation is that one's position on an issue is
rarely if ever completely articulated and pinned down as
well as it could be. The process of dialogue, then, can
be valuable if it takes statements from the dark side and
brings them into the light side of an arguer's position.
One's position can be expanded and deepened on a topic of
dispute.

Hence dialectic is not a trivial or merely formal undertaking, empty of real value or content in practical terms.
Accused of employing similar or worse practices in the
treatment of dissent than those we criticize for the same
faults, we can reply in argument by many different ways
advocated in the treatment of the ad hominem fallacy in the
previous chapter. But the deepest value of such an allegation may arise from our reflection on what there might be
of substance in it. Perhaps, for example, there may be real
limits on the sort of dissent we are prepared to tolerate.
A clearer articulation of these limits may result, then, in
a fairer and more realistic position on dissent that we can
advocate in better conscience. The idea that a position can
be better known, as expressed by JBV, opens the way for a
partial vindication of ad hominem criticism in dialogue.

VALUE OF POSITIONAL ARGUMENTATION

A critic of positional argumentation might say, "I think
people (and philosophers in particular) often worry too
much about defending their own views or attacking somebody

else's. Instead, they should examine the facts and see
whether in fact the proposition at issue is true or false
in light of the evidence. Positional disputation is not
in itself wrong, but it is ultimately unproductive in
arriving at the truth. Consistency of position is not
sufficient for truth, nor is victory in argument any
measure of progress toward the truth or substitute for
scientific inquiry." This criticism raises the question
of the value of ad hominem argumentation, and raises the
specter of whether there might always be something inherently fallacious about engaging in it.

In reply, a number of points need to be made. First, few
would deny that ad hominem argumentation has at least a
negative place in logic as a necessary defense against
unfairly aggressive ad hominem attack, a common enough
phenomenon in many forms of inquiry and argument. To
understand enough about what your attacker is doing to
be able to dismantle or repel the attack by circumstantial
ad hominem is a skill of undeniable value. But over and
above this negative or protectionist value of ad hominem
analysis as a known form of argument, it remains to be
seen whether there is a positive value in positional argumentation.

Before that, however, it needs to be said that, as the
criticism above alleges, people do often spend more energy
on worrying about whether a view is attackable or defensible than whether it is true or false. That is a common
failing of argumentation, but one whose understanding is
deepened by the analysis of the structure of ad hominem
refutation and fallacies. The main ad hominem fallacy is
just that: arguing from positional indefensibility of
preaching a proposition and practicing the opposite to
the falsehood of that proposition per se. Thus the fault
of an excessive preoccupation with attackability or defensibility as a substitute for truth or falsity is the very
thing marked out by the ad hominem fallacy as worthy of
avoidance. Thus nothing in the positional analysis of
ad hominem argumentation runs contrary to the criticism
levelled above. Rather, the analysis provides a basis
for support of the contention alleged by the criticism.

But apart from that, is there positive value in positional
argumentation itself? I think there is, for several
reasons. First, often one does not know what the truth
is, or one has no way of arriving at the truth of a matter.
Therefore one has to operate on the basis of assumptions

or presuppositions. Such provisional assumptions are
particularly needful when deliberating on how to act,
for the future is rarely or never known, and moral or
prudential principles are rarely or never confidently
established as nondisputable. Consequently, the best
one can do is to seek out the most plausible subset of
a given set of principles to forge a defensible position
to act upon. Adoption of such a provisional position
for action should always be open to revision and correc-
tion, and it is indeed the function of dialectical argumentation to guide the improvement of one's reasoning
in positional refinement. Thus positional argumentation
is valuable and appropriate when the truth is not to be
had by other means.

Second, although dialectical argumentation may not be
the only means of reasonably trying to arrive at truth,
it by no means follows that any other means altogether
excludes or replaces dialectical and positional reasoning. For example, formal classical deductive logic does
not by itself in many instances uniquely determine truth
either. Deductive logic will tell you whether given sets
of propositions are consistent, or whether a conclusion
is true given that designated premises are true. But
it will not normally tell you by itself whether a proposition is in itself true or false. Deductive formal
logic, in this regard, is no better off than positional
argumentation. So there may be different ways of arriving
at the truth, and neglect of one way by inappropriate use
of another is to be deplored. Yet it does not follow that
any particular way is inherently useless. In particular,
then, positional argumentation may be used inappropriately
or excessively in certain situations, but it does not
follow that it is inherently useless as a way of working
towards the truth of a matter.

Part of the value of positional reasoning is its propen-
sity to make hidden assumptions surface by forcing an
arguer to articulate his position better in the face of
criticism. Another benefit is the deepening of the coherence of one's position by forcing an arguer to relate
pairs of propositions that he did not previously see as
related to each other. Another benefit may be the realization that one's position is deeply inconsistent and
consequently needs to be revised and improved, or possibly
even rejected. Those particular benefits and others all
flow from the assumption that having, defending, or attacking a position is itself productive in inquiry. Can this

assumption itself be justified?

Ultimately the justification, indeed the necessity, for
taking a position on many disputable subjects stems from
the pragmatic nature of the human condition. We are in
the world and we have to act or do nothing. Either
course must often be justified if one is to have any
pretensions at all to being a humane, civilized, or
reasonable being. Hence one is constantly obliged to
adopt a position, or to defend oneself against the
adoption or concession of a position imposed by some
other source of authority. One in fact cannot avoid
positional disputation except by being a moral and intellectual vegetable. If you have to engage in positional
disputation anyway, it is useful to learn how to do it
well, or at least try to do it as well as one can. And
in fact many of the practical arts like moral reasoning,
prudential decision making, political argumentation in
democratic parliaments, congresses, and legislatures,
and virtually all forms of deliberation and argument in
natural language inevitably take the form of positional
disputation. Hence the assumption that having, defending, and attacking a position as a productive and worthwhile activity can easily be justified.

Different philosophies of science, however, do vary
greatly in the importance placed on dialectic as a method
of scientific inquiry. Those postulating truth as a
relationship between a proposition and some fact that it
corresponds to are less likely to see dialectic as important. Those who see truth as a relationship of coherence
among a set of propositions are of course much more
friendly to the notion of positional connectedness and
defensibility. Most prominent among recent defenders of
plausibility, dialectic, and coherence has been Nicholas
Rescher. His idealistic framework comprises all these
notions in a way that systematically supports the central
claims of dialectical argumentation as a scientific
method of working towards truth. But those, like Sir
Karl Popper, who believe that we have no direct access
to the truth but must work towards that elusive goal by
the indirect method of falsifying our hypotheses and
conjectures, place the greatest importance on dialectic.
Because, on this view of the progress of science, dialectic is all we have. All intellectual progress comes
through the negative route of discarding the theories
and positions we find to be inconsistent or fallacious.
We get to the truth through exposing our errors, as it

were. I am not prepared to endorse either Rescher's or
Popper's views on these matters, even though I may be
criticized for being positionally inconsistent in admir-
ing both of them.

NOTES

1. A tableau is really much more than a record of
commitments. But for a fuller account of the use of the
tableau method, the reader should look to Hintikka and
Saarinen (1979).

2. A player's position is directly inconsistent if
a statement A and its negation ⅂A are both in his commitment-set. A player's position is inconsistent if it
contains any sets of statements that imply a directly
inconsistent position by the rules of the game. A
player's response 'No commitment A' is directly ambivalent
if A is already in that player's position. In Hamblin
games like (H) with retraction allowed, ambivalence never
arises, because 'No commitment A' simply erases A if it
was previously in the answerer's position. In the games
outlined in the next section, however, ambivalence will
become significant and interesting as a sign of something
questionable in a player's position.

3. The characters in the Socratic dialogues often
congratulate themselves for having made this sort of
progress of "coming from the cave into the light."

4. "Fouling Up: Taxes and Babies Dog Two Pols,"
Time, August 2, 1982, p. 29.

5. For the more negative side of political debate as
a model of argument appropriate for the theory of argument, see Woods and Walton (1982b, ch. 1).

APPENDIX 1

Just How Ethical Are the News Media?

Gerald McAuliffe

It was late on an April evening in 1978 when the telephone rang in the home of Mr. and Mrs. Alfred Greene in
St. John's, Newfoundland. The voice on the other end was
reporter Randall (Randy) Stevens of Toronto radio station
CFTR. He introduced himself through a Greene family
acquaintance. After exchanging pleasantries, he asked
Mrs. Greene if she was aware that her daughter Barbara
had given birth to a baby girl in England. Mrs. Greene
did not even know that her daughter was pregnant. But
more important, she did not know that her conversation
was being tape-recorded. Mrs. Greene's daughter Barbara
is best known as Controller Greene of the Metropolitan
Toronto City of North York. No, she was not married.

Six weeks before, Ms. Greene had told the press she was
taking a two-month holiday because she was suffering from
hypertension and was in need of a rest. But her absence,
particularly at budget time, was uncharacteristic of her
normal dedication. Reporter Stevens, young (then 23) and
very aggressive, was suspicious. He eventually chased
her down to a London, England, apartment where she was
enjoying postnatal recuperation and trying to decide how
she was going to break the news to her family and make
the announcement to the outside world.

The telephone rang. It was reporter Stevens. Ms. Greene
refused an interview and hung up. He called back not once
but several times and each time tape-recorded the call.
When that didn't work, he went to her apartment and knocked
on the door for 10 minutes. Ms. Greene refused to answer
and then made two decisions. First she called Scotland
Yard to get rid of Stevens. And then she called the
Toronto Star and told a reporter about her newborn child.

Reporter Stevens returned to Toronto. The story was out
but CFTR broadcast the conversations of Ms. Greene's
repeated refusal of an interview and the interview with
her mother. The Broadcasting Act prohibits the use of a

This appendix originally appeared in slightly different
   form in Quest (February-March 1980), 51-58.

taped interview without the person's knowledge and consent. Ms. Greene filed a complaint with the Canadian
Radio-television and Telecommunications Commission. Nine
months later the station was fined $1,000 in provincial
court when it pleaded guilty to a breach of the act. The
station regarded it as a technical breach but Provincial
Court Judge Harold Rice said the station was guilty of a
"flagrant violation" of the law.

Controller Greene is a public figure. There are those
who rightly argue that because she said she was going
abroad for a rest while in fact she was a pregnant public
official, she became fair game for substantial press
attention. But Ms. Greene claimed she was harassed by
Stevens and that her privacy had been invaded. What is
most important about the Greene case is not the fine at
all, but the fact that the only places she could turn to
for adjudication or even retribution were a government
agency and the courts.

There are no enforceable ethical or professional standards
in [Canada] governing the conduct of journalists or the
newspapers, radio and television stations that employ
them. Consider this: A doctor or lawyer can be brought
before his professional discipline committee on a complaint
of incompetence by a patient or client and, if found guilty
of misconduct, can face punishment ranging from a public
reprimand to disbarment. But people who have been abused
or wronged by the press can turn to no one with any guarantee of an independent or fair hearing or public redress.
(Many serious and justifiable complaints do not fall within
the provisions of the various provincial libel and slander
acts. Often when they do, people are not prepared to go
to the time and expense of pursuing the matter.) The
press considers it front-page news when it is revealed that
the common-law wife of a cabinet minister was given a free
ride on an airline. Yet many publishers, editors, news
directors and reporters think nothing is wrong with taking
anything free and do their best to hide it from the public.

Conflict-of-interest rules that require federal and provincial cabinet ministers to place their stock portfolios
in blind trusts came about as a result of numerous news
stories and editorial page pressure from the press. Yet
those same editors who lobbied for the regulations in some
cases cannot guarantee their readers or listeners that the
reporter covering the business beat does not hold stock
in the companies on which he is reporting. If a member of

Parliament were to rise in the House and ask a question
of the government about a company he had an indirect
business interest in, even as a former employee, his
name would be spread across the front pages and airwaves
for a breach of conduct. Yet journalists and editors
can see no wrong in the reporter on the medical or travel
beat receiving thousands of dollars in "award" money from
private industries and government bodies for making the
readers and listeners more enlightened about their vested
interests.

What the press in Canada is saying is this: There should
be strict codes of discipline governing the conduct and
competence of doctors and lawyers, and strict guidelines
for politicians and bureaucrats--and the public should
know what they are. But the press is beyond such rules.
Journalists are not swayed or influenced so easily--rules
would interfere with the freedom-of-the-press doctrine.

The press does have codes of ethics and statements of
principles. But they are weak, ignored and unenforceable.
They would be funny if the subject weren't so serious.
Take the Barbara Greene case once again. She claims her
privacy was invaded and that she was rudely treated. The
code of ethics of the Radio Television News Directors
Association of Canada states that "broadcast newsmen shall
at all times display humane respect for the dignity,
privacy and well-being of persons with whom the news
deals." And, it says, "the association shall actively
censure and seek to prevent violations of these standards
and members shall actively encourage their observance by
all newsmen, whether of the RTNDA or not." Despite the
decision by the court, the RTNDA has never dealt with the
matter. Dick Smyth, news director of CHUM radio and the
association's president, said he believes it is the role
of the CRTC to act as policeman. He has never known the
RTNDA to censure anyone.

Or take Article 5 of the code: "Broadcast newsmen shall
govern their personal lives and such nonprofessional
associations as may impinge on their professional activities in a manner that will protect them from conflict of
interest, real or apparent." Norm Jary was the news
director of CJOY radio in Guelph, Ontario, for more than
15 years. He was mayor of Guelph for nine of those years.
He sees no conflict of interest between the two jobs.
"I didn't or I wouldn't have done it," says Jary, who is
still the mayor but now sports director for CJOY and its

sister FM station.

In 1975 the editorial division of the Canadian Daily Newspaper Publishers Association set out to draft a national
code of ethics. Two years later it determined the task
impossible. It couldn't get agreement. Instead, it
drafted a "statement of principles"--motherhood and apple
pie principles that were approved by the association in
April 1977. "I think we did well to get agreement as we
did. There are a lot of people who didn't wish to go
along with it and it was watered down, but not exten-
sively," said Louis D. Whitehead, the committee chairman,
who is now president of the CDNPA and president, publisher
and editor of The Brandon Sun.

The question of ethics is dealt with in 39 words: "Newspapers have individual codes of ethics and this declaration is intended to complement them in their healthy
diversity. As individual believers in free speech they
have a duty to maintain standards of conduct in conform-
ance with their own goals."

If you were to ask most reporters about their newspaper's
code of ethics, they wouldn't have the slightest idea what
you were talking about. I have 20 years' experience as
a newspaper, radio and television news reporter. I have
never seen a code of ethics nor have my superiors ever
held in-house workshops to discuss a code of ethics--if,
in fact, such existed. Is it not fair to assume that if
you don't tell your staff what the rules are, you can't
expect them to follow them?

Newspapers, radio and television news departments hold a
position of public trust. The CDNPA Statement of Principles describes it this way: "The newspaper should hold
itself free of any obligation save that of fidelity to
the public good. It should pay the costs incurred in
gathering and publishing the news. Conflicts of interest,
and the appearance of conflicts of interest, must be
avoided. Outside interests that could affect, or appear
to affect, the newspaper's freedom to report the news
impartially should be avoided."

What about conflicts of interest? Just how aggressively
do publishers work to keep their publications and staff
free of outside interests that could appear to affect a
newspaper's freedom and news impartiality? An examination
of the facts leaves one wondering if the CDNPA's Statement

of Principles isn't really more window dressing than anything.

Take, for example, the question of newspaper awards. The
very purpose of the awards is to create an incentive for
journalistic excellence. Who could have a bigger stake
than the newspapers themselves? The National Newspaper
Awards, the most prestigious in the country, are sustained
by interest on a trust fund that has not been added to by
the individual newspapers or chains in 10 years. There
are nine awards worth $500 each for a total of $4,500 a
year.

But journalists all know that the more lucrative awards,
which can amount to thousands of dollars, are provided by
large corporations and government agencies. Among the
best bankrolled are the National Magazine Awards. Fifteen
major corporations, including Comac Communications Ltd.,
which publishes this magazine, and the Reader's Digest
Foundation, along with the University of Western Ontario,
contribute some $25,000 for 16 awards handed out annually
by the National Magazine Awards Foundation. But an important distinction should be made between this type of award,
which is judged by an independent body, and those awards
that are made directly by large corporations and government agencies that have a vested interest in getting good
press. Examples: the Canadian Petroleum Association
National Journalism Awards, worth $750 each, for stories
on the development of the petroleum industry; the Canadian
Grocery Distributors' Institute Press Awards, which total
$2,550, plus an expense-paid trip for winners to the
presentation dinner in Edmonton, for journalists who
demonstrate a high degree of professionalism by research-
ing and writing accurately on any aspect of the Canadian
food industry; the Eastman Kodak Company's Run for the
Money Contest, with $7,000 awarded in five categories for
the best newspaper color reproduction; the Ministry of
State for Science and Technology Award, with a $1,000
prize for science journalism; the $450 Greg Clark Outdoor
Editorial Writing Award, sponsored by the Ontario Ministry
of Natural Resources; and the $2,250 annual Business
Writing Awards funded by the Royal Bank of Canada.

The Western Ontario Newspaper Awards have been sponsored
by private industry for 26 years. B. F. Goodrich Canada
Limited has supported them since the start and the Ford
Motor Company has been a cosponsor for the past eight
years. The awards and dinner cost more than $10,000.

B. F. Goodrich and Ford pay 80 percent; the remaining
$2,000 is contributed by some but not all of the partici-
pating newspapers.

That is not all private industry does for the press.
There is the Imperial Oil Limited fishing derby held at
Indian Harbour just outside Halifax, which has been an
annual event for 17 years. Last year it attracted almost
130 journalists from all over the Maritimes. It is just
a fun time with the press--"No company business is talked
about," said Greg MacDonald, an IOL spokesman. Then there
is the annual Broken Broom Media Curling Competition held
in Toronto and last year sponsored by Coorsh & Sons Ltd.
Posters hung in newsrooms proclaim it "The curling event
of the year for Metro's working press." It is open to
journalists, broadcasters, photographers and cartoonists.
"Be our guests . . . no registration fee. Enjoy fabulous
free refreshments courtesy of Coorsh Specialty Meats.
Great prizes courtesy of various friends of the Metro
media." Special prize categories include the Klutzes,
Meatheads, Hotdoggers and the Best-Dressed Team awards.
The highlight of the day is four lucky draws. The prizes?
Four free tickets from Air Canada to anywhere the airline
goes.

The number of freebies, as they are called in the business,
has diminished over the past five years because an increasing number of journalists and corporate public relations
people don't approve. As a matter of policy some newspapers now forbid them. Editorial employees of The Globe
and Mail are subject to dismissal if they violate the
policy and for many years The Toronto Star has insisted
on paying for all services received by its staff. The
fact is, however, freeloads are still numerous and well
attended. The reason is simple: not enough broadcast
owners and publishers have taken a firm stand against them.
Saying you don't approve of them and then doing nothing to
enforce the rule is no different from not having a policy
at all.

The relationship between the press and industry is one
thing. What is even more revealing is the kinship that
exists between many members of the press and politicians
at the federal, provincial and municipal levels. Watching
The National at night leaves many Canadians believing the
press and politicians are antagonistic adversaries. It
is more a myth than a reality. What they are really wit-
nessing is pack journalism. Everyone is after the same

story. There are no Jack Andersons in Ottawa. Most news
bureaus, even those of the large daily papers, are not
large enough to permit their creation: working on Parliament Hill for many reporters is like working in a sausage
factory or on the assembly line at General Motors. You
spend your day churning out copy and film for that night's
newscast or the next day's paper. Everyone is onto the
same story. There is little originality. What happens
is that journalists become part of the process. They no
longer cover the system; they are part of it. The fact
is, many journalists and politicians are close friends.
They eat and drink together in the parliamentary dining
room, they play cards together (MPs get honorary social
memberships in the National Press Club) and they holiday
together. The canoe trip through the Canadian North that
Pierre Trudeau went on after losing the May 1979 election
was organized by CTV's Craig Oliver.

Geoff Scott, the Progressive Conservative MP for Hamilton-
Wentworth, was a reporter on the Hill for 20 years before
he entered the world of "formal" politics. "Parliament is
a club, the press gallery is a club and they intermingle.
There is a cross-pollination,' explains Scott. This is
best exemplified by the annual spring bash sponsored by
the Parliamentary Press Gallery. It starts with dinner
in the parliamentary dining room and is followed by an
evening of frivolity in the Railway Committee Room. Press
gallery members must bring a politician as their guest.
It is firmly understood that the evening is private and
off-the-record, and that nothing may be reported.

Once again the double standard creeps in. When a cabinet
minister gives up politics to return to "private" life,
government guidelines require that he cannot sit on a
board of directors or act for a firm in dealings with the
government for a period of two years. Yet many journalists
float between jobs in government and jobs in the press.
Neither they nor their editors acknowledge that there
could be the same type of conflict of interest.

It is probably the "club" rules more than anything that
have left the press owners at the public trough in a style
and degree the media would find unacceptable in any other
industry. Radio, television and newspaper reporters
covering legislatures across the country get free government office space and an assortment of free services:
messenger service, duplicating facilities, free parking
and stationery, telephones (in B.C., free long-distance

phone calls within the province) and cut-rate bar services.

There is the question of government hospitality. In
Ontario alone, the provincial government has spent more
than $40,000 in the past five years buying breakfasts,
lunches and dinners for various media functions. When
the Canadian Community Newspapers Association and the
National Newspaper Association of the U.S. held a joint
convention in Toronto six years ago, the taxpayers bought
their dinner one night. The bill came to $10,218--1,027
showed up.

Whatever ethical problems exist for journalists and media
owners should be solved on an individual basis, says
Brandon Sun publisher Whitehead, who is this year's chief
spokesman for Canada's newspaper publishers. He, like
many but not all of his colleagues, does not believe in
press councils or nationwide rules: "Publishers are
pretty responsible--a pretty aware bunch of people. I
would not be in favor of any national body. I think any-
body who has been maligned has access to the courts. I
feel if we keep dumping more and more regulatory bodies
on top of the press we are going to end up with a thing
we don't want; we are going to have a press that is no
longer free. The housekeeping thing should be kept within
the house. If someone does not perform to acceptable
standards, then he should not be a journalist," Mr. Whitehead said.

The conduct of journalists and the performance of the press,
however, is becoming a subject of greater public debate
than the media owners either realize or care to admit. In
fact, there are some who actively attempt to stifle it.
The Spectator in Hamilton, Ontario, has been running a
steady stream of stories on the number of closed Board of
Control and Board of Education meetings and the need to
open them to the press and the public. The Spectator
argues that those in public life hold a position of public
trust and as such should have their debates and deliberations open to public scrutiny. But it does not believe
those same rules should apply to itself.

The Spectator revealed in a front-page story last summer
that Mayor Jack MacDonald had gone on a free fishing trip
as a guest of Nordair, which operates flights out of
Hamilton Civic Airport. The story continued to attract
major attention in the news pages for a week (MacDonald
eventually paid for the jaunt).

The irony of the situation, however, is this: for years,
The Spectator's travel writer roamed the world on free
airline passes. The Spectator claimed it could not afford
to pay his way. When a complaint was brought before the
Ontario Press Council, The Spectator first succeeded in
insisting the hearing be held behind closed doors. Then
Spectator publisher John Muir successfully blocked the
council from hearing testimony from Norman Isaacs, the
continent's leading expert on press ethics. Mr. Isaacs
is on the teaching staff of Columbia University's Graduate
School of Journalism and is a distinguished American publisher and editor. He was at the time also adviser to
the National News Council of the United States. Unfortunately, the stance and attitude taken by The Spectator is
not peculiar to that paper.

Insisting that ethics and standards are best dealt with by
the individual news organizations may have been acceptable
10 or 20 years ago. It is not any longer. Canadians want
and have a right to expect a well-informed, ethical and
unimpeachable press free from all external influences.
The public is not blind to what is going on.

The credibility gap between the press and the public is
continuing to widen at an alarming rate. Unless media
owners and journalists start to recognize that the double
standard is no longer acceptable, people will quit buying
papers or stop watching and listening to the news. If
they don't do that, they will do something much worse:
they will stop believing us. The tragedy is that many of
them don't now.

The Myth of Szasz

Gordon R. Lowe

The derisive titles of Szasz's books proclaim that he
enters the psychiatric cathedral not to pray but to jeer.
Medicine is "theology," psychiatry is "slavery," psychotherapy is "a myth" (like mental illness), and schizophrenia is "a sacred symbol." These trumpet blasts
herald Szasz's determination to shatter not only the hal-
lowed psychiatric silence but also the holy icons.

His chapter headings prick the skin and draw blood.
"Psychiatry and the syphilitic mind"; "Anti-psychiatry
and the plundered mind"; "Psychiatric remedy: rhetoric,
religion, and repression"; "Schizophrenia, a scientific
scandal": these thrusts are intended not merely to goad
but to slaughter psychiatry's sacred cows.

Hurling himself at the high priests of psychiatry, Szasz
goes straight for the jugular. And one after another,
they go down: Freud, the Jewish avenger; Jung, the pastor
without a pulpit; R. D. Laing, the canting, blaming
preacher. Szasz cuts a wide swathe through the psychiatric
priesthood, from Benjamin Rush to Karl Menninger, until no
one of any importance is left standing.

Now we may as well admit that Szasz's onslaught is perfectly justified. He is right that many current medical
practices are ritualistic ceremonies, designed more to

Thomas Szasz, Schizophrenia: The Sacred Symbol of Psychi-
    atry. New York: Basic Books; Toronto: Fitzhenry &
    Whiteside, 1976.
Thomas Szasz, The Theology of Medicine: The Political-
    Philosophical Foundations of Medical Ethics. New York:
    Harper & Row; Toronto: Fitzhenry & Whiteside, 1977.
Thomas Szasz, Psychiatric Slavery: When Confinement and
    Coercion Masquerade as Cure. New York: Free Press;
    Toronto: Collier-Macmillan, 1977.
Thomas Szasz, The Myth of Psychotherapy: Mental Healing
    as Religion, Rhetoric and Repression. New York: Anchor
    Press/Doubleday; Toronto: Doubleday, 1978.
This appendix originally appeared in slightly different
    form in Queen's Quarterly, 86 (1979), 485-492.

enhance the prestige of the guru-doctor than to benefit
the suffering patient. He is right that the typical
psychiatric hospital is a prison where people utterly
innocent of law-breaking are incarcerated like criminals,
reclassified as subhuman, and forced to conform to the
behavioral prejudices of the Establishment and its
psychiatric agents.

He is right that schizophrenia is not factual, but facti-
tious; that it is not an empirically observable illness,
but a concept created by psychiatrists to justify their
particular form of people-abuse; and that so-called
psychiatric treatment is merely the manipulation of the
non-existent by the deluded, or worse, the coercion of
the helpless by the disingenuous. And he is right that
to call psychotherapy a medical treatment even by analogy,
is immoral.

But given that Szasz is right, why has his siege against
psychiatry, which he has maintained relentlessly for
almost twenty years, been so ineffective? Why do all
these psychiatric malpractices still flourish? For the
fact is that psychiatry, however bloody, is still unbowed.
And it would appear that Szasz, for all his savagery, is
not lethal.

We must of course recognize, and allow for, the fact that
the medical profession has developed over the centuries
a massive indifference to its detractors. Medical response
to the need for improvement has always been a masterly
inactivity. Now doctors meet public criticism with silent
denial and a wondering stare of monolithic vacuity. They
no longer insist that they are superior; they simply assume
that everyone else is inferior. Doctors have come a long
way from their original role as caretakers of the sick:
now they see themselves as "healers," and delegate care-
taking to nurses, ward orderlies, social workers, and
other para-medics, so as to leave themselves free to
"cure" by the laying on of hands. The modern doctor, as
born-again cure-monger and faith-healer, is now as well-
defended against criticism as any other religious zealot.

Even so, part of the reason for Szasz's peculiar ineffec-
tiveness lies in his unique method of attack, and not
only in what he says but also in what he does not say.
His criticisms are so vociferous that they distract us
from his tacit concessions. He decries mental illness
as mythical, but accepts the reality of physical illness

and the medical model. He castigates involuntary psychiatry as criminal coercion, but accepts voluntary psychiatry as a game played by consenting adults. He ridicules
the idea that the doctor is the patient's agent, but
accepts the doctor as altruistic healer.

Quite often, when Szasz has wounded psychiatry he himself
staunches the blood. Consider for example how brutally
he hacks to pieces the so-called classic symptoms of
schizophrenia--delusions, "such as the belief that Jesus
is the son of God who died, but has been resurrected and
is now still alive"; inappropriate behavior, "like invad-
ing Vietnam, or having long hair or short hair or no hair";
hallucinations, like believing oneself to be in communication with deities; over-activity, the lifestyle of a
typical doctor, or under-activity, the lifestyle of a
typical television watcher. Szasz is being provocative,
but his point is perfectly valid. Calling behavior
"unusual" involves a value judgment, and almost any
behavior is unusual to somebody. So who is to decide
what is unusual? Psychiatrists, convinced that their
diagnoses are not value judgments but facts, hasten to
offer themselves as final arbiters.

Szasz sees that once this is accepted the diagnosis-treat-
ment process becomes circular. Psychotic patients typically do not make sense. So, if the psychiatrist is successful in interpreting the psychotic symptoms, then
either the patient is making sense and is not ill, or the
psychiatrist is mad in the same way. Again, the psychotic
patient typically does not seek or want treatment. The
psychiatrist interprets this as "lack of insight," meaning
that the patient does not see himself as the psychiatrist
sees him; or as "loss of contact with reality," meaning
the psychiatrist's reality. Even if the psychiatrist
claims to be representing the reality of society, then
either society is sick (as R. D. Laing would argue) or
the psychiatrist is merely a flunkey-warder for society's
rejects.

Szasz knows that the subjectivity of psychiatric diagnoses
has been proven many times over. The readiness of psychiatrists to call a patient schizophrenic varies not clini-
cally but geographically, from east (less likely) to west
(more likely) across the Atlantic; and politically, as
shown by Wing's study of British as against Russian
psychiatric diagnoses. Given all this ammunition, why
does Szasz, having fired his broadside, pretend that he

aimed to miss? No genuine critic of psychiatry would
first demonstrate that diagnostic categories represent
a psychiatric delusional system, then back off with an
ingratiating "but seriously, folks . . . ," asking pardon
for having been provocative.

For all his cut-and-thrust criticalness Szasz manages
somehow to avoid psychiatry's vital spots. There is no
one more viciously retaliatory than a psychiatrist whose
authority is genuinely being questioned; yet psychiatry
pays less attention to Szasz than an emperor to a court
jester. His tirades fall on ears still plugged with
unimpaired self-satisfaction. Psychiatry can allow
Szasz to go on wringing his hands so long as its own
withers remain unwrung.

This situation is not new. Throughout history those
would-be iconoclasts who tacitly accept the unspoken
assumptions of the system they attack always have been
tolerated. In fact, the advocate of harmless and superficial change is positively welcomed by the Establishment, since the noise and dust he raises create the
impression that something has actually been done. It is
only when critics do promote real change that they are
taken seriously. Joan of Arc, Jesus Christ, and Socrates
were respectively incinerated, crucified, and poisoned
the moment their criticisms began to bring about genuine
change in the status quo.

Szasz not only makes concessions to orthodoxy; he teaches
psychiatry how to nullify his attacks. For example, when
he denounces involuntary psychiatry while supporting
voluntary psychiatry he is almost openly inviting psychiatrists to make involuntary treatment "voluntary," simply
by getting in advance the patient's "informed consent."
Any psychiatrist worth his salt can soon terrify a patient
into giving his consent to the most gruesome treatments
imaginable. Every day psychiatrists persuade patients to
have their minds forcibly changed by surgical assault and
mutilation (lobotomy and leucotomy), by electrically
induced epileptiform brain convulsions (ECT), and by
poison cocktails (drugs).

In any case, where coercion, threats, and persuasion fail
psychiatrists can always bypass the patient's healthy
resistance to treatment by subterfuge and deceit. Many
psychiatrists, like their medical brethren, use placebos

as a matter of course. And their staff follow suit.
One head nurse, infuriated by a patient's refusal to
take oral medication, surreptitiously injected his milk
carton with the drug. She was subsequently applauded
by her colleagues, including the doctors, for her ingenu-
ity. The patient's "right to refuse treatment," made
much of by Szasz, is meaningless so long as psychiatrists
retain the power to administer treatment anyway.

Nor does it help the patient, as Szasz would have us
believe, to be granted the right to choose his own psychiatrist. To offer a choice between this psychiatrist and
that psychiatrist conceals the enforced "choice" of a
psychiatrist of some sort. "Choose your own psychiatrist"
is the clinical equivalent of "vote for your own political
candidate" (but vote), or "worship in the church of your
choice" (but worship). The patient may reject a given
psychiatrist, but he must never reject the psychiatric
profession.

Szasz shares with psychiatrists the hidden conviction
that, when you get right down to it, doctors always know
what's best for the patient. He also believes that doctors can "allow" the patient his freedom. This is perhaps
the most dangerous of all the doctor's delusions. When
a doctor forbids a freedom to a patient, then removes his
veto, this does not "legalize" the freedom; it merely
restores to the patient the freedom he had in the first
place, which he always had, and of which he should never
have been deprived. There is a subtle but crucial difference between doing something because it is "permitted" or
"allowed," and doing it because one is free to do it.
Szasz's psychiatric "permission" is the impertinent
officiousness of superfluous medical middlemen who have
forced themselves between patients and their freedom.
Psychiatrists, like governments, do not stand in loco
parentis to patients.

Szasz's self-defeating concession to psychiatric arrogance
shows in his discussion of suicide. He noisily abuses
the therapist who uses physical treatment to intervene,
because "suicide is not an illness," yet he regards
psychotherapy as "unobjectionable, and indeed generally
desirable." Now Szasz cannot have it both ways. If the
patient is not ill, as Szasz insists, why should any
attempt be made to intervene? In advocating psychotherapy
for a non-illness Szasz reveals, ambivalently but unmis-
takeably, his own psychiatric sense of outrage that a

person might feel himself capable of choosing life or
death without the sanction of a duly qualified member of
the medical profession. He admits openly that suicide
is "medical heresy." To "allow" this heresy would
threaten the whole psychiatric edifice. What else might
people want to decide for themselves?

Szasz ostentatiously contrasts psychiatry with medicine.
He exposes psychiatric decisions as essentially moral,
political, and theological; psychiatric terminology as
a smoke-screen for malpractice; and psychiatric diagnosis
as mere value judgment. Why then does he keep attacking
psychiatric concepts as if they were facts, and thereby
enhancing their credibility? If psychiatry is such a
morass of idiosyncratic interpretation, where the rules
of the game are forever being arbitrarily redefined, how
can Szasz ever give the game away? Where doublethink
prevails, doublecross becomes impossible, and Szasz
becomes Alice in Wonderland.

Psychiatry need never fear Szasz so long as it can define,
and redefine as necessary, its own self-sustaining professional delusions. Indeed psychiatry daily extends its
scope. Alcoholism and drug addiction are no longer self-
indulgences but psychiatric sicknesses. Even gluttony is
now redefined as "the illness of obesity."

We should notice here that the psychiatrist's psycho-
semantics not only extend his own power but also cancels
his patient's culpability. When psychiatry has abolished
sin by calling it sickness the patient (just by being
called a patient) is no longer responsible for being fat,
drunk, or stoned out of his mind. This prompts the question: is the doctor-patient relationship really a villain-
victim relationship? Szasz makes a good case for the
psychiatrist as villain, and simply assumes that the
patient is a victim, and a helpless victim at that. But
is he? There are advantages to the patient, however carefully hidden or vehemently denied, in being a patient.
Are psychiatric patients willing victims? At first sight
the idea seems monstrous. But any experienced therapist
watches constantly for "secondary gain" in his patients.
He knows that people play patient-games, actively resist
constructive change, then revert through "repetition-
compulsion" (i.e., sheer perversity) to the conditions
that made them crazy in the first place. Many so-called
neurotic interactions are collusive relationships in
which all parties have a concealed vested interest in

maintaining them.

Careful observers, as different from one another as Jay
Haley, William Barrett, and Ken Kesey, have pointed out
that even deteriorated psychotic patients show an animal
cunning that enables them to adapt perfectly to the sick
society in mental hospitals. Patients may be crazy but
they are not foolish. They learn very quickly how to
qualify themselves for continued perquisites and extended
welfare care. To many people being a sick prisoner is
preferable to the arduous responsibilities of a healthy
freedom. To many, being a patient is better than being a
person.

If the patient, a willing victim, is not really a victim
at all, it might be argued that the doctor is not a
villain. Unfortunately, the patient's malingering merely
underlines the doctor's malpractice. The doctor, already
colluding with the Establishment by acting as its paid
hireling to force social deviants to conform, becomes a
villain double-dyed if he also colludes with someone who
wants to be classified as "a patient with an illness" in
order to avoid the stresses of social living. The psychiatric delusional system cannot be justified by the patient's
voluntary complicity. Even three wrongs do not make a
right.

There are in fact several guilty parties, not just one,
as Szasz would have us believe. There is the Establishment, the social subgroup with whom the patient-person
cannot get along, and who shanghais him by force or fraud
into a mental hospital. This is the psychiatrist, willing
to do anything for money, prestige, or power, even if it
means hitting a man when he is down. And there is the
patient-person himself, voluntarily abdicating from effort-
ful living by resorting to illness as a way of life.

The very most that can be said for psychiatrists is that
when they volunteer to take responsibility for the unjustifiable incarceration of social dissidents they simultaneously render themselves scapegoats for both the Establishment and the patients. In this respect the psychiatrist
stands shoulder to shoulder with the policeman, the soldier,
and the common hangman.

For, either we let the psychiatrist be our scapegoat for
punishing dissidents and stop blaming him for accepting
the job, or we stop him doing it and take the responsibility

ourselves. And there's the rub. It is our own disin-
clination for that kind of responsibility that gives
psychiatrists their ace-in-the-hole. In return for
imprisoning and assaulting society's troublesome citi-
zens under the guise of treatment they demand more money
and more power. So far, society has kept the psychiatrists happy and looked the other way, secure in the knowledge that the patients will keep letting themselves be
called schizophrenic for fear of losing the protection
from social stress that goes with the label.

But that still does not get the psychiatrist off the hook.
It is true that, faced with an Establishment and a citizenry
both clamoring for collusive treatments for mythical ill-
nesses, the doctors are caught in the middle. But even
middlemen may behave honorably. Granted, the first doctor
to take a stand, openly accusing the Establishment of
political subversion and the patients of collusive malingering, would get little sympathy from either. But he
would win respect.

Is Szasz that doctor? Not by a country mile. He manages
never to hit psychiatry where it might hurt. Not only do
his surreptitious concessions leave psychiatry triumphant;
they leave it more degraded. For example, he says "it
hardly matters" whether those who curtail other people's
liberties act with complete sincerity or utter cynicism,
and that "what matters is what happens." But surely that
is not all that matters. Surely motives matter too; not
only when one curtails but also, and especially, when one
professes to defend other people's liberties?

Not to Szasz, apparently. While shouting at the pitch of
his voice that people have the right to refuse treatment
if they don't want it, he silently implies that people
who do want treatment should get it. With a cynicism that
can only be described as disgusting, he explicitly advocates voluntary treatment as a game played by consenting
adults, namely the doctor and the patient and the Establishment. According to Szasz collusion, however repulsive,
does not matter so long as it is voluntary.

Szasz always assumes that patients need doctors. He describes the typical contemporary Western psychiatric scene
as "pre-patients and ex-patients in desperate search of
psychiatrists who will make them well (happy), and psychiatrists in equally desperate search of patients whom they
can save from mental illness." He never considers the

equally plausible likelihood that doctors need patients, and need them for other than altruistic reasons. (The hidden psychological needs of doctors are the best-kept secret within that secretive profession.) And of course Szasz never considers that the Establishment might need both doctors and patients to collude in order to maintain its own political status quo.

We have to remember, despite Szasz's dazzling pyrotechnics, that he launches his attack on psychiatry from a unique and special position. He is an M.D., Professor of Psychiatry at the State University of New York Upstate Medical Center in Syracuse. He is on the editorial board of at least four medical and psychiatric journals, and on the board of consultants of a psychoanalytic journal. That is, he is not only a practicing psychiatrist and a teacher of psychiatry, but a veritable pillar of the psychiatric community.

What on earth can he tell his students? What can Professor Szasz, M.D., say to the average resident struggling through the medical steeplechase, trying desperately to hew to the party line, and terrified of any view that might be tainted with heterodoxy? If Szasz teaches in his classes what he writes in his books he guarantees that any student who follows his teachings will fail his finals.

How can Szasz reconcile what he professes with a professorship? He sees the whole psychiatric subculture as "a medical tragedy" and "a moral challenge," insists that it must be improved, then adds "but we cannot do this so long as we remain psychiatrists." Why then is Szasz still a psychiatrist? The more telling his criticisms of psychiatry the more obvious his own conflict of interest. To remain in psychiatry while snarling at its evils is about as graceful as a dog biting the hand that feeds it.

The blurb on the dust-jacket of Szasz's books commends him for his "relentless logic." His logic is relentless only when he applies it to his colleagues. He appears to regard himself as exempt from his own criticism merely because he is critical. Nowhere does he justify his own position. He quotes the French proverb, "Qui s'excuse, s'accuse." He would have made a better, or at least a more honest, case for himself if he had said instead, "Qui accuse, s'excuse."

Szasz must have thought of getting out of psychiatry, for
he quotes the example of Jaspers who, when disillusioned
with doctoring, turned philosopher. Szasz writes as
though psychiatry turns his stomach; but he suffers the
nausea and takes the money. There is a sense in which
this single fact reduces the whole of Szasz's writings
to a Bernean whine of "Ain't it awful?" There is perhaps
some excuse for a psychiatrist who believes in his own
delusional system (although Szasz would give him no mercy):
but what excuse is there for a psychiatrist who exposes
the delusion, sneers at it for twenty years, but keeps
practicing it with his tongue in his cheek?

How can Szasz indict Bleuler for preaching freedom for
schizophrenics while practicing psychiatric slavery, without adding "me too"? The only place where Szasz comes
close to admitting the fatal weakness of his own position
occurs in his discussion of psychiatry and matrimony.
Even here, and it is surely significant, the master of
vigorous assertion makes his point only in the form of a
question. "The point, of course, is that one cannot
simultaneously maximize freedom and security, independence
from matrimony or psychiatry, and also avow dependence on
these institutions. That is, one cannot have one's cake
and eat it, too. Or can one?" He leaves his sly question
unanswered.

The fact that Szasz asked that question makes his subtle
sell-out to psychiatry inexcusable; and it makes it
impossible to explain away his writings as some kind of
personal expiation. He never complains to psychiatry,
"Look what you made me do"; he does it voluntarily.

When he likens the psychiatrist-patient relationship to
a marriage enforced by a shotgun wedding he never sees that
the shotgun wedding is enforceable only when the bride-
groom is a coward. If psychiatry is a delusional legal
system, then Szasz is an amicus curiae disguised as an
inimicus curiae. If psychiatry is theology, then Szasz
in the psychiatric cathedral is a petulant altar-boy.
Whatever the system, Szasz is its paid servant, enjoying
to the full the honors it bestows, and surreptitiously
supporting by personal example the basic assumptions of
the institution he rails at. Surely the world is already
too full of people who say, like Szasz, "Don't do as I do,
do as I say"?

In the end, écraser l'infame is to Szasz only a game. If

Voltaire were alive, all he could say to Szasz would be,
"I approve every word you say, but you do not have the
right to say it." Szasz the mythoclast is himself a
myth.

Bibliography

Anderson, Alan R., and Nuel D. Belnap, Jr. 1975. Entail-
    ment: The Logic of Relevance and Necessity, vol. 1.
    Princeton, N.J.: Princeton University Press.

Anscombe, Elizabeth. 1957. Intention. Oxford: Blackwell.

Apostel, L. 1982. "Towards a General Theory of Argumenta-
    tion," in Argumentation: Approaches to Theory Formation,
    ed. E. M. Barth and J. L. Martens, 93-122. Amsterdam:
    John Benjamins.

Åqvist, Lennart. 1974. "A New Approach to the Logical
    Theory of Actions and Causality," in Logical Theory and
    Semantics, ed. Sören Stenlund, 73-91. Dordrecht:
    Reidel.

Aristotle. 1928. The Works of Aristotle Translated into
    English, ed. W. D. Ross. Oxford: Oxford University
    Press.

Barth, E. M., and E. C. W. Krabbe. 1982. From Axiom to
    Dialogue. New York: De Gruyter.

Barth, E. M., and J. L. Martens. 1977. "Argumentum Ad
    Hominem: From Chaos to Formal Dialectic," Logique et
    Analyse, 77-78, 76-96.

Barth, E. M., and J. L. Martens, eds. 1982. Argumentation:
    Approaches to Theory Formation. Amsterdam: John Benja-
    mins.

Batten, Lynn M., and Douglas N. Walton. 1979. "Graphs of
    Arguments," Abstracts of the 6th International Congress
    of Logic, Methodology, and Philosophy of Science, vol. 5,
    15-19. Hanover, Germany.

Brand, Myles. 1971. "The Language of Not Doing," American
    Philosophical Quarterly, 8, 45-53.

Carlson, Lauri. 1983. Dialogue Games: An Approach to
    Discourse Analysis. Dordrecht: Reidel.

Copi, Irving. 1972. Introduction to Logic, 4th ed. New
    York: MacMillan.

Crossley, David J., and Peter A. Wilson. 1979. How to
    Argue. New York: Random House.

Danto, Arthur. 1966. "Freedom and Forbearance," in Free-dom and Determinism, ed. Keith Lehrer. New York: Random House.

Davidson, Donald. 1966. "The Logical Form of Action Sentences," in The Logic of Decision and Action, ed. Nicholas Rescher, 81-95. Pittsburgh: University of Pittsburgh Press.

DeMorgan, Augustus. 1847. Formal Logic. London: Taylor and Walton.

Eemeren, Frans H., and Rob Grootendorst. 1984. Speech Acts in Argumentative Discussions. Dordrecht: Foris Publications.

Ellul, Jacques. 1972. Propaganda. New York: Knopf.

Engel, S. Morris. 1976. With Good Reason: An Introduc-tion to Informal Fallacies. New York: St. Martin's Press.

Epstein, Richard L. 1979. "Relatedness and Implication," Philosophical Studies, 36, 137-173.

Epstein, Richard. 1981. Relatedness and Dependence in Propositional Logics, unpublished manuscript.

Finocchiaro, Maurice A. 1974. "The Concept of Ad Hominem Argument in Galileo and Locke," The Philosophical Forum, 5, 394-404.

Finocchiaro, Maurice A. 1980. Galileo and the Art of Reasoning. Dordrecht: Reidel.

Finocchiaro, Maurice A. 1981. "Fallacies and the Evalu-ation of Reasoning," American Philosophical Quarterly, 18, 13-22.

Fogelin, Robert J. 1978. Understanding Arguments. New York: Harcourt Brace Javanovich.

Goldman, Alvin I. 1970. A Theory of Human Action. Englewood Cliffs, N.J.: Prentice-Hall.

Govier, Trudy. 1981. "Worries about Tu Quoque as a Fallacy," Informal Logic Newsletter, 3, no. 3, 2-4.

Govier, Trudy. 1983. "Ad Hominem: Revising the Textbooks," Teaching Philosophy, 6, 13-24.

Green, Romuald. 1963. An Introduction to the Logical
    Treatise 'De Obligationibus' with Critical Texts of
    William of Sherwood and Walter Burley. Thesis,
    Catholic University of Louvain, 2 vols.

Grice, H. P. 1975. "Logic and Conversation," in The
    Logic of Grammar, ed. Donald Davidson and Gilbert
    Harman, 64-75. Encino, Calif.: Dickenson.

Groarke, Leo. 1982. "When Two Wrongs Make a Right,"
    Informal Logic Newsletter, 5, no. 1, 10-13.

Hamblin, C. L. 1970a. Fallacies. London: Methuen.

Hamblin, C. L. 1970b. "The Effect of When It's Said,"
    Theoria, 36, 249-263.

Hamblin, C. L. 1971. "Mathematical Models of Dialogue,"
    Theoria, 37, 130-155.

Hansard. Canada: House of Commons Debates. Ottawa:
    Queen's Printer.

Henry, Desmond P. 1967. The Logic of St. Anselm. Oxford:
    Clarendon Press.

Hinman, Lawrence M. 1982. "The Case for Ad Hominem Argu-
    ments," Australasian Journal of Philosophy, 60, 338-345.

Hintikka, Jaakko. 1962. Knowledge and Belief. Ithaca:
    Cornell University Press.

Hintikka, Jaakko. 1976. The Semantics of Questions and
    the Questions of Semantics, vol. 28 of Acta Philosophica
    Fennica. Amsterdam: North-Holland.

Hintikka, Jaakko. 1979. "Information-Seeking Dialogues:
    A Model," Erkenntnis, 38, 355-368. Reprinted in Becker,
    Werner, and Wilhelm K. Essler (eds.), 1981. Konzepte
    der Dialektik. Frankfurt am Main: Vittorio Klostermann,
    212-231.

Hintikka, Jaakko, and Esa Saarinen. 1979. "Information-
    Seeking Dialogues: Some of Their Logical Properties,"
    Studia Logica, 38, 355-363.

Hughes, G. E. 1958. "Moral Condemnation," in Essays in
    Moral Philosophy, ed. A. I. Melden, 108-134. Seattle:
    University of Washington Press.

Iseminger, Gary. 1980. "Is Relevance Necessary for
    Validity?" Mind, 89, 196-213.

Johnson, R. H., and J. A. Blair. 1977. Logical Self-
    Defense. Toronto and New York: McGraw-Hill Ryerson.

Johnson, R. H., and J. A. Blair. 1980. Informal Logic:
    The First International Symposium. Pt. Reyes: Edge-
    press.

Johnstone, Henry W., Jr. 1970. "Philosophy and Argumentum
    Ad Hominem Revisited," Revue Internationale de Philoso-
    phie, 24, 107-116.

Johnstone, Henry W., Jr. 1978. Validity and Rhetoric in
    Philosophical Argument. University Park: Dialogue
    Press of Man and World.

Kahane, Howard. 1976. Logic and Contemporary Rhetoric.
    Belmont, Calif.: Wadsworth.

Kahane, Howard. 1978. Logic and Philosophy. Belmont,
    Calif.: Wadsworth.

Kanger, Stig. 1972. "Law and Logic," Theoria, 38, 105-132.

Kasher, Asa. 1979. "What Is a Theory of Use?" in Meaning
    and Use, ed. Avishai Margalit, 37-55. Dordrecht:
    Reidel.

Kielkopf, Charles. 1980. "Relevant Appeals to Force, Pity,
    and Popular Pieties," Informal Logic Newsletter, 2, no. 2,
    1-5.

Krabbe, Erik C. W. 1982. "Theory of Argumentation and the
    Dialectical Garb of Formal Logic," in Argumentation:
    Approaches to Theory Formation, ed. E. M. Barth and
    J. L. Martens, 123-132. Amsterdam: John Benjamins.

Kripke, Saul. 1965. "Semantical Analysis of Intuitionistic
    Logic I," in Formal Systems and Recursive Functions,
    ed. J. N. Crossley and M. A. E. Dummett. Amsterdam:
    North-Holland.

Lenk, Hans. 1976. "Handlungsgraphen: Graphentheoretische
    Modelle in der Analytischen Handlungsphilosophie,"
    Grazer Philosophiche Studien, 2, 159-172.

Lorenzen, Paul. 1969. Normative Logic and Ethics. Mannheim:
    Hochscultaschenbucher-Verlag (Bibliographisches Institut).

Łukasiewicz, Jan. 1957. Aristotle's Syllogistic from the Standpoint of Modern Formal Logic, 2d ed. London: Oxford University Press.

Mackenzie, J. D. 1979. "How to Stop Talking to Tortoises," Notre Dame Journal of Formal Logic, 20, 705-717.

Mackie, J. L. 1964. "Self-Refutation: A Formal Analysis," The Philosophical Quarterly, 14, 193-203.

Massey, Gerald J. 1981. "The Fallacy behind Fallacies," Midwest Studies in Philosophy, 6, 489-500.

Perelman, Chaim. 1982. The Realm of Rhetoric. Notre Dame: University of Notre Dame Press.

Pörn, Ingmar. 1970. The Logic of Power. Oxford: Blackwell.

Pörn, Ingmar. 1974. "Some Basic Concepts of Action," in Logical Theory and Semantics, ed. Sören Stenlund, 93-101. Dordrecht: Reidel.

Pörn, Ingmar. 1977. Action Theory and Social Science: Some Formal Models. Dordrecht: Reidel.

Rescher, Nicholas. 1976. Plausible Reasoning. Assen-Amsterdam: Van Gorcum.

Rescher, Nicholas. 1977. Dialectics. Albany: State University of New York Press.

Salmon, Wesley. 1963. Logic. Englewood Cliffs: Prentice-Hall.

Segerberg, Krister. 1982. "The Logic of Deliberate Action," Journal of Philosophical Logic," 11, 233-254.

Simon, Herbert A. 1977. Models of Discovery. Dordrecht: Reidel.

Slupecki, Jerzy, Grzegorz Bryll, and Urzula Wybraniec-Skardowska. "Theory of Rejected Propositions I," Studia Logica, 29, 75-123.

Tarski, Alfred. 1944. "Semantic Conception of Truth," Philosophy and Phenomenological Research, 4, 341-375.

Toulmin, Stephen. 1958. The Uses of Argument. Cambridge: Cambridge University Press.

Vanderveken, Daniel. 1980. "Illocutionary Logic and
    Self-Defeating Speech Acts," in Speech Act Theory and
    Pragmatics, ed. John R. Searle, Ferenc Kiefer, and
    Manfred Bierwisch, 247-272. Dordrecht: Reidel.

Van Dun, Frank. 1972. "On the Modes of Opposition in
    the Formal Dialogues of P. Lorenzen," Logique et
    Analyse, 15, 103-136.

Van Dun, Frank. 1982. "On the Philosophy of Argument and
    the Logic of Common Morality," in Argumentation:
    Approaches to Theory Formation, ed. E. M. Barth and
    J. L. Martens, 281-294. Amsterdam: John Benjamins.

von Wright, G. H. 1963. Norm and Action. London: Rout-
    ledge & Kegal Paul.

von Wright, G. H. 1968. An Essay in Deontic Logic and
    the General Theory of Action. Amsterdam: North-
    Holland.

von Wright, G. H. 1972. "On So-Called Practical Infer-
    ence," Acta Sociologica, 15, 39-53.

von Wright, G. H. 1983. Practical Reason. Ithaca:
    Cornell University Press.

Walton, Douglas N. 1976. "Logical Form and Agency,"
    Philosophical Studies, 29, 75-89.

Walton, Douglas N. 1977. "Performative and Existential
    Self-Verifyingness," Dialogue, 16, 128-138.

Walton, Douglas N. 1979. "Philosophical Basis of Related-
    ness Logic," Philosophical Studies, 36, 115-136.

Walton, Douglas N. 1980a. "Why Is the Ad Populum a Fal-
    lacy?" Philosophy and Rhetoric, 13, 264-278.

Walton, Douglas N. 1980b. "On the Logical Form of Some
    Common-Place Action Expressions," Grazer Philosophische
    Studien, 10, 141-148.

Walton, Douglas N. 1980c. "Ignoratio Elenchi: The Red
    Herring Fallacy," Informal Logic Newsletter, 2, no. 3,
    3-7.

Walton, Douglas N. 1980d. "Petitio Principii and Argument
    Analysis," in Informal Logic, ed. R. H. Johnson and
    J. A. Blair, 41-54. Point Ryes, Calif.: Edgepress.

Walton, Douglas N. 1981. "The Fallacy of Many Questions,"
    Logique et Analyse, 95-96, 291-313.

Walton, Douglas N. 1982. Topical Relevance in Argumenta-
    tion. Amsterdam: John Benjamins.

Walton, Douglas N. 1983. "Enthymemes," Logique et Analyse,
    103-104, 395-410.

Walton, Douglas N. 1984. Logical Dialogue-Games and Fal-
    lacies. Washington: University Press of America.

Whately , Richard. 1836. Elements of Logic. New York:
    William Jackson.

Woods, John, and Douglas Walton. 1974. "Argumentum Ad
    Verecundiam," Philosophy and Rhetoric, 7, 135-153.

Woods, John, and Douglas Walton. 1975. "Petitio Principii,"
    Synthese, 31, 107-127.

Woods, John, and Douglas Walton. 1976a. "Ad Baculum,"
    Grazer Philosophische Studien, 2, 133-140.

Woods, John, and Douglas Walton. 1976b. "Fallaciousness
    without Invalidity?" Philosophy and Rhetoric, 9, 52-54.

Woods, John, and Douglas Walton. 1977a. "Ad Hominem Contra
    Gerber," Personalist, 58, 141-144.

Woods, John, and Douglas Walton. 1977b. "Ad Hominem," The
    Philosophical Forum, 8, 1-20.

Woods, John, and Douglas Walton. 1977c. "Composition and
    Division," Studia Logica, 36, 381-406.

Woods, John, and Douglas Walton. 1977d. "Petitio and
    Relevant Many-Premissed Arguments," Logique et Analyse,
    77-78, 97-110.

Woods, John, and Douglas Walton. 1978a. "Arresting Circles
    in Formal Dialogues," Journal of Philosophical Logic,
    7, 73-90.

Woods, John, and Douglas Walton. 1978b. "The Fallacy of
    Ad Ignorantiam," Dialectica, 32, 87-99.

Woods, John, and Douglas Walton. 1979a. "Circular
    Demonstration and von Wright-Geach Entailment," Notre
    Dame Journal of Formal Logic, 20, 768-772.

Woods, John, and Douglas Walton. 1979b. "Laws of Thought
    and Epistemic Proofs," Idealistic Studies, 9, 55-65.

Woods, John, and Douglas Walton. 1982a. "Question-Begging
    and Cumulativeness in Dialectical Games," Noûs, 4,
    585-605.

Woods, John, and Douglas Walton. 1982b. Argument: The
    Logic of the Fallacies. Toronto and New York: McGraw-
    Hill Ryerson.

Woods, John, and Douglas Walton. 1982c. "The Petitio:
    Aristotle's Five Ways," Canadian Journal of Philosophy,
    12, 77-100.

Wilcox, Lance. 1983. "The Ad Hominem Rides Again," The
    Humanist, 43, 20-23.

Index

About the Author

Douglas N. Walton is Professor of Philosophy at the University of Winnipeg. His works include *Logical Dialogue—Games and Fallacies, Topical Relevance in Argumentation, Argument: The Logic of the Fallacies,* and *Ethics of Withdrawal of Life-Support Systems: Case Studies on Decision Making in Intensive Care* (Greenwood Press, 1983).